PRAISE FOR *PUNK*

"Set in the glittering ruins of late-seventies Hollywood, MacDonell's coming-of-age tale tracks the rise and folly of LA punk. Searing, comic, and self-immolating, *Elegies* ultimately becomes a love letter to lost time."

—Evan Wright, author of *Generation Kill* and *Hella Nation*

PRAISE FOR *PRISONER OF X*

"A luridly entertaining memoir...MacDonell strives to balance the sleaze with dry wit and genteel wordplay—and often strikes gold."

—*Rolling Stone*

"Entertaining...as former *Hustler* editor MacDonell's memoir makes clear, the porn mag exists in its own alternate universe."

—*Spin*

"Hours of guilty pleasure that pass like seconds...Indulge before the restraining orders pull this great book off store shelves."

—Chuck Palahniuk, author of *Fight Club* and *Beautiful You*

"MacDonell gives us a keen, witty, and unflinching look inside his psyche, without resorting to money shots."

—Mike Seely, *Seattle Weekly News*

"Scabrous, cleverly funny new memoir...MacDonell lays the whack-off industry bare...all that's missing is a scratch-and-sniff centerfold."

—*BlackBook*

"The first must-read book on porn."

—Luke Ford, author of *A History of X: 100 Years of Sex in Film* and *XXX-Communicated*

PUNK

ELEG

True Tales of
Death Trip Kids,
Wrongful Sex, and
Trial by Angel Dust

Allan MacDonell

A Barnacle Book | Rare Bird Books
Los Angeles, Calif.

THIS IS A GENUINE BARNACLE BOOK

A Barnacle Book | Rare Bird Books
453 South Spring Street, Suite 531
Los Angeles, CA 90013
rarebirdbooks.com

FIRST TRADE PAPERBACK ORIGINAL EDITION

Set in Minion
Printed in the United States

10 9 8 7 6 5 4 3 2 1

Publisher's Cataloging-in-Publication data
MacDonell, Allan.
    Punk elegies : true tales of death trip kids , wrongful sex , and trial by angel dust / Allan MacDonell.
    p. cm.
    ISBN 978-1940207612

1. MacDonell, Allan. 2. Punk rock music—California—Los Angeles—Biography. 3. Punk culture—United States—Biography. 4. Subculture (United States). 5. Los Angeles (Calif.)—Social life and customs—20th century. 6. Music and youth. I. Title.

HQ796 .M33 2015
306/.10973—dc23

To everyone who was there.
To the ones who remember it like I remember.
To anyone who remembers something else.
And to everybody who didn't make it through.

CONTENTS

PROLOGUE: A CHILD'S HISTORY OF FUN

I'll start in the dirt, on my back, bleeding from my face, and staring at the hot California sky from the bottom of a shallow ditch. I am nine years old. This is a long time ago. It would take forever to stop and count all the intervening years. The front spokes of my Sting-Ray bicycle spin up above my face, passing in a whir, ten at a time. The handlebars are twisted in the dry soil beneath my shoulders.

A tinny transistor radio is propped in the shade beneath a slab of sandstone. The raw beats of "96 Tears" by Question Mark and the Mysterians are shaking the radio to pieces.

"You're gonna cry... / You're gonna cry, cry, cry..."

A eucalyptus breeze gives a scent of medicine to the clouds crossing high above the ditch. Knuckles scraped, this boy's hand reaches up, pulls a piece of doctored cotton out of the yellow sky, and holds it to his nose. I breathe in the mentholated rush.

I can tell you exactly how I came to be crashed beneath the pulsating sun.

My every busted intention and perverted ambition trace back to this dusty trench. You'll see. The wayward carnal ignorance, the signpost overdoses, the hostile campaign for world conquest, the scorched-earth emergence where I stand steely and hollowed out as the sun stumbles toward the first shaky dawn of the rest of my life—I'll connect the dots. It's all plotted out by forces and choices as innocent as a child's whims.

For starters, nine years old, I am not alone out in the burned-lawn suburb of Covina, California. Three of us have met up at our neighborhood bar—the rec room of a bachelor's starter house.

A skinny, redheaded tomboy whose cop dad dropped his Harley under an eighteen-wheeler and is on perpetual disability has joined me for drinks, along with a pensive, creepy kid whose older sister is the fattest girl in the entire school.

Richard's sister is so far outside the accepted weight norms that the regular kids taunt Richard for being related to her. The bus stop mockers wag their asses and chant: "Regina waddles when she walks; she gobbles when she talks. Regina waddles when she walks; she gobbles when she talks."

The brother needed a drink.

"Try this one." I wiped tears from my eyes and extended a bottle of bourbon. I'd developed a partiality to the stuff, but Richard declined.

"It burns." He didn't like the way any of it tasted: vodka, gin, schnapps, even beer, they were all too much for him.

Redheaded Deena snapped the bottle from my hands. She was a year behind me—in third grade—but we were the same age. I'd skipped second grade, and was now the youngest kid in fourth. Like me, Deena had an advanced appreciation for all the flavors of the bar.

Right around here, a respectable narrator might clarify how, at age nine, Deena and I had found one another and discovered our shared passion. A responsible writer might point to the developmental blunders, family failures, and systemic breakdowns that had turned two scrawny kids in a parched, sixties housing tract into cocktail party prodigies. Let's agree not to go all sappy with the spoon-feeding? How many times do I need to say early sixties? The signs were everywhere. A plaque on the back mirror of Mr. Kirby's bar showed a parrot sipping a tropical drink: "It must be five o'clock somewhere," said the parrot. It was closer to 3:30, but Deena and I were, as previously noted, prodigies. An early start was in our natures.

Her red hair and her angularity in a California of soft blondes and round brunettes weren't what made Deena different. Fury set her apart. Something had pissed her off, probably in the past five years or so. Her nine-year-old's rage lived in her clenched twiggy fists, in the smashed front teeth of her Chiclets sneer, in her sore-looking freckles, and in her yellow eyes, squinting behind a triangle of orange hair pulled down to conceal them.

Deena took a brave slug from the bourbon, and thrust the fifth back at me. "I want the bottle with the bat," she gasped. "Give me the bottle with the bat."

"Be careful!" Richard put his hand on Deena's pink, freckled forearm. "Don't drink too fast."

Deena jerked her arm from Richard's grasp. "We don't have all day, queer bait."

She was starting to relax, though too late for Richard's feelings. Deena had violated our tacit agreement not to use any of the pet names our classmates hurled at us—queer bait, rotten crotch, scab face, and the name they had for me. Richard took some distance, sitting alone at Mr. Kirby's kitchen table, keeping watch on the driveway while Deena and I topped off with Mr. Kirby's Bacardi.

The rum did, in fact, burn going down, just like the bourbon and anything else worth drinking. But these fluids had a trick of expanding outward from the stomach, as if some fictional being, some spirit or genie, had breathed happiness into you. It was like you were sharing the same air as the kids in the Mickey Mouse Club, like Annette Funicello was blowing on your skin, like you had inhaled the life that you saw on TV or driving through some rich neighborhood.

I took a gulp of Bacardi; Deena took a gulp. A balance flipped. We were no longer the skulking creatures hoping to navigate from classroom, to cafeteria, to playground, and back home unnoticed and unscathed. That had all dissolved like a cube of sugar. In the bar-back mirror, beside the boozing parrot, our wincing lips shifted into cock-sure grins. We were better now. Better than them, better than you, better than we'd been moments earlier.

Richard, of course, was still hurt, but he was loyal. He hissed "Kirby" when the homeowner's car pulled in; he tidied up our hasty abandon of Mr. Kirby's array of bottles; he followed Deena and me out the never-locked back door as Mr. Kirby stamped his feet at the front.

Deena, Richard, and even young Allan, I guess, are why I try to live in neighborhoods without any of those young families. You see these kids. They're breaking your heart. Maybe you've been one of them. Somehow, you have a notion of what they'll be going through. You know from experts, or experience, a lot of them will tumble into the obvious pitfalls ahead of them. Then you find some dirty thief child from up the block in your garage, and you pull back your foot to kick the little crap ass into the pit. That's how it goes with these younger versions of the advanced self.

Those toddlers, even the brightest of them, grow up to be troubled adolescents, felonious teens, too dumb and chicken to break into any house that's not on their own home grid. It's not that I'm opposed to the family principal or am antichild. I nearly had one, one time. You'll hear about that if you stick it out, if we don't get too nosy and ahead of ourselves with a lot of why and how-can-this-be-happening dithering.

If the delivery here seems out of sync, pretend what I'm telling you is music. Think of it as an LP side that's never made sense to you until you decide to play it for one last time before throwing the record away. Suddenly, you move with it, and you know what's in those grooves is tuned in on some unexpected harmonic that you had never heard before as melodically true, and you reshelve the disc—filed under "off key, but worthy of continued investigation." That's something like what was going on with these kids, my friends and me: Our continued investigations were following a dissonant harmonic.

Deena owned the radio. In a plastic casing no bigger than a blackboard eraser, transistor powered through a stressed, three-inch speaker, strapped to the handlebars of her boys' Schwinn Sting-Ray bicycle, the radio rattled with all the charms of a big-beat Peter Pan: Boss Radio 93 KHJ brought us "House of the Rising Sun" by The Animals, The Kinks doing "You Really Got Me," The Seeds singing "You're Pushing Too Hard," The Who smashing out "My Generation."

"Psychotic Breakdown" by the Count Five, "I Had Too Much to Dream Last Night" from The Electric Prunes, "Paint It Black," the Stones, "Dirty Water" by The Standells, "Wild Thing," The Troggs.

Never losing track of the radio behind him, Richard pedaled out front, hewing to a straight line, announcing the approach of cars from cross streets and driveways. Deena and I lagged five or ten yards back. We obeyed the discordant commands of Boss Radio's switchback melodies. Tuning in on "I Fought the Law," we wove our bicycles in erratic and hazardous circles. Our handle grips dipped inches from the pavement. Gliding back on ourselves, we chanted the chorus: "…and the law won."

The adults were all at work, in offices and retail showrooms, on construction sites and telephone lines, or at home, staying inside, away from the sun, or out in the backyards soaking up heat next to a pool.

Three kids with scabbed knees, gritty fingernails, and swoony, lidded eyes, we pedaled out of the ranch-style cul-de-sac that housed us and onto a single lane of rutted blacktop that ran along a row of dilapidated horse stables. Towering eucalyptus lined the asphalt. Past the stables, we swerved onto packed dirt roads that bisected flats of scrub brush that were a few years away from being cut up into housing lots. Once off the pavement, even Richard rode recklessly.

We headed to a ridge of ratty sumac. Storm drain runoff had scraped a two-foot ditch into the sand and rock. We propped the bikes on boulders beside the ditch, and Deena wedged her radio into a patch of sandstone shade.

Three-minute anthems stoked the uneasy temper that anyone, if they'd looked, could have seen behind our eyes when we peered out at the adult world, or at the bulk of the kids around us. You didn't need a lyric sheet to know what the words were saying in your twisted gut.

"Breakin' rocks in the hot sun / I needed money 'cause I had none / I fought the law / and the law won."

Older kids had set up plywood ramps at a spot where one side of the ditch was a foot higher than the other. We sat on the high side of the gulch beyond the sun break of the eucalyptus. Three pairs of skinny legs dangled over the ledge. The three of us shared a can of Hamm's beer, contemplating our private dilemmas of home and schoolyard and what the radio had to tell us about them.

"Wild thing, you make my heart sing."

Buoyant with carbonation and alcohol, Deena and I took turns sprinting our cycles to the ramp and jumping our bikes across the narrow ditch from the higher bank to the lower. We glided through the air, our faces concentrated and exultant, landed on our back wheels, and swerved in the dirt with our front wheels popped toward the sky.

After splitting that beer, our landings became deliberately rocky. Skidding and crashing were a kind of artistic endeavor. We flipped extravagantly in the dirt, flinging our bikes as if exploding fuel tanks were blasting them through the air.

We pissed as partners. I stood on the high bank and aimed. A golden arc glimmered in the sun and splashed down on the lower side of the culvert.

Deena pulled her cutoffs down to her shins, and squatted beside me, facing away from the ditch. She lifted her hips, looked back between her legs, aimed her boney cheeks, and shot a glistening stream straight out off the raised ledge. Her puddle fell far short of mine.

Side-by-side boy-girl urination, and outdoor nudity: Do these kids have no parental oversight? Where is the social worker safety net?

This story could end right here, right now, with a deft intervention and a rigorous course of family court and juvenile counseling.

*Shhh…*don't disturb my children.

We don't know anything is wrong with our behaviors. We're too busy learning what's wrong with the world around us, with everything around us.

This drinking, crashing the bikes, treating our genitals to the after-school sun, this is saving our lives, this is numbing the cruel pricks—some of the cruel pricks.

Richard, poor, unfortunate teetotaler, was still stinging from Deena's queer-bait slip back at Mr. Kirby's bar. "Deena pees like a girl," he observed, out loud.

Deena glared at me as if I'd pointed out her shortfall. Measuring me in her yellow squint, she hissed: "At least I'm not a kak."

At Barranca Elementary School, the social system broke down into two factions: surfers and kaks. Surfers wore blue Keds tennies like the Beach Boys did and butch-waxed their blond hair into short-cropped imitations of Jan and Dean.

Me, I had pointy black leatherette shoes with metal strips to preserve the heels, some sort of peg-legged slacks that were remnants of Catholic school aspirations, and my hair was long over the collar due to a crimp in the family grooming budget. I'd transferred to the school district less than a year ago from another country, a foreign, exotic, far-off place…Canada. For this, I was lumped in with the kaks.

There were no other kaks at Barranca.

That word—*kak*—was flung at my back and to my face with the relish of a derogatory term. No one would tell me what a kak was.

Day after day, I felt as if my darkest, most shameful secrets had been uncovered, discussed widely, and labeled kak. The word might mean anything. It applied to everything. I had no safe, kak-free place inside me, no kak-proof sanctuary. My hope for a brighter day was all covered in kak.

I shouted at Deena: "You don't even know what a kak is!"

"Yes I do." She pulled up her cutoffs over her twin-blade pelvis. "A kak is you."

Deena gripped Richard by the neck and pointed at me. "He's a kak!"

Richard joined her chorus, a little too eagerly. "A kak, a kak, a kak."

I tucked my sad wiener back into the shadows.

The avenging redhead picked her radio out of the dirt and reattached it to her handlebars. She stood high and pale in her stirrups. She wheeled her bike around to face the ramp. She was screaming actually, as if she were a drunken child in an emotional frenzy. "Kak, kak, kak, kak!"

That effervescent air I'd burgled and stolen and guzzled to breathe in blew away. Deena had kicked the happy wind right out of my guts. I snorted something furious. It was like I inhaled all the cruelty ever carried in the hot breeze. That free-floating nastiness mingled with an atmosphere of hurt waiting inside me.

"Kak, kak, kak, kak, kak." Deena was blind in her fit, swirling her bike on the higher ground.

I hunched over my handlebars on the lower bank. The radio played Question Mark and the Mysterians. "You're gonna cry."

This is how it happens. This is how the place where love should be is filled with the bigger-than-life vibrations of brash, speaker-straining music. Sad songs, defiant songs, taunting songs, songs distorted with distraught and overwrought emotion, they come to overlay your everyday life. If you're the kind of kid who feels a need to change into somebody else, the songs shape the anticipation of the person you yearn to become. "You're gonna cry, cry, cry."

Deena's legs pumped with potent fury as she zipped her bike, radio blaring, to the launch ramp. She cackled "kak" and looked behind her to clock my reaction to her flying gloat. Only I was not behind her.

I had moved with stealth and purpose to the low ground. I approached the landing ramp at full gallop to meet the flight of her bike. I sped front wheel in the air and launched my bike into the empty space across the ditch. The blot of my urine passed in the dirt beneath me. Deena was coming down fast; I flew up hard. She figured out where I was coming from just before we hit. Her face twisted forward, mouth open, eyes locked with mine.

"You're gonna cry, cry, cry."

Our bikes clacked together and seemed to interlock and hang in the air. It was as if we had a moment to reach out beyond our kak differences, through the pee discrepancies, and grasp each other at depth. We hugged there, elevated over the ditch bed, embraced like a couple of dear friends.

Without transition, I was on my back, marveling at the nearness of the clouds. Blood seeped from my nostrils. The scent of eucalyptus wafted in. My front wheel spun inches from my nose, in silence. Laughter broke the quiet. Deena sprawled beside me in the culvert's bottom. Then I heard Bobby Fuller, or the Mysterians.

"I peed my pants!" Deena gasped for air. "Let's do it again."

We straddled the bikes. The songs wound their guitar strands into our DNA; the radio was with us in our cores. We crashed head-on, and I loved the redheaded, rotten-crotched, scab-faced tomboy I was colliding with—even as our blood splashed her white, button-up blouse, and she struggled to crawl away, her bony limbs entangled in mine. Her elbows struck out as she clambered from under me and left me on my back.

Prologue

Prone in the grit, staring at the sky from the bottom of a shallow ditch, dirt turning to mud in my sweat and blood, guitars and drums clattering in my pulse, exhausted and flush with alcohol—where will my bleeding soul ever know such release and companionship again?

That, my presumed friends, is what I am here to tell you.

PART ONE: HARDCORE PARTY PEOPLE

"Hey ho, let's go"
—The Ramones, "Blitzkrieg Bop"

SCENE ONE:
FUTURE-SLASH-SELF

I n 1977, we felt that we were pretty great. All of us did. This was before we even knew we were a "we."

Most of us were stumbling from our tragic teens into our terrible twenties. One on one, we might have been toxic, strung out, slutty, unemployable, overprivileged, socially retarded, grandiose, needle-dicked, porky, pock-faced, boneheaded, delusional, depressed, and demented. We'd been rejected. We'd been ostracized. We'd been diagnosed.

Still, each of us was pretty certain, deep down, of greatness—individually and, suddenly, as a group. At any moment, the world would be forced to acknowledge what we'd suspected all along. The secret was coming out: We were pretty great.

One hundred or so of us, stoned and smashed, had been lured into an alley-entry loft off of Pico Boulevard to witness the reinvention of rock and roll. It was May 28, 1977, the public debut of the Screamers. The event had been hyped as the first appearance of the future—an unprecedented future, a climactic, orgasmic future to change everything.

Careers and magazines and record companies will come out of this night. The next few hours will spawn media empires that will be bought up by bigger media empires. People will become obnoxious millionaires. Not many people, but all of us will believe we are in the running.

Four of us arrived in an MG Midget, a car about the size of a bathtub. Johnny drove. The MG was his car. He had a history degree, a history of DUI arrests, and a mixed hillbilly American Indian heritage. His younger brother, Larry, rode shotgun and drank 151 rum. Larry's singing drowned out the cassette. Roxy Music, David Bowie, Grace Jones: All of them made secondary by Larry's blown-out croon.

Johnny turned the car at random and spilled his beer. We seemed to be lost. The wife and I made out in the cramped confines of the luggage space behind the Midget's seats. We were young, we were high, we'd been fighting earlier, and we were making up for lost time.

Tommie, the wife, was ten months ahead of me, twenty-two years of age in May of 1977. Lean, brunette, short-cropped, she dressed like an updated heroine from a Ronettes song. She had lowrider brothers and hidden-razorblade attitude.

Between them, Tommie and a half dozen other girls who would just as soon spit at you as be flattered by you created the punk-chic template that shows up so fresh and original to this very day—this is true; ask anyone who was there. I liked looking at her.

A violent impact wedged the wife and me together in the MG's luggage nook. When the car stopped sliding, I put my throbbing mouth to Tommie's lips and tasted blood. Johnny had just gotten into his second collision in twenty minutes. Johnny wasn't a particularly cautious, or safe, or arrest-free driver. He *was*, however, a great driver. A lesser driver in his condition wouldn't have dared to take the wheel.

Johnny's greatness aside, the MG had stalled out, and the cassette music went dead. Larry declared the car parked, and we abandoned it on foot.

Eight or ten stragglers of our ilk detoured around the MG and pointed out that it was in the middle of a sidewalk. The wife and I disavowed any connection with the car and blended in.

The Screamers were being unveiled in the headquarters of *Slash* magazine—a storefront loft two doors beyond a liquor store. In we went…to the liquor store. The weathered black man behind the liquor counter had seen everything, but not this odd strain of white persons.

We all had poignant cheekbones and pallor. Straight-legged trousers, pointy-toed shoes, salvaged thrift-store spike heels. Animal prints, torn T-shirts, extra eye shadow, sex lube as hair gel, safety pins, and cock rings as accessories. This crowd made pretty great out of pretty much nothing.

Tommie and I, Larry, and Johnny, we had not been invited to the Screamer's coming-out party.

Crashing the alley was easy enough. Clumps of party people shambled in the dark, from pothole to pothole. Bumping into strangers with casual disregard was a skill I had mastered, but a doorman—some thuggish cliché in a black leather blazer— blocked the entryway to the loft itself. The doorman concerned me. My experience with doormen wasn't great.

I put a grip on Tommie and surveyed the approach.

"What about that guy?" I said.

Obvious lames—in bellbottoms or Earth Shoes or UCLA sweatshirts—were being turned away.

The wife took a draw on her cigarette, squinted an eye, tilted a hip. It was a balletic stance. Tumbles of smoke framed her face.

"Do you hear that?" she said.

A voice came from within the brick-framed doorway: a soaring, cock-up voice—Larry singing.

We shoved past the lout in the leather.

The loft was about the size of a two-car garage, painted gallery white, with sparse and powerful lighting. Music industry snobs and guttersnipes formed a ring of spectators in the center of the cement floor. This impromptu audience looked sideways at one another, leery of being jostled, of being taken for fools.

Nothing had been happening for so long that nobody anticipated anything real or new to ever happen again. The mud of Woodstock, The Beatles' breakup, the Altamont murder: just three historical disappointments of trying to make rock and roll into something more than music to pop your cherry to.

So no one who'd assembled for the Screamers' highly amplified paradigm shift had been lured in by high hopes. Skepticism—a provoked, aroused skepticism—had circled up this full spectrum of Los Angeles disaffection on *Slash* magazine's cement floor. Now, a single voice had ambushed the muted expectations of these habitually unimpressed onlookers. A cluster of hushed seen-it-alls stood stock-still with their mouths stalled.

Tommie and I knew exactly what we would find in that crowd's center.

Larry had yanked the front tail of his metallic thrift-store blouse up through the garment's neck, baring his midriff. Alcohol lit him from inside. He danced in place, singing full-throated. His voice filled the performance space from floor to ceiling, drowning out any incidental chatter and the David Bowie playing through the JBLs.

Undulating, flexed-lips narcissism was Larry's standard show any time he'd finished his third Coke and 151. At the

Slash loft, cocaine sophisticates and Boone's Farm brats alike were astonished by the performance.

In the next couple of years, Larry will front a band, Wild Kingdom. It will astound and confound fans, mentors, and managers, and the band will collapse. Misfortune, head trauma, and seizures will render my friend unrecognizable.

Back on May 28, 1977, Larry is still pretty and great, and his future possibly will be spectacular. So let him show off while we wait to usher in the Screamers.

The world was a dead musical place in 1977. The glitter promises of Bowie and T-Rex had gone the way of my late teens, with very little worthwhile following along. The trendiest young minds of the LA basin were ready to blow out our brains from boredom and schmaltz. Patti Smith and the Ramones had flown in from New York, bringing signs of salvation. Even better, a two-chord defiance wafted over from England—the Sex Pistols, The Damned, The Clash. We saw pictures of these bands before we heard their songs. The pictures helped, but we needed something at home, of our own.

The Screamers looked like they might be it. They strolled into a far corner of the loft: Like The Beatles, there were four of them, but with no guitar or other stringed instruments. They had two keyboard players, a drummer, and a singer.

The musicians flexed and shrugged in front of a white wall, a wall decorated with larger-than-life photos of the Screamers. The hair was spiked, and the jaws were clenched. The singer wore a white jumpsuit stitched together from plastic trash bags and tailored to his limbs by slimming strips of electrical tape. His synthesizer player shed a conservative suit jacket to reveal a blouse crafted from clear bubble wrap.

Abruptly and abrasively, the music started. The Screamers were more aggressive and louder than The Who. Pictures show me standing in the front row, skinny, scowling, pasty white dressed in faded black, transfixed. The face is twenty-one years old. It has the vacated stare of an obstinate child who refuses to answer the question of what it had been thinking to do such a thing. This is a face that has not been denied inclusion since grade four. If there is a chance of being blackballed or snubbed or passed over, then fuck off: This face won't stoop to join any clique that might reject it.

The Screamers were not in the business of rejection. The band was in no position to look down on that twenty-one-year-old, or any of the other faces straining eyeball-to-eyeball with the band in those photos. There was no stage; the musicians cleared a space with their noise, with songs that sounded like we felt—undervalued, wronged, and arrogant about it all. *Jarring, discordant, frenetic*: Words did the onslaught justice. The Screamers were wise enough to keep the set short.

The performance was like a hit of amyl nitrate. You took a huff, and your head exploded for a minute. Then you wandered around with your mind blasted out, wondering what to do next.

People were forming bands to the left and to the right. Germs, X, Alley Cats, Skulls, Weirdos, Plugs, Mau Mau's, Deadbeats, The Go-Go's, Black Randy's Metrosquad, and on into absolute obscurity, everyone was in that loft or a phone call away from having been there. Two fussy members of Devo circulated in an isolated way; their first album would come out in mere months, it might as well have been half a lifetime away. Everyone knew who Devo were, of course. Devo made sure of that.

No one was paying attention to me. Slighted, I dragged a bin of empty liquor bottles to the loft's industrial shower. One by one, I shattered six bottles on the cement basin. *That will show them!*

Part One

Breaking glass did something for Tommie, or so I believed. The pop of impact, the gleaming whole splintering into countless glittering shards, this transformation of a useful object into a hazard, I told myself, spoke to Tommie like a broken phrase of jagged poetry; not to incite or soothe her complex and volatile soul, but to mirror its reflection of mine.

Shrapnel from a Michelob bottle flicked past my cheek. I was attracting attention. For instance, Steve Samioff, founder and publisher of *Slash*, noticed me. He lived in the loft. It was his shower.

Samioff was an old guy, closer to thirty than twenty, wearing a Humphrey Bogart hat and some kind of forties gangster drag. Suddenly, he stood too close to me. His eyebrows looked like they'd been feathered on with a laundry marker. He pushed a small pistol into my gut. The weapon, I assumed, had to be a toy, a BB gun.

The fact that it was his place, that he owned *Slash* magazine, even his very presence as a human being, all those crap details were unavailable to me. Samioff was talking, pressing some forceful point, but I was off in a Screamers after-rush, lost in the grandeur of being intoxicated me.

I tossed another bottle.

The prop gun jabbed into my solar plexus. Still, I couldn't pay full attention. The wife had circled around, and she was laughing. Her entire face lit up! That mouth. I'd been alone with her naked, and I would be astounded by her nudity again, but this instant was as much raw beauty as I could absorb. The gun moved up to punch into my heart, and my wife's face convulsed in gorgeous laughter.

Samioff's brows flexed. He sensed that Tommie was laughing at his expense. I touched the gun barrel, to shove away the silly toy. The barrel was metal, cold oily metal. Beyond looking just like a real gun, it was a real gun.

I'd been high, why try to deny it? So my perceptions and emotions were exaggerated and subject to abrupt reversals. Suddenly somber and contrite, I might cry.

"This isn't a joke," Samioff said.

Tommie's face said otherwise; she was seeing comedy. Which perspective was I obligated to believe, really?

Tommie composed herself, prepared to take this serious man with his serious gun seriously. She doubled over, spat out laughter, pointed at me.

"Your face!" Tommie roared. "Look at your face!"

I'd seen her like this before. I'd been fresh out of college, fry cooking at a family hamburger place, feeling the sweat of injustice rolling down my bent spine, and a laugh broke through the lunch-rush clatter. It silenced the place.

One of the waitresses—I'd swooned every time I'd pictured her in my car—stood beside a booth of diners with their mouths ajar. Gleaming teeth split the waitress's face, and laughter spat out of her. No one at the table was amused.

Grim and accusatory, the restaurant's manager stood in front of the waitress, shoving a plated burger combo toward her. A dirty Band-Aid had been located in that burger. A family of five squirmed in the booth, gagging and outraged.

All those faces turned from the offending burger toward me, behind the counter, at the grill. Reflexively, I fingered a cut knuckle on my hamburger-making hand. The wound was rough, scabbed and—my face clenched—exposed. Above the heads of the suddenly invested diners at the counter, I slipped a glance toward the waitress.

If only she would ride in my car, I thought, *this unfair, humiliating, exhausting mistake of a life wouldn't be so bad.*

Laughter burst out of her all over again.

She couldn't have stopped if she'd wanted to. She couldn't have stopped if Samioff had shot me.

I pictured me sinking, curling up in the shower basin's carpet of shattered glass. Samioff's bullet resting uneasy in my guts, and Tommie's teeth flashing in her ruby lips.

She was right to laugh. Would this guy shoot me in his own place? Absurd! I scanned the room. We had roughly 200 witnesses, all riveted.

The adult with the gun saw Tommie's point of view; he didn't see any humor in it.

I raised another empty Michelob from the bin and let the bottle drop. The wife and I locked eyes, waiting for a pretty great shattering.

SCENE TWO:
A PRETTY COOL GUY

I stood hesitating on the front porch of my own home, picking pieces of lawn out of my hair, unsure. Should I move forward into the living room and let the screen door shut behind me?

The wife was indoors, and she was unhappy. She wouldn't even open her mouth. I knew not to say good morning. There were some things I was unable to picture from the night before, things that I had done. My head held more ache than information. The mind had not sorted the ugly details, not yet.

You may presume that alcohol was involved, just as I presumed it. Whatever spontaneous behaviors the juice had enflamed and blotted out since my last conscious memory, whatever that last conscious memory might turn out to be, would—when revealed to me—surely inflict shame rather than instill pride. Those were the general truths that had me dreading the dawning of the specifics.

There were clues. For one thing, I was missing my shirt. Telltale claw marks crossed my chest. I'd woken up in the front yard, face pressed into the dead grass. The day was young, not yet eleven. With the wife's help, it would all come back to me.

Tommie was housecleaning in a fury, shifting from broom, to mop, to sponge. Her flurry intensified my uncertainty. I could not face her.

Squinting back, out to the driveway and Huntington Drive and the town of Pomona beyond, it was almost like I could see a shimmer of the high spirits we'd traveled in the day before. Things had started out well enough, from what I remembered on my own. My first issue of *Slash* had come out.

A pang of pride disrupted me on the Pomona front porch. I was a *Slash* insider.

After the Screamers' debut, where I'd stood out by shattering beer bottles in the publisher's shower stall, I'd sent *Slash* a letter introducing myself as a person of great independent wealth and investment potential who, incidentally, desired to write for the magazine. Somebody wrote back and suggested we should meet.

A few nights later, I talked some Pomona lowriders into driving to a new wave music marathon at the Whisky a Go Go on the Sunset Strip. Once in the club, Tommie and I had crammed into a booth with the *Slash* people. They were older, sophisticated, traveled. Maybe they bought me drinks, maybe I'd stolen my own, who can be sure?

The magazine's editor, a Frenchman with a greasy ducktail and a cracked leather jacket, lolled his head. Clearly Tommie and I were nonexistent beyond the smokescreen of his chain of cigarettes. An Englishwoman with an angular haircut pronounced her four-syllable name in precise, boarding school diction—a few times. Still, it escaped me. Another four or five art-damaged adults filled out the crew. They tapped cigarettes and tended drinks on the table separating us and regarded the wife and me as though we were curios.

Evidently, I had been talking. The place was loud; music was being played on the stage. The effort to be heard above it all had carried me away in my own exuberance.

Samioff, the publisher, made a V of the thick, solid bar of bristle across his brow.

That stopped me.

"You do not really come from great independent wealth, do you?" he said.

Right there, the wife had started to laugh.

"He hasn't mentioned the gun," she said. "The one he jammed in your stomach." Only I heard that, but Tommie's laughter went up a notch and shared itself with the entire booth.

The Frenchman picked flecks of tobacco from his teeth and studied them as though they held serious meaning. "What's funny?" he said. He had a funny way of saying funny.

"He doesn't recognize us!" Tommie said, louder now, audible to perhaps half the booth.

"No, no," said the British lady. "We recognize, from the writing, and from meeting you, that you are serious about the scene."

The wife, just as I knew she would, erupted in laughter. There was some mockery to it, musical and light, but loud.

I'd suspected Tommie's hilarity had blown the deal, but I played it off and persuaded the Frenchman to consider publishing a write-up of the Whisky's new wave music marathon, since we were there.

Standing outdoors on the Pomona front porch, I scoffed at those unfounded worries, weeks old, not sure if I were allowed to cross the threshold of my home.

The wife regarded my naked, clawed chest as if I were some sort of stain that would not rub out.

I saw her decide to speak to me, and I kept my hopes down.

"First of all," she said, "do you even remember who you were with last night?"

I said, "Of course." I had to think about it.

Larry and his acting boyfriend had pulled up in a Volkswagen Bug around seven. The fresh issue of *Slash* contained roughly thirty percent of what I had written about the Whisky marathon. The waitresses at work saw me only as a grumbling fry cook with stooped posture and stunted attitude, but a new social order was rising. I was in with the originators, a shaping force of it. Sunlight was still in the sky. The Volkswagen had no radio, but it had an open bar policy.

So we started driving and drinking and bickering. Standing in the glare of the wife's shriveling estimation, I couldn't remember why the quarrel had come about. In Pomona, all hope for a glamorous future centered on Larry's vocal gift and his imminent wealth and fame. Tom, the Volkswagen's driver, the current hometown boyfriend, was in a band with Larry—Wild Kingdom. All the girls and any other friends that hung around, it was agreed, would be in bands produced by Larry's band. Sometimes these future arrangements caused intense present-time squabbles.

It was fully dark by the time the Volkswagen reached Hollywood. I could not have pinpointed just when night had happened. The show we'd intended to catch was canceled, or we'd missed it while getting lost and arguing, but there was an after party at Joan Jett's apartment. Half of the Germs would be there.

I'd seen Joan Jett's band, The Runaways, maybe twice, both times at the Whisky. Once, unless I've confused events, they'd opened for future stadium icons Van Halen. Joan Jett was the standout; I have no confusion about that. Her brunette insouciance seemed to come from some actual aspect of the actual her.

We reached the party, in a West Hollywood apartment complex. I'd already overshot the mark. I was drinking on pure momentum, pouring it down. So I was encouraged by the sight of a breakfast nook stocked with tubs of beer. A liquor-bottle skyline spanned the kitchen countertop from the sink to the stove. I would be free to express myself.

There, in that same kitchen, stood Joan Jett, looking like she could be Tommie's cousin, splashing alcohol into a glass, slouched, casual, bare shoulders in a wifebeater, probably nineteen years old, although the publicists were claiming sixteen.

Claude and Philly from *Slash* suddenly hemmed me in. Claude, the paper's primary editor, was the Frenchman. He called himself Kickboy Face, and so did several other people. His hair was greasy and worn ducktail style as if he were from a previous generation, which in fact he was. Philly, short for Philomena, gave the impression of growing up in a big English country manor filled with family retainers and posh accents. She had nonetheless become Claude's concubine. Claude was a crawling, hands-and-knees lush; on many nights the worst lush in Hollywood.

Claude and Philly wanted to know if I had any drugs, which is exactly what I had intended to ask them.

People my age, my peers, wielded mixed drinks and moved me aside to complement old Claude on the new issue of *Slash*. Did they realize that my precious words immortalizing the Whisky's new wave marathon were the issue's highlight?

I solicited agreement on that opinion from Joan Jett's party guests, solicited and obtained, all around.

"I really am quite talented, and the voice is unique in its absolute authenticity and authority. We can all agree on that, can we not?"

"Sure," agreed some guy. I blocked him from moving on.

"And can we agree that the scene belongs to the authentic? Also, I am very funny. You must have laughed out loud."

"Whatever you say."

"No, I really mean it. Don't fuck with me on this."

The wife can't keep up with my transcendent throes. One minute I'm like a moth or a butterfly breaking free from the fabric of my confining insecurities; the next moment, I'm in Joan Jett's kitchen scuffling with three heavyset girls who wear a lot of makeup. We're all soaked in alcohol, and our clothes are shredded.

In Pomona, the wife mops around the spot where I stand. "Do you remember fighting with girls?"

Joan Jett's kitchen floor slides beneath my feet. I sense spectators. I sense a spectacle. I wouldn't have known how to stop it if I'd wanted to.

"There's a pattern with you," the wife observes, holding two fingers an inch apart. "You're always this close to getting your ass kicked."

A bruiser in torn fishnets and cha-cha slippers comes at me across Joan Jett's linoleum with an open switchblade knife. And I feel sympathetic to her, for her feelings, for her plight. Next thing you know, my bruiser scowls, cursing me from the sink, a wet cloth to her swelling eye.

Her knife is in my hand, closed. A lot of people are yelling at me.

Part One

"Get out!"

"Fucker!"

"Fuck you!"

"Get out!"

"Don't let me hear you say life's taking you nowhere…."

I hear singing. It's from another room. The voice is live, and it adds timbre to the entire kitchen.

I have no shirt. My torso is soaked in beer, spit, and sweat. Joan Jett is basically under my arm, propping me up, amused.

"Last night they loved you, opening doors and pulling some strings…angel!"

Larry is singing. Bowie's voice spinning on the record has no chance against Larry's world-conquering swell. I could picture people paying attention to Larry in the room adjacent to the kitchen, and Larry paying attention to the people paying attention to him. He will notice that not everyone attending the party is paying attention to him. He will be unhappy. He will leave the room he is singing in and investigate.

"Wish upon wish upon day upon day…"

Joan Jett is the only one in the crowded kitchen not yelling at me. She asks for the knife back. She talks to me through a smirk. Draped shirtless across Joan Jett's bare shoulders, I listen hard. What is she telling me? The noises of "fuck you" and "asshole" are in the way.

"Nothing's going to touch you in these golden years—"

A record scrapes to a halt, and silence.

Larry and the wife stand in Joan Jett's kitchen doorway, Tom the driver pressing in behind them, all with the look on their faces. Maybe you don't know *the look.*

I focus on the movement of Joan's lips. She doesn't want me swooping in too close to her mouth.

"I can tell you what Joan Jett said," offers the wife, in Pomona, wringing out the mop. "She said you might be a pretty cool guy, if you didn't drink so much."

Tommie paused to let that sink in. What I absorbed wasn't so bad.

Picture Joan Jett shouldering the wet, shirtless burden of me—a shot snapped and motionless. It frames up an entertaining memory. If the story ends right there, why this press of descending doom?

Tommie's face said that she had a postscript, and it would include none of her famous laughter.

She tells me the lost bits, the entirety. Claude had fired me from *Slash*, for being drunker than him. Maybe he would not remember. There is more.

"Larry doesn't want to see you, not for a long, long time."

"I remember," I said. I feel like I might throw up. I raise a hand to stop the retelling.

Larry's acting boyfriend is behind the wheel of his Volkswagen at the side of the freeway, headed east toward home, Pomona. It's after 3:00 a.m. A highway patrolman's flashlight flits across the vomit in my lap. The officer is too disgusted to arrest us.

My hips hurt. My head is bouncing. Tom and Larry wrestle one of my ankles each, dragging me across the ground. A moon, stars, all those celestial things orbit up in the sky beyond the faces of strain and disgust. The faces bend closer. One on each side, they have me under the armpits and lift.

"You need to go into the house."

I reject their pity. I punch free, and my naked chest hits the dirt.

"Explain again why you stay with him?"

"You might as well tie a big brick to yourself and jump off a pier."

I crawled down from the voices, away from the front porch, and dug my face like a mole into the turf.

From there, I'd come to, the sun high, my nose pressed into a patch of burned-out front yard. The smell in my nostrils made sense. I knew what it was. I'd known all along, but I'd blotted out knowing. It is vomit and dog shit.

"You're sure you remember everything?" said Tommie. "Come inside. You're going to throw up."

I allowed the screen door to close behind me, and I made it to the bathroom before the consequences heaved out of me in a series of dry spasms and a mouthful of wrenched bile.

We were partitioned from Larry's favor, displaced from the luxury liner of the smooth-sailing golden years. We'd been put off the ship in a crap port. The rich sunsets ahead would saturate one enviable panorama after another, none of them including us.

Let's finish with Larry: Four years on, Larry will be hit by a car while stumbling drunk onto Santa Monica Boulevard, land on his head fifteen yards away, come out of a coma, and be told that drinking alcohol on top of his antiseizure medication will induce convulsions. Larry will drink on top of the medication, and he will collapse in a fit. His right leg will snap beneath his weight. The limb will be pinned by his body for six hours before someone bashes in his bathroom door and drags him onto a stretcher.

An infection contracted in the hospital will necessitate amputating the snapped leg. No one warned Larry that his brain would shrink twenty percent under the twin influences of trauma and medication. He will be hobbling in a walker, dragging along a fake leg as he hits fifty, with no way for anyone to look at the tragedy he has become and be able to picture the promise he had been.

I didn't know any of these disasters were on the way, but as I gripped the toilet seat to pull myself off the floor, I had a feeling Tommie and I wouldn't miss much by being cast out from Larry's lifeboat.

I plant my feet under me, and notice that Tommie has come into the bathroom. She's been there for a moment, maybe more. Now she is looking me in the eyes.

"Nothing a beer wouldn't fix," she says. I'm not seeing laughter, but something wry is in the delivery. "You need to eat. I'll make something."

Relief floods in. She still cares.

Steadied, in the shower, I played the previous night through again. The wife has given me some solace. In my mind's replay, my sequence of ill-conceived actions tracks out much as I imagine it truly did. At the end of the trail of follies, I peel my face off the prickly, dog-crapped turf of the Pomona front yard, and all dignity is not lost.

Joan Jett has said that I might be a pretty cool guy.

SCENE THREE:
JAMMED UP AT THE WHISKY

Complaints were being voiced about Johnny Cougar, voiced at a volume that his singing didn't quite drown out. Johnny Cougar was up at the microphone, in the spotlight at the Whisky a Go Go.

Four of us, Claude and Philomena, the wife and I, were seated at a table beneath the stage lip.

Johnny Cougar could have stepped across the footlights and put his boot down on our ashtrays, if he had been more theatrical.

Tommie and I had moved from Pomona to Venice Beach, overshooting Hollywood by twenty miles and lodging where the debris meets the sea. Venice Beach: the last seaside resort for petrified old junkies, Charles Bukowski, police brutality, and predatory, shoreline hobo clans. Impetuous and independent, the wife had scooted out to Venice ahead of me, staying with Claude and Phil. Claude was the editor of *Slash*, and Phil might as well have been married to him.

The wife was charming the pants off Claude and Phil's more-worldly circle of acquaintances. Like I never tire of saying, they were a little older, a little further traveled, and they had allowed the wife to move into their apartment. Why they housed Tommie, who did nothing for them, and did not house me, who was a contributing writer, made perfect sense to me.

My fear was that I would be stranded all on my own in Pomona, fry cooking and collecting rejection slips. My solution was to pick a fight with the lead chef and take my termination check out to Venice to reclaim the wife.

She and I rented a ground-floor shotgun flat at 40 Brooks Street, half a block from the tetanus sand of Venice Beach. We'd landed jobs selling shoes. The Venice dump was the first place I'd ever lived in that had cockroaches, but it was a short stumble down the strand to Claude and Philly's better place, which is where the wife and I had toddled to mooch a ride out to the Sunset Strip. Destination: the Whisky.

We'd come to see The Jam making their first appearance from England.

British magazines printed The Jam's photos. Rodney on the Roq's radio show had played their demos. Some of us, the ones whose money wasn't tied off elsewhere, even owned The Jam's album. The evidence pointed to The Jam being an actual thing, and we'd taken the drive from Venice to Hollywood's Sunset Strip to test that evidence.

My type always went to *see* the band. We wanted to witness the sounds being made. We wanted to observe their faces, the twitches and involuntary jerks of limb and torso. We wanted to verify that the music meant to them what it meant to us—that the songs came out of a physical necessity. We craved visual proof.

And here we were, mired in an opening act that looked just as contrived as it sounded. Johnny Cougar was a few years shy of a beautiful future of hit songs and accolades, but authentic stardom would only come under his real name, John Cougar Mellencamp. Until then, his act was vulnerable to basic criticisms.

Claude was leading the conversation.

"*Fuck me!* This man is disgusting. He is a product squeezed like sausage into the skin of the intestine. What other byproduct is squeezed into the skin of the intestine? Oh, yes, how could we forget: *shit.*"

All Claude's pronouncements were delivered with a soused Frenchman's queerly stressed English. Who could take that accent seriously? Still, I kept mostly quiet. The soapbox, for the moment, belonged to Claude. He had unfired me from *Slash* a few times throughout the summer; so on this October evening in 1977, I was showing that I had learned some deference.

"These man Cou-gar is a joke and a sham and a masquerade." Claude said *Cou-gar* as if he were speaking of some exotic species of parasite. "There is no art here. There is no soul. There is only the desire for the millionaire mansion in Malibu and the groovy chicks in their Porsche cars. This dream will never happen. *These* man will be back washing the cars by the end of the year. Mark my words, Johnny Cou-gar."

One thing we liked about Johnny Cou-gar was that the drinks were free during his set, so long as we sat at the table to receive them. A management firm was pushing the singer as a fresh voice of the new wave music. His handlers were desperate for Johnny Cougar photos, headlines, and all the credibility a thriving, trusted counterculture publication might bestow.

That meant free drinks for *Slash*. We hadn't fooled everybody, but we'd fooled someone who could run a tab.

Claude used his cigarette to fire up a new one and squinted in the direction of the bar, looking for our waitress with her rack of no-cost doubles.

"There is no culture in America. There is only a confluence of Mafia urges." Claude pronounced Mafia so it partially rhymed with bas-relief. *Mas-fia.* He jutted his scarred nose toward an oily, middle-aged man glowering at the other side of the stage. This guy's shirt was open down to his hairy belly. He had been watching our table with distaste.

Claude pursed his lips toward the guy. "Johnny Cou-gar's manager: *Mas-fia.* The Whisky a Go Go: *Mas-fia.* The record company: *Mas-fia.* The radio stations: *Mas-fia.* The trash trucks that drive away and leave this garbage named Johnny Cou-gar at the microphone: *Mas-fia.*"

Well, nothing lasts forever, to state the obvious. Still, I wasn't so sure that Johnny Cougar's set would ever end, or that Claude's rant would wind down, or that the intermission was not interminable. I did have faith that our free drinks would be cut off, and we were refused a final round just as The Jam came onstage.

The band had an album out, *In the City*, which seemed like it would forever rank next to The Who's *My Generation* as the two best long player debuts in the history of percussive British velocity and volume—at least, that's the kind of phrases I was scribbling on my napkins as the first chords launched off the back of the room.

Singer Paul Weller and the other two guys came on so strong that the drinks weren't really missed: Three mod punks in an electric charge jammed across the stage like pinball people. To say that The Jam changed the atmosphere in the club would be to settle for understatement. It was like the entire venue had been picked up and spun through space and dropped down in a land of infectious excitement where the first great thing of the rest of your great life was happening, to be followed in rapid succession by an ever-extending string of great things.

The club was suddenly packed, and every punk on the floor surged forward.

Tommie puked.

She threw up under the table, mostly unnoticed. She'd been fine through Johnny Cougar, which had been something to heave about.

Tommie raised her head. She had the eyes of the puppy that has just peed on the bed. She took a seat.

"All better?" I demanded.

Her face paled. *Scared looking*, I'd have to say upon reflection.

Philomena spotted the wife's fear and worry; she took Tommie under the arm and they disappeared with it.

The stage lights seemed to refract brighter from The Jam than they had from Johnny Cougar. Even the speed of light was susceptible to their brilliant play.

Philly came back from the women's bathroom.

She pulled my ear down to her mouth. "I'm worried about Tommie." She turned to watch the band.

This is about forty-five seconds into The Jam's second song. Already, you don't want to miss a minute of a show like this. People will be talking about The Jam at the Whisky for the rest of their lives, even if they make it to age thirty. But I am a romantic at heart, with a compelling sense of loyalty and duty; so I surrendered my stage-side vantage and pushed through my friends and contemporaries for the women's bathroom.

The accommodations were less than pristine. Beneath its thinly maintained veneer as a dive, the Whisky was a sewer. My memory paints the walls of the bathroom all in red, with a dim red light over the scratched mirrors and the off-white sinks.

Three of the Whisky's reigning groupie princesses were grouped in front of the mirror and sink. These weren't our type of girls, punk girls, or I would have known them all, by name or by sight, and we would have exchanged chatty banter. These three were established Sunset Strip house girls. They carried themselves—at least in the cramped, smelly shitter at the Whisky—with the pomp of Hollywood rock royalty. They had clustered in the bathroom to escape the noise in the club proper.

These snobs would rather inhale the acrid pinch of vomit and feces than hear The Jam! Our encounter was immediately confrontational.

"Asshole. You can't come in here."

"But here I am, in here. You must be wrong."

My irrefutable logic—and not for the first or the last time—met only outrage.

"Fucker. Get out, fucker."

"Someone's going to kick your ass, fucker."

I behave rashly when I've been drinking. Four or five black Russians make me retaliatory. But the situation was grave. My wife might be imperiled. So even though the free drinks had kicked in, I pleaded: "Show some mercy. Can't you see this is an emergency?"

I squeeze in next to Tommie in the stall. It's smelling bad in there, in the close quarters; I don't have to tell you. The wife seems to have been sapped of all strength. Although her wrist is draped over it, she can't even pull the handle to flush the toilet.

I work around. It's a tight squeeze. Her shoulders are heaving; she's sobbing, then she heaves, then sobbing again. I've seen this girl throw up before, never with the sobbing. I try to reach her face, to let her know that I am at her side. Help has arrived. We are together. I manage to flush the toilet, and the whole atmosphere changes.

The stale, tight air swooshes out, and the sound of The Jam swooshes in. Obviously, the door to the bathroom has opened. I look back, one quick glance, and see for myself. The Whisky princesses are filing out of the shitter, like three glittering turds in platform heels.

I wedge myself astride the toilet so I can observe and comfort Tommie. Barfing is only one of her problems. She's borderline delirious, chanting and pleading and making broad apologies to deity and family.

"I didn't want to lie. I don't want to die. I didn't want to lie."

If I were to listen closely, Tommie might be trying to unburden herself of heavy, crushing secrets, compromising realities hidden from me. A private moment of shared drug ingestion, very recent, that had excluded me might be begging confession.

Or, unlikely as it seems, her self-recriminating supplications might have been directed at someone or something not me at all. How would I have known the difference?

My thoughts are on the princess groupies. Once the three of them are back in the club proper, there's a chance that the little redhead with the lazy eye might break off from peer-pressure consciousness and have a thought of her own, a thought about me. Perhaps she will perceive a depth to me. She will admire the tenderness and compassion with which I tend to Tommie. The female perceives these as arousing qualities. It is only a matter of moments before the squinty redhead returns to the ladies lounge and discretely passes me her phone number while I dab vomit from Tommie's cheeks with wads of dampened toilet paper.

A new gush of real air bursts into the bathroom, along with unfiltered sounds of The Jam. I look back over my shoulder.

A suit comes charging forward. He's younger than the suit who works the door of the Whisky, but he may actually be the older suit's boss. He has a commanding presence. The commanding presence comes from blown-dry hair layered down to the collar of his velvet jacket, from stiletto-trimmed sideburns, and from fat, gold links of chain flashing at the open neck of his shimmering shirt.

The three princess groupies press in behind the suit, honking like a flanking chorus of slattern geese:

"Go ahead; get wise now, fucker."

"Suddenly you're not so smart, asshole."

"Someone's here to *kick your ass!*"

The Whisky suits are not suits as in record company suits or movie executive suits. These are suits as in *Mean Streets* suits.

"I'm going to break his fucking arm."

He means me. I'm not just some perv in the girls' toilet. I'm an underground pop journalist who was drinking free drinks only half an hour ago. But I know the suit means me. He has grabbed me by the neck and pulled me out of the stall.

"That's him," confirms the redhead. "That's the asshole who tried to finger fuck me."

There are times when I have lost hours, half days, whole nights, but I am reasonable and sure, even now, that I made no attempt to finger this woman. The suit has no interest in my credibility.

The redhead mewls: "He's an ass*hole*."

"Calm down, baby. I'm going to break his arm. I told you already."

My skull thuds against some hard and unyielding structural element. Behind me, in the toilet stall, a groan from Tommie underscores the absurdity of my circumstances.

"Break my arm!" I offer the suit. "Then how do you get her out of here?"

He glances at Tommie's lurching back and understands the situation immediately: "What did she take?"

"She only had one beer."

He looked at me and did a simple calculation: Did I think he was a moron? Or was I the moron?

He recognized my idiocy, and his manner softened a bit. He helped me drag Tommie through the bathroom and out the back door. We landed in the familiar parking lot.

"Keep going," said the suit. "Off the property."

Out we go, the suit and me working shoulder to shoulder, rolling the wife to the sidewalk along Clark Street. Tommie projected a stream of vomit, and it ran down the Clark sidewalk toward the Sunset Strip gutter. Where she was finding the fluid, I don't know.

I sat her up against the wall of the Whisky and squatted beside her. We looked natural enough to the environment that the police cruised right past us.

The suit looked down toward Sunset and ran a hand over his hair. Not a strand was out of place. "Was it quaaludes?"

Quaaludes were a coveted soporific manufactured for the legitimate treatment of an inability to take off your clothes in public. I posed the question: "Tommie, did you take two quaaludes when you should have shared one?"

The wife showed no intention of answering.

"She just had one beer. Maybe she ate something rotten."

Tommie could not have been more distant if she'd flat-lined.

"Don't let her choke," advised the young suit. That was the closest thing to a display of kindness that guy had in him. He faded back into the parking lot, and a shadow of loneliness descended in his absence. I tried to pass it off as the October chill. I thought, *Why am I always the outsider? Why am I always the person who misses out?*

I heard the clatter of cha-cha heels and raised my head, intuitively looking for a sign of hope. Little Viva rushed down the Clark Street hill toward us. I loved the wife, but I dreamed of Viva; so I tried to interject some nonchalance between the drooling woman at my side and me.

Viva stopped in front of us on the slanted sidewalk, every inch a self-styled superstar. She stood with her legs apart and one hip jutting. Her boobs jutted as well. Along with her staggering heels, Viva wore the shreds of an oversized T-shirt, clamped at the waist by some style of improvised S&M corseting, and a sense that she'd lost interest in her outfit before coming up with a trouser strategy. My chin was level with her crotch. Everywhere my eyes went, they landed on crotch or boob.

She shook a boob over in Tommie's direction. "What happened to her? I just jerked off an old guy in his car, and he gave me twenty dollars."

Viva flashed a twenty and her imp smile. She winked and hurried on toward the front of the Whisky.

I was scandalized, in a way, feeling sad for Viva, the tragic figure of an exploited waif, and titillated. She'd been very open about possessing that twenty. An offer to share was implicit in revealing the money and in confessing how she'd come to possess it. *In what further ways*, I wondered, *ways to be touched and tasted, might Viva's generosity of spirit express itself?*

During the next forty minutes or so, while my thoughts were variously occupied, a trickle of friends capered by.

They paused in front of Tommie long enough to voice their concerns: "Is she all right?" "What did she take?" "Is there more?"

Then they hurried on to The Jam, reminding me of what I was missing and that I was always missing something.

When would it be okay for me to leave Tommie here on the sidewalk and go back in and see the band? The bass and the drums shook the plaster against my back. It wasn't the same as being in there.

I would look at Tommie. She would seem almost composed enough to leave alone. Then she'd flop sideways onto the sidewalk, and I'd pull her back into position just in time for another pass by the LAPD.

She firmed up as the last encore ended. People straggled out of the club, blissed, and bombed, and slightly deaf. I didn't need to hear a word anyone had to say. I pulled Tommie to her feet, and she steadied herself with one hand on the Whisky wall. I could see in the faces coming from the club that musical history had been witnessed, and I needed to blot out the awareness that I had missed it.

When I opened my eyes again, I was in a car that smelled of gasoline with Daryl Dumb behind the wheel. Problems, or transportation dilemmas at least, solved themselves almost magically in those days. Tommie was in the backseat, more asleep than awake, but stabilized. It seems that while in a blackout, I had browbeaten Daryl Dumb into driving us all the way to Venice.

I turned around in my seat and faced down Tommie.

"What did you mean back there while you were barfing? What was the lie? What was the lie that made you want to not die? What was all that about?"

Her eyes rolled back in her head, but I could fill in that blank stare. Her toilet stall unburdening might have been all about the misty looks I'd seen exchanged between her and Larry's acting boyfriend back in Pomona. Maybe she'd been agonizing over the innocent explanations that showed up every time she wandered off with some wayward gamine or another.

I stewed in silence, traveling the freeway along Pacific Avenue. Daryl Dumb drove right past 40 Brooks.

The new morning, the sales floor at Kinney Shoes, the day's first customers, the store manager, the district supervisor, all these were mere hours away. Daryl Dumb was squandering my precious sleeping moments by trolling the block at two miles per hour.

"Why are you driving around and around? Just stop the car. Let us out."

"I need to find a parking spot," said Daryl Dumb.

God, he was annoying. This pointless driving around pisses me off even now, and Daryl Dumb has been dead for thirty years; so imagine how aggravated I was then.

"You'll never find a parking spot," I explained. "Even smart people don't find parking spots around here. A parking genius couldn't find a parking spot."

Just then, a pickup truck pulled away from the house next door to 40 Brooks. People stopped their cars all hours of the day and night and rushed into that house, then emerged all slow and cool after not a lot of elapsed time. The pickup truck merged like narcotic molasses into the traffic, and Daryl Dumb drifted into the newly vacant space. His tires crunched across the glass of a shattered window.

Part One

I'm out of the car before it's even turned off. I'm pulling Tommie out onto the sidewalk.

"Can I come in?" asks Daryl Dumb. "To use the bathroom?"

"No," says Tommie, finally speaking up. "Out of the question."

A biker couple wanders out from the house next door. They have a child with them, a boy of about five. He's on a leash. It's about 3:00 a.m. Their pickup truck has just been stolen. They don't even ask us if we can describe the thieves. Why waste their breath? The biker dude does slug Daryl Dumb a few times because Daryl has taken his parking place.

We locked Daryl Dumb out of the apartment and fell into our evening routine, turning on the oven to ward off the cold Venice fog and crawling into bed fully clothed.

In the morning, Tommie and I put ourselves together and leave for work. Daryl Dumb is sleeping all twisted up in the back of his car. From what I can see, his face is swollen and bruised. I feel that I am the loser here, between the two of us, because I am wearing one of my father's discarded suits, and I'm on my way to sell cheap goods at Kinney Shoes on Lincoln Boulevard in Venice.

Unconscious in the back of his car, Daryl Dumb had the day off. Again. And he had seen The Jam.

Tommie stands at the bus stop across Pacific Avenue, mirroring me. We are headed in opposite directions. Cars and light trucks hurtle by in the roadway between us.

If I didn't know Tommie, I might have glanced over as her bus sighed to a stop. I might have imagined a rich and leisurely life with her.

The wife's bus steamed away. I watched, furious about what I was wearing and where I was headed to wear it.

SCENE FOUR:
DRAG QUEEN HALLOWEEN

Waking life dragged me back from a dream of thwarted escape and dropped me in the morning murk. I had a headache, nausea, and no memory of going to bed. The sheets were clinging. My body was naked and wet. A smell I didn't recognize lingered for a whiff and quickly fled.

Again, the eternal questions chattered while I shivered: Where am I? Am I alone? How did I land in a dump like this?

When you start asking the eternal questions, the answers always lead to deeper discouragement. These questions only pop up when dismay is certain. Have I pissed the bed? Will somebody ever, please, help me figure out what is wrong with me?

Jesus stared down from a crucifix on the nearest wall. I was at the place called home.

The wife and I had rented a cold, dim, cramped flat in Venice Beach, California. We'd moved there from the sunny and spacious Inland Empire, and we drove out nightly from our shorefront residence to Hollywood punk shows and parties.

The orbit of our acquaintances had expanded in a big bang way. It was as if the shady sun of some shadowy new solar system was at the place where Tommie, and I, and the *Slash* people and the first six or seven LA punk bands, and the people hanging on with those bands, all spun on our peculiar axis. The wife and I were part of the originating nucleus, at the center of the sphere of influence. We were learning what it felt like to be part of an inner circle.

Most evenings spiraled out during the early morning at the Plunger Pit, a one-room apartment just off Santa Monica Boulevard, behind Circus of Books. The Plungers—Trudie, Trixie, Mary Rat, Hellin Killer, and Viva—were so punk they didn't need to form a band. Their place was trashed beyond salvage.

Fifty of us would squeeze into a space designed for single occupancy. No one ever had any money. Touring bands that played the Starwood would swagger over. They'd be from New York, or Ohio, or occasionally from London, and they would have record deals and singles that commercial radio stations were refusing to play and albums that stores couldn't sell.

Sometimes we let them in. The Plunger Pit was a place you really didn't want to venture into unless you belonged there. If you passed out, you ended up cuffed to the bed frame. Some kids, you sensed, passed out on purpose.

So, upon awakening in Venice, I could assume that the truant portions of the previous evening had contained some small Hollywood adventure, an adventure I would now pay for. A trace of fragrance hinted at exotic encounters just beyond recall.

Drinking and blacking out from drinking, once it starts happening, becomes familiar right away. You never really get used to it. Lying there, twisted in the stomach and the brain, knowing after a bit where I was, I searched for stray sense memories that might fill in the blank of where I'd been.

Some things were open to deduction. Tommie had slid out of the bed ahead of me. I was able to figure that out.

Our apartment was all in a line, two small rooms, plus a sliver of a kitchen and a closet where they'd stashed a shower and toilet.

Listening hard, I tried to pinpoint Tommie in that layout and determine what she was doing and her present opinion of me. I couldn't quite.

The windows at the head of the bed looked out onto the sidewalk of Brooks Avenue. Except we had been advised to keep the windows covered; so they didn't look out onto anything. The street view lacked charm, and intruders had been climbing in through ground level windows and carrying off electronic goods and other portables through the front doors.

Venice had problems beyond its pests. Dampness from ocean fog was a morning constant. Every day's outlook was literally dampened.

While a guest of *Slash*'s Claude and Philomena, Tommie had rejected this apartment a few days prior to when, on my own, I'd handed over the cash for our first and last. In the months of our 40 Brooks occupancy, a bitter glaze was always close to her eyes.

Somewhere in that small, confined space, Tommie was lost to me. Just like the details from six hours earlier were somewhere in my mind, but beyond my access.

"Get up," called the wife. I placed her in the kitchen.

The Kinney Shoes sales floor had an appointment with me. The sales floor didn't like me being late.

I needed underpants.

I gazed down into the clothes hamper. I sensed hostile organisms mixed in deep with the laundry. Apprehension shivered through me. Even if, let's say, I'd woken up cognizant and optimistic, clothes at 40 Brooks were always cold and clammy with morning fog, even clean clothes. I was out of clean clothes.

I grabbed a pair of used boxer shorts from the top garment layer. There was trouble with the boxer shorts. I saw a brown streak along the seam of the crotch. I groaned.

"What's wrong now?" demanded Tommie from another room.

Had I started shitting my pants?

People I couldn't be bothered to hang out with anymore had warned me that I was losing my grip; that things would only get worse. They'd cautioned me that I was slipping away, that I didn't recognize them when I was drunk, that I was forfeiting my potential future to drugs and alcohol.

Fuck those people. I had business to attend to, the business of becoming the new me.

But no one had hinted that I might take a drink and shit my pants.

I snuck the spoiled boxers into the bathroom. What was my plan? Flush the evidence? Throw the shit britches out the window, the window that had been nailed shut? I took a breath, for calmness—a deep breath.

The smell coming up from the underwear was musky, not fecal. Emboldened, I rubbed the brown smear between my fingers. The color spread evenly. It was mascara! No, shit! I recognized the stink—*patchouli!*

Today, the patchouli scent is universally reviled as the smell of hippie. Back then, the pungent body oil was wafting off of all types of sexually adventurous, empowered women of all ages.

The wife bumped around on the other side of the bathroom door. She never wore that patchouli shit, and she wanted answers, starting with, "Are you ever getting out of there?"

Sometimes an odor brings back an entire experience whole—like it or not. Poor Tommie. Pounding on the hollow toilet door, and the bathroom was empty. I'd been hooked by the nose and whisked to the night before:

I was walking along Santa Monica Boulevard with Claude Bessy and some handsome and virile compatriot of Claude's from France. The French dude wore a skintight, striped T-shirt with the sleeves rolled high to showcase the erectile set of his biceps. He had lifted the T-shirt from the wardrobe chest of a TV show he built sets for.

Penis Arms, Claude, and I were strolling to a liquor store—I could feel the destination in my step.

We were on a supply run for the Plunger Pit. The Frenchman had offered to make the run, and I'd volunteered to accompany. The Germs were at the Plunger Pit, giving out their Germs burns, a sort of initiation mark applied by a member of the Germs with the hot tip of a cigarette.

The Germs had pressed a record with the song "Forming" on one side, and something less than a song on the other side, and impressionable kids, of twenty or whatever age, desperate for belonging, were lining up to have Terry or Bobbi push the glowing tip of a lit cigarette into the flesh under their wrists. This Marlboro branding produced a round welt and scar—the Germs burn!

The branding process also produced a heightened frenzy around the arrival of any alcohol. If you wanted to snare a drink in this environment, you accompanied the Frenchman with the penis arms on his booze run.

I urged the Frenchies to hurry and keep up with my pace. Far more women than usual flexed for attention in the 1:00 a.m. West Hollywood crowd. West Hollywood was called Boys Town, and not due to charity institutions renowned for housing youthful male delinquents. Delinquent young males were, in fact, a prominent West Hollywood demographic, but the boys played right out on the streets, working those streets, working especially the stretch of Santa Monica Boulevard between the Plunger Pit and the closest liquor store.

Except this night, oddly, the delinquent female form seemed to be resurgent. The gay boys, as if to compensate for the oddly abundant female presence, had draped themselves in outlandish ensembles, beyond their extravagant norm.

Halfway to the liquor store, I passed Anita Bryant.

Anita Bryant was an apex celebrity in 1978. Her name was synonymous with a sweeping national movement to demonize homosexuality. I had never seen the former Miss Oklahoma outside of TV commercials for Florida orange juice, or denouncing homosexuals on news shows.

Here she was on Santa Monica Boulevard, in West Hollywood, in the flesh. And costumed all slutty and raped and ravaged. *Costumed* is the key word here.

"It's Anita Bryant!" I accosted Penis Arms and Claude. "We've got to take her back to the Plunger Pit!"

"Get a grip, Basho," shouted Claude. "For fuck's sake! It's Halloween."

That explained so much. I muted my response to all the flamboyant characters of stage and screen passing by. The Village People, for instance, were just regular Boys Town boys in masquerade. Still, the surge in delinquent female forms along the boulevard was unusual.

Part One

The French dude picked up the bill at the liquor store. He worked on TV shows; so he had money. He also had quaaludes, and I mooched one.

Have we talked about quaaludes and what they did? This about sums it up: I blinked my eyes, and it was later.

I was in a doorway near the Plunger Pit, sitting on a step. The scent of patchouli swirled around me. In hindsight, with wisdom, I realize that the hippie stench had jarred me out of a methaqualone blackout.

Since taking the Quaalude on Santa Monica Boulevard, I'd been walking around doing things that required decisions being made, with no awareness that I was walking around, never mind that decisions were being made. I was acutely aware, now, of the circumstances those decisions had put into place.

My pants were around my ankles, with my boxers spread at my shins. A head of long, blonde hair dipped and rose in my crotch. My cock was being blown. Patchouli waves dipped and rose with the blonde hair. My eyes adjusted. The blower was not Tommie. Imagine my delight!

If you'd asked me while I was in the right mind or chemical mood, I was deeply infatuated with my wife, in love even, but variety is the great sexual enhancer. I was rigid and thrumming and ready to pop.

I pawed the hair of my fellator. I stroked the lucky and generous lass's cheek. My fingers rasped on stubble. Like in a beard.

My cock responded with immediate wilting. A moment later, the rest of me caught up with my penis and processed this grave disappointment. That face in my lap was a man's. Halloween costuming, it dawned on me, had steered me wrong.

The blower, not wanting to lose the moment to limpness, worked harder, sucking with clearly male pops and slurps. I pitched in, rocking my hips and thrusting. I put more into the motion than I felt.

Dude or not, I didn't want to hurt anyone's feelings, especially not the feelings of someone who had agreed to put my dick into his mouth. I wanted to finish this exchange on friendly terms. An erection would go a long way to remaining pals.

I pictured all the girls that were on my current masturbation wish list. There was Viva, of course, and Alice and Patricia from the Bags, and the ones we called the Doublemint Twins. The other four Plunger girls; I couldn't forget them. What a great quantity of fantasy seductresses I'd harbored! A Cuban coworker from Kinney shoes tangoed into view; her pelvis did some kind of samba-limbo toward my chin.

I lined up all my mind's-eye prospects, single and in combinations, stark naked and in outfits like that which Anita Bryant had paraded out onto Santa Monica Boulevard. I visualized them resisting, aggressing, assisting. None of it did any good. *Flaccid* is the word that sprang to mind.

As a last resort, I pictured Tommie. If I didn't shoot a load soon, I pictured her coming out of the Plunger Pit for a little quiet and air and catching me with my penis being mouthed by some skeeve in a ratty wig. Still, no tumescence.

I felt like an idiot. What kind of wheedling had placed this earnest cocksucker and myself into this false position? Surely, I hadn't paid actual money!

I consoled my slurping friend: "Hey, look, it's not your fault. It won't work. I've been selling my dick up and down the Boulevard. I shot five wads in two hours. There is just nothing left."

My wigged lover accepted this excuse at face value. Even then, I wondered what it said about me that a free-loving drag queen believed without hesitation—with a sigh and a crooked smile—that I had been prostituting myself to multiple anonymous men.

I returned to the Plunger Pit to look for the wife. The quaalude I'd taken seemed to make me friendly. I talked to people I didn't like, and was convivial and interested in what they said. I'd have to be careful with that stuff.

I remembered standing at the refrigerator, disappointed that all the beer was gone, talking to a guy who I thought was Cliff Hanger, the Germs drummer of the moment. The guy had hidden two quarts of beer in a produce drawer, and he split one with me. Someone nearby smelled of patchouli.

"Why do you keep calling me Cliff?" he said.

He insisted we'd already met, and he acted surprised that I failed to recognize him.

Sometime after that, I'd taken the wheel of our car, and then I was at home the next morning, stalling on the toilet, clutching a pair of soiled and smelly underpants.

"Allan, whatever you're doing in there, do it faster!" The wife! "We're late for work!"

Slobber. Mascara. Patchouli. I girded myself and pulled on the dirty boxers.

PART TWO: TWO-BEER MORNING

"I'm okay. I'm all right."
—Daryl Dumb's last words

PREMONITION SCENE: SCAB IN THE BARREL

A party isn't really a party until you've splintered off and locked yourself away in someone else's bathroom with one or two special friends. This is as true at ten on a Thursday morning as it is at 3:00 a.m. on a Saturday night.

I was downstairs from my apartment at the Canterbury Arms Hotel, barricaded in the bathroom of an abandoned unit. In half an hour, I had a meeting with executives from A&M Records to discuss guerilla promotion for a band called The Dickies.

A&M had agreed to come to me. Our phone rapport had been strong—things were looking up, I sensed. Within weeks, I might have a secretary, new clothes, better drugs.

The wife awaited the arrival of the A&M executives upstairs, at my home, while Russ, Hellin Killer, me; we knelt on discolored tile one story below, keeping our heads only a whisper away from one another.

Our elbows touched on the toilet seat. It's not as sordid as it sounds. The abandoned bathroom was appreciably cleaner than the active bathrooms of our Canterbury Arms friends, those likeminded neighbors who we had shut ourselves away from.

Nobody cool shoots up angel dust. The angel dust is why we were being quiet, embarrassed, and secretive about our shared activity, without having discussed it. I pressed down on the plunger. Something weird could happen here.

SCENE ONE:
INTO THE CANTERBURY ARMS

A few more months of morning fog, and living at the beach didn't seem like a bright idea. Only our Venice shoe store careers anchored us at the shore. The real business of living drew us night after night to Hollywood's Masque.

The Masque was not a nightclub in the accepted sense. There was no marquee out front. Inside, no booths, no tables, no bar, no waitresses, no amenities or comforts whatsoever. The "club" was located in a brick maze of storage rooms below Hollywood Boulevard's XXX Pussycat Theater.

Entry was through a steel door in a dark alley. A sleepy, 300-pound security guard, belly hanging over his gun belt, would take your two bucks—or absorb your spiel as to why you were exempt from shelling out the two bucks. From there on in, it was every surly and bruised twenty-something adolescent for him or herself.

The Masque was like a closed secret; a defended enclave for one hundred or so people whose previous experience of exclusivity was to be excluded. Even then, when the seventies were as modern as it was humanly possible to be, you should have known the cachet wouldn't last for long.

Venice Beach was too far from the action.

Russ had moved into the Canterbury Arms Hotel, a thirties garden-court building north of Hollywood Boulevard, about two hundred yards up Cherokee Avenue from The Masque.

Everybody we knew from The Masque and the other places we went to knew Russ, too. He wore a leather jacket, square, dark sunglasses and straight leg black jeans, and he sometimes treated his hair with peroxide. He'd lived in New York and seen the Ramones at CBGBs. Everywhere everybody went, Russ went there, too.

The wife and I were at his housewarming. We were the whole housewarming.

"Let me show you around the place," said Russ. "No, don't get up."

The single room had come furnished, including the sofa we sat on. A bed pulled out from the wall. Russ had taped a row of *Slash* magazine covers across the paneling that hid the bed. We admired the kitchen from where we were sitting. A bathroom was behind the only doorway. The windows from the living room looked down on the flagstones of the courtyard, three floors below. We'd played the one Stranglers album three times through.

"Venice seemed nice," said Tommie, "but everywhere you step, it's dog shit and junkies."

"I was on the bus," I said, "and somebody shot out the window right in front of my face."

Russ had heard this story already; everybody had heard it.

"We have a car now," said Tommie, moving on.

"You'll never get shot in this building," said Russ. He'd been living at the Canterbury for less than a week. "Last night the manager stabbed a burglar."

"Did they arrest him?"

"Too late. He bled to death, right there in the lobby." Russ pointed to the windows overlooking the courtyard and the entrance gate. "The cops came and called someone to take the body away."

Whatever drugs we were taking to celebrate the homecoming ran out. We walked south from the Canterbury and passed three distinct hubs of prostitution—one each for dudes, the trans spectrum, and born women. Everyone had something nice to say to us. We crossed Hollywood Boulevard and arrived at The Masque.

Suddenly, I became aware of myself behind the wheel of the car, driving the long haul back to the Venice shore.

The wife looked skeptical in the passenger seat. By the time we'd found a place to park the car and crawled in between the damp sheets of 40 Brooks, it was 4:00 in the morning. Our sales floors expected us at nine.

Two days later, 10:00 a.m., we were back at the Canterbury, dressed in our shoe-selling best. Tommie stood over a discolored patch in the lobby floor.

"This must be where the burglar bled to death," she said.

The Canterbury manager joined us.

"He's an animist," Russ had warned us. "Do you know what that is?"

Evidently, an animist was some sort of African American religious zealot. The Canterbury manager wore a beaded skullcap, loose, plain garments, and an air of grave reserve behind a gray-specked beard. When he spoke, the big surprise was that his accent was not foreign.

"Why do you want to move in here?"

"The location is central," answered Tommie. She'd prepped for the question.

He sized us up quietly for a moment. "Have you any children?"

Tommie and I looked to make sure we were still ourselves. Our eyes carried mismatched sets of bursting luggage, and it wasn't some procreative responsibility loading us down. *Children!* Who was he kidding? Maybe the guy was insane as well as religious.

In the tiny elevator, we got a close-up of the animist. The gray-specked beard did a good job of covering a jagged scar from one corner of his mouth back to the clench of the corresponding jaw. The elevator door opened. We stepped into a hallway and away from the scar.

"Do you want furnished or unfurnished?"

I didn't know what he was talking about.

"We have a kitchen table," said Tommie. "The rest we'll need furnished."

The first apartment he showed us had smoke damage all along the back wall and a stack of wigs in one corner. I suspected movement in among the wigs.

"Can we see it with the lights on?"

"The lights are on."

"I don't really like the way this room smells," said Tommie.

This information caused the slightest ripple in the animist's grave reserve. "You consider yourselves a fancy couple."

He took us up to a one-bedroom suite on the fourth floor, on the outer corner of the building, giving excellent surveillance of Hollywood Boulevard to the south and west. All three local hubs of prostitution could be monitored from here.

The manager selected a passkey from a ring, unlocked the door, and pulled aside a strand of yellow police tape. The wife and I balked at the tape.

"This tape is routine. Really. A girl has fallen from the windows. Naturally, the police investigate."

A raspy, deep voice boomed from inside the suite: "You know what's good for you, you best stay out."

The wife and I backed away. The manager showed no patience. He looked at me in a way that was meant to belittle. His attitude was at odds with the religious bent of his skullcap.

Somehow, I'd failed to grasp the significance that the Canterbury's manager had fatally stabbed an intruder in the lobby. The avenging knife-man and the grave animist showing us apartments were the same human.

We settled on a single apartment on the top floor, the fourth floor, just up the hall from the police tape, with a bed that pulled out of the wall. We were moved in by dark.

That first night, after drinking to excess, we walked home from The Masque. Drugs also were involved. Rather than driving across town and out to the shore, the wife and I took the tiny elevator up to our new home, congratulating ourselves on a smooth move.

The elevator lurched and stopped at the fourth floor. The door rattled open.

Maybe five feet beyond our apartment door, a white girl scuttled across the carpet on her back with her legs in the air. A black man was trying to move close to her. She kept him off with well-placed up-kicks. Both parties were very angry, and vocal about being angry. You couldn't really make out the words.

The girl wore boots up to her knees with thick cha-cha heels. She was in her twenties; if her parents had been looking for her, they'd given up by now. The man was from an earlier generation; he might as well have been forty. He wore a long coat and a pair of platform shoes that had outlived their time by at least five years.

The man crouched and sprang forward, weaving his hands out between his face and the kicking girl. Beneath the screeching, she seemed calm and proficient. A cha-cha heel flashed through the man's snaky arms and caught him square under the jaw.

Tommie and I moved deep back into the elevator. I hit the close door button, but it had stalled out. We stepped out into the hallway, casually, minding our own business.

Catching a second heel in the face changed the tone of the event for the guy. Despite his previous death threats and vile vocabulary, clearly he had only been playing. He lunged at the flat-backing woman, ignored a boot square in his crotch, and caught her by the hair. That grip was the advantage he needed.

Coat flapping, the black man dragged the white woman by the ponytail. She slid down the hall, away from our door, struggling, crying out in pain and outrage, clutching her head. Her feet kicked at the empty air behind her.

Tommie and I were scared. It was also an awkward social moment.

With a sick, ripping sound, the woman's hair tore loose from her skull and came away in her companion's hands.

"He's scalped her! Allan! Do something!"

Shock stopped me midbreath. Then I saw...

"It's not as bad as it looks," I said.

The woman's wig had come unhinged. For an instant, the man stood baffled, the tresses lax in his fist. Then he began whipping his girl with her wig.

The verbal exchange escalated. Tommie and I stood frozen outside the door to our apartment. It was impossible to make out anything in the screeches and recriminations, other than "bitch" and "cocksucker." Really, there wasn't much else.

"Don't you look over here, bitch," the man said. It was the voice that had rasped from within the apartment with the police tape. He was talking to Tommie or to me.

The girl clawed her companion's face. Over her shoulder, she sneered. "Mind your own fucking business!"

We slid inside our apartment and wedged our combined weight against the door. The walls shook—the hallway combatants had evidently risen to their feet and were body-slamming the walls. Our deadbolt rattled, and the doorframe seemed flimsy.

"What if we need help?" said Tommie. There was no phone in the apartment. No way out except the one door into the hall, or through the windows and four stories below.

It had gotten quiet out in the hallway.

"Shhh. Maybe it's okay." I put my ear to the door and listened for sounds of muffled death. "Should we make a run for it?"

Tommie returned my whisper: "Where would we go?"

She opened the windows to the courtyard. The drop was no way out, and not even high enough for a certain suicide. The summer night air was thick and still out there. Perhaps our screams for help would be heard.

Cautiously, we pulled the bed down out of the wall, keeping the creaking of the mechanism to a minimum. Tommie yanked a blanket and a sheet from one of our moving boxes. Clearly, our high had been blown. We took off some of our clothes and settled in, too afraid to let the crusty mattress creep us out.

Our last two hundred dollars had been put up for the Canterbury security deposit. The animist would never refund them. And we'd stiffed the Venice place for a month on our way out. Prone in the murk, Tommie and I looked into each other's frightened, wide eyes. There was no moving back.

A deep voice boomed from the courtyard: "Danny."

The voice was different from the one in the hall, not raspy but nasty nonetheless. From four floors down, it sounded like a large, angry man was craning his neck at our window and shouting directly in. "Danny, come out here. I'm not daring you. I'm telling you."

A steady *clack, clack, clack* came up from the courtyard stones, moving away, pacing toward the street, and back again. Heel strikes.

I slipped out of bed. On hands and knees, I moved to the courtyard window.

"Get back here!" hissed Tommie. She was worried about what might befall me at the window. She cared. Plus, she didn't like being left alone.

I peeked above the ledge. The noise was coming from a heavyset, middle-aged white guy. He commanded a German shepherd on a short lead. Tommie's face popped up next to mine.

"Is he a cop?" I whispered.

"Don't let him hear you," whispered Tommie. Her cheek touched mine.

The man in the courtyard paced back and forth—*clack, clack, clack.* His gruff voice reasoned with this unseen Danny character.

"I'm not coming in there, Danny. You're coming out." His eyes scanned the windows that overlooked the courtyard. Tommie and I ducked our heads and crawled back to bed.

The voice was louder. "Danny! You're making me angry."

Danny said nothing in return. The wife and I cowered under our blanket. I smelled the fog and mildew of Venice Beach in the bedding, the beloved fog and mildew of Venice.

"Are you so selfish, Danny? Are you so selfish and small? Danny! Will you really be so selfish and small?"

The guy in the courtyard stopped his guttural baiting. The silence was unnerving. I couldn't fix a position on the man and his dog until he was joined by, I guess, Danny. The dog barked two or three times, yelped, and was quiet. Two voices went lower, conversational, receding. The dog man's heels clacked on the flagstones, moving off to the courtyard gate and—I assumed—beyond. Finally, quiet.

The wife and I relaxed a bit. We touched one another's faces. A gunshot sounded, right around the corner from the courtyard gate. Neither of us mentioned it.

The *click, clack* of the dog man's heels moved back through the courtyard and into the building.

Over the weekend, four or five of our friends would move into the Canterbury. In two weeks time, there would be fifty of us. Everybody knew they were going to be famous before the year was out.

SCENE TWO:
MARKETING GENIUS

The old tightwads at *Slash* refused to cough up a dime for my writing, no matter how hard I squeezed. All I wanted was some token payment, just enough for a couple of quaaludes every week. But *Slash* would let me quit before they'd give me fifty bucks a month. I know this to be true because publisher entrepreneur Samioff and his soused French editor Claude kept their wallets in their pockets and watched me walk away, an ex-*Slash* writer hacking out my solitary path.

A path to where, I couldn't tell myself. It's not like I was a fan, the lowest type of life form; so what was I doing being stoned every day at all these punk rock venues and living at the Canterbury, where everyone was always forming another new band?

I wondered: *Would I still get into The Masque for free?* I wasn't even in possession of a guitar. In truth, I looked down on people who formed bands. They were trying too hard; they needed to prove something. They might as well be in college, studying for careers.

Proving anything was a waste in my mind. I comprehended that I'd forfeited my relevance by quitting *Slash*. Why not reject that tired, false concept of relevance? Being relevant was a thing hippies out to save the planet did. I had myself to consider.

Principles aside, I was sad, dejected, despairing of ever being paid for the word. Conditions were perfect for giving up, but a publicity assistant at A&M Records called in with an assignment! I'd been smoking hash oil when the phone rang, and the conversation went on without me for a few minutes.

Who is this woman, I said to myself, *and who gave her my phone number?*

"You're the guy who calls himself Basho Macko. The one who writes for *Slash*, right?"

I grappled with how to clarify that relationship, and she closed the deal, ordering three fanciful pages of copy about what The Dickies meant to Los Angeles.

The Dickies were a local novelty band that played Saturday morning cartoon theme songs in the hyper tempo and pitch of England's Buzzcocks. The Dickies meant to LA whatever drivel I might type out in half an hour. That's what I mailed off to A&M, and a record company owed me 150 dollars, almost my entire month's rent. I'd lived to see the day—I was a professional.

A few weeks later, an A&M publicity assistant alerted me to drop by the record company offices, on La Brea just south of Sunset, and accept my check by hand.

Less than two miles beyond the Canterbury's perimeter of yellow police tape, the A&M world lay in some unknown corner of space alien to mine. I was reluctant to visit on my own; so I enlisted Viva to join the excursion. She was adventurous and bold, the kind of girl who hitchhiked on a whim and plucked twenty bucks off the driver with a spur-of-the-moment handjob. She and I were coworkers.

Tommie had met a pair of wild black girls wearing blue blazers and navy slacks on the bus and chatted herself into a job as an attendant at the traveling Treasures of Tutankhamen exhibit, currently on show at the LA County Museum of Art. The position offered a temporary career in crowd control guaranteed to terminate in a series of unemployment checks.

Tommie dragged Russ and Viva into King Tut's personnel office, and the museum hired them on. The work consisted of lurking among priceless golden artifacts unearthed from an ancient Egyptian king's tomb and bullying patrons who dared to touch the display cases. I ditched the shoe selling and followed my peers. The museum job perfectly fit my greatest ambition: to ultimately be paid for not working.

Each of us had a day off during the week, occasionally mine coincided with Viva's, so while Russ and Tommie stood guard over the treasures of King Tut's grave, on loan from Egypt, I steered the car south on La Brea.

The car was out of date, a square, blue Ford fit for a modest family of four. Viva splayed across the passenger area. She lit a joint, and I opened my second beer of the journey. Beer foam bubbled in my nose. Viva was my favorite Plunger at that moment. All five Plungers had been evicted from the Plunger Pit and were having sleepovers at the Canterbury. Plunger Trudie had an actual residence there, and a live-in boyfriend who paid for it.

Viva flung an arm across the back of the seat and cocked one leg up on the armrest. "You sure you don't want any of this?"

She meant the weed. I was sure I wanted none of it. The stuff made me nervous. I needed confidence.

Viva sucked the joint down to her nails. She wore a sheer, clinging thrift-store dress and a pair of twenty-year-old glamour heels. She also wore angular slashes of makeup across her cheeks and a sheen of KY lubricant in her spiked hair. That is absolutely everything she was wearing. I am sure.

Like so much else, Viva affected my nervous system. She may have been the wrong choice as companion to A&M Records, a destination freighted with anxiety all its own.

More than an office complex, the A&M headquarters was a compound—there were recording studios, a private cul-de-sac, armed guards, and bungalows full of people so socially adept that I needed a security badge just to be allowed in their midst. These people knew things beyond what I knew, and they would know better than I knew precisely what I did not know.

I veered toward a parking spot on the street.

"What are you doing?" said Viva.

"The parking meter. I'm taking it to the parking meter."

"What's wrong with you? Do you think your car isn't good enough for the security guard?"

The faded-blue Ford had two doors and a roomy back seat. It was old, by about a decade, and would never be a collector's item. Record company people, it was common knowledge, drove impractical classics.

"I don't know what you're talking about," I said.

A meter opened up right next to the A&M driveway. We were closer to where we needed to go than if I'd parked inside on the lot. Things could only be looking up. I finished off that second beer with one pull. Prudently, I had not brought along a third can.

Out in the sunlight, Viva's dress worked its charm. The clingy wrap clearly illustrated it was all she had on. The man in the security booth walked us to the door we needed. He stood and watched while we hesitated.

"You don't have to knock. Just go right in."

I couldn't have anticipated an office setting—with its hierarchy of desks, cubicles, private rooms, and bustle of workers—to be a familiar one. The atmosphere in the A&M publicity pen came from another planet. A party seemed to be in progress. No actual music was to be heard, only Supertramp. Hatred of Supertramp was strictly enforced in the circles that Viva and I revolved in, but any discerning human with ears should know to despise that band's entire catalog without being told. The A&M employees appeared to be dancing to Supertramp at their workstations.

The girl at the reception desk looked like she had never worked a day in her life, and would never be forced to, just based on her looks. She hit me with a smile that was perhaps amplified with irony, maybe lightly medicated.

I dropped the name of the guy who was supposed to supply me the check; let's call him Chuck.

"Give a little bit," harmonized Supertramp, "give a little bit of your love to me."

The front desk girl spun in her chair, 540 degrees.

A fellow of thirty-plus in a suit was dancing silently behind her, on a trajectory to a corner office. His hair was razor-cut, over the collar, neither blond nor brown. His dance was some hybrid of the twist and the hustle, in slow motion. My impression was that this was the way he moved from place to place at all times. He was too cool for simple walking.

"Hey, Chuck," said the girl. "These people are here to see you?"

"What do they want!" Chuck demanded.

"I'm here to pick up a check," I said.

"They want a check," said the girl. She started her chair spinning again.

"There's so much we need to share," sang Supertramp. "So send a smile and show you care."

Chuck stared at the spinning girl: "Why do they think we owe them a check?"

"I wrote the Dickies story," I said.

"This one says he wrote a Dickies story," relayed the girl.

Chuck thought it over, maintaining eye contact with the girl in the spinning chair.

"I remember that," he told her.

"Should they see you now?" she asked.

"So give a little bit," sang Supertramp. Chuck sang along. "Give a little bit of your time to me."

Chuck waved us off. "Lindsay will handle them."

Chuck shuffled into what I assumed was Chuck's office. Was he truckin'? Was he a truckin' hippie in a suit?

"Have a seat," said the girl at the front desk. But there were no chairs.

Viva sat on the front girl's desk and gazed upon me as if I were a major talent. The receptionist continued performing her tasks—answering telephones, filling envelopes—working around my friend's ass.

Bringing Viva along had been the right choice after all. The two-beer preparation had also been correct, as had refraining from anxiety-inducing marijuana. I was juiced at exactly the right voltage. The dancing tools at A&M Records might make me wait, but they couldn't make me awkward.

The wait wasn't long.

Lindsay came out from Chuck's assumed office. Lindsay was my age, maybe two years older, with social skills a decade ahead. Women have so many more opportunities for sophistication at that age. Lindsay wore low-waist flared slacks, and her hair was layered in an unruly shag. The message of her hair was obvious: she'd just finished fucking Chuck in his office.

Viva had a question for Lindsay: "Have you people been listening to that Supertramp album for the entire year?"

"Mr. MacDonell!" Lindsay extended a hand. "Finally we meet!" We shook on it.

She was the picture of all-business propriety. Except that she was wearing panties on the outside of her slacks.

Viva and I followed Lindsay's panties deeper into the party atmosphere. Assistants and interns danced in place and stared at Viva, then at me, with wide-eyed, grinning wonder.

"They do a lot of coke here," observed Viva.

"Sit down," said Lindsay. She indicated a pair of chairs adjacent to her desk. She mounted her chair, legs spread like a cowboy, and wheeled out to face us. Was I supposed to not mention the underpants outside the slacks?

Lindsay treated me to a huge smile and an enthusiastic testimonial about how much she had enjoyed what I'd written. She was looking forward to reading more from me. She was certain that we would work together frequently and long into the future.

Almost as an afterthought, she produced the check, slid it into an envelope, licked the flap, and left her tongue hanging out. She sealed the check inside.

She led Viva and me out of the party. I couldn't keep my mind off those panties. Lindsay waved from the doorway, and the sunlight hit us. We were out on La Brea. My car came into sight.

"Lindsay is already back in there blowing Chuck," said Viva. "And snorting more coke."

Viva laughed it all off, but something like a fixation took hold in my mind.

I started the car, took a hit on some weed, and then the Canterbury hove into sight.

"You got your money," said Viva, interrupting me. "So why are you thinking so much?"

"I am not thinking."

I took my check upstairs and waited for Tommie.

The wife came in from crowd-controlling King Tut throngs. She was pissed, having stood on her feet all day. The Tut exhibit was in its last weeks. We'd worked there long enough. When the artifacts moved on, and we were laid off, we would luxuriate in our unemployment money. The doper lottery!

I showed Tommie the A&M check. It didn't make her as happy as I would have liked.

Black Randy arrived unannounced. Black Randy was a white guy, not as old as the *Slash* people, but a few years beyond my mean age. Randy was chubby; he was also a performer and a big thinker. He carried a bag of beer. See? He thought of everything.

Randy's arrival didn't make Tommie any happier. She disguised her displeasure by going into the kitchen and frying up a dozen potato-and-pickle tacos.

I cracked a beer, and Randy cracked a beer, and he suggested I should refrigerate the rest of them. I never would have thought of that. Not counting open bottles, barely a six-pack and a half remained. Keeping them on the couch between us appealed to my love of efficiency, but Randy was a guest; so I carried the bag of beers in through the kitchen.

I paused at the open refrigerator door, sucking down a bonus beer, watching grease pop in a pan under Tommie's supervision. It seemed as though tears were bubbling up in Tommie's eyes and plopping into the grease popping around the tortillas folded in the pan.

This sadness was alien and contrary to Tommie's characteristic ebullience, to her natural enthusiasm and raw curiosity, all the up qualities that had plucked me out of my gloomy depth of self and into love with her in the first place. Tommie's bruised beauty pained me, as an observer and as a suspect.

I returned to the sofa. While Black Randy talked, I tried to not think about what I had thought in the kitchen.

Tommie deserved happiness. If I had more A&M checks, like a stack of ten, surely she would be obliged to perk up?

Tommie plated the food, and Randy acted all giddy about potato-and-pickle tacos. You believed he really wanted those tacos—because he was chubby. His first record, an epic punk paean to a mythic pitched battle between the LAPD and the feral boy hookers of Hollywood Boulevard called *Trouble at the Cup*, had been released to unanimous critical acclaim. Unanimous acclaim from me in *Slash*, that is, where I would acclaim no more.

Randy had ideas about how to make money. Aside from being a recording artist, he was a principal in Dangerhouse Records. Unlike A&M, Dangerhouse didn't have a compound, or an office, or a phone number even, but it had issued *Trouble at the Cup.*

"We will have street teams," Randy boasted and envisioned. "We will go down to the Gold Cup and round up our runaways and hustlers. We'll organize them and disperse them throughout the suburban sprawl to invade the ice cream shops, high schools, and malls. Dangerhouse street teams will be trained to spot youths susceptible to peer influence. For a pack of cigarettes and some well-tended candy bars, the harnessed rebel energy of the Gold Cup will spread the obviously superior aesthetic of punk music throughout Oxnard, Torrance, Huntington Beach, and the world."

"You expect the hustlers to work for you without pay?"

"Dangerhouse is actively formulating a plan of fan diffusion similar to Mary Kay Cosmetics or Amway."

Dangerhouse was actively formulating nothing of the kind anywhere outside of Randy's mind.

All night I thought over Randy's scheme to mobilize the corrupted urchins of Hollywood Boulevard. It boiled down to sending young male prostitutes and their girlfriends on a mission of conversion to the surrounding wholesome districts. I couldn't come up with a single reason why it wouldn't work.

I thought about me. I wanted an expense account. I wanted an office door I could close for on-the-job coke parties. I wanted a secretary who would wear her panties on the outside of her flares.

There was no sleeping. I was out of bed, away from Tommie, and making notes. I wrote down everything I could recall from Randy's improvised guerilla marketeering.

In the blue Ford, during the drive to the museum, I rehearsed the scheme's high points, silently, in my mind. When 10:00 a.m. rolled around, I took my cigarette break at a pay phone next to the museum café and called the A&M Records executive, Chuck. Lindsay intercepted me.

"Do you remember who I am?" I asked.

Lindsay paused, as if stumped, then laughed and said, "Certainly. I've been thinking about you all night."

This response, which I judged to be in jest, threw me for a moment. I recovered and told her the purpose of my call.

"I have a plan to make The Dickies the most popular band in high school America."

"Terrific," said Lindsay. "What's your plan?"

My mouth went very dry. I should have bought something to drink. I saw Tommie and Viva walking toward the café. Viva said or did something, their shoulders bumped, and Tommie laughed.

At a distance, I saw the laughter fire up Tommie's eyes. Her spirit hadn't died out after all. It only needed to be sparked back into full flame. My calling, I realized while struck mute at a public pay phone, was to save my wife from bitterness—and to satisfy myself at the same time.

I pulled the notes I'd written the night before from the pockets of my blue blazer and stacked them atop the phone. I would do whatever it took to revive Tommie's faded happiness, so long as what it took satisfied me as well. I made myself be brave.

"Listen, Lindsay," I said. I sketched out Randy's concept of the street teams. I depicted the hustlers recruiting susceptible kids from the suburbs and organizing them into punk rock ambassadors. The young prostitutes would select outsider kids, but not cowed kids. The Dickies wanted leading-edge kids rather than kids who had been dumped behind.

Lindsay stopped me for clarification.

Yes, of course we would seed the recruits with free tickets to see the band. Yes, if a rich enclave of potential influencers were found, we might send a Dickies punk bus to pick up a batch and return them home safely after the show.

Lindsay sounded like she believed what I was talking about. Who was I to doubt it?

I pictured her underwear, outside the slacks. In truth, I had been picturing those panties even before I'd picked up the phone. The panties had been a fabric of my entire scheme.

Suddenly, the slacks under Lindsay's panties fell out of the picturing.

Lindsay was saying something over the phone. But every time I heard her, I saw her. And I'd seen her taking off her flares.

My brain stumbled.

Lindsay asked a couple of questions, simple ones. Who knows what they might have been? My mind refused to wrap around anything that wasn't wrapped in panties. I was flustered, a loser. The dropping panties had done me in.

"Are you okay?" she said.

"Sure. I'm fine."

"You don't sound fine. Well, it was okay to hear from you."

The line went dead.

SCENE THREE
DRUGS AND GLORY

I'd traveled to El Monte with an amateur stripper friend of mine. El Monte is the third or fourth major barrio to the east of Hollywood. In 1978, it was a place of lowriders and gang graffiti, a proud neighborhood with a rich, multigenerational heroin culture. If you were white and driving a ten-year-old Ford through El Monte after dark, there was no concealing what you were up to. My amateur stripper friend had a dope connection there, a *vato* gone all gray and round at the middle.

We were in the *vato's* living room. It was his mom's house, or the house of an ex-wife or the ex-wife's mom. Saints and a Madonna looked on from the walls, and sheets of plastic protected the flocking of the furniture from our lasting imprint. I smelled a faint scent of tortillas past, homemade ones. I sniffed them out with the nose of a connoisseur.

The kitchen, half visible, contained three *vatos* young and old, washing down tortillas with Coors beer from the can, silent partners in our transaction.

The dealer sat just outside the circle of light from the living room lamp, enthroned in a regal lounger. He faced a TV that partitioned him from whoever sat on the plastic-covered sofa. The shifting TV light played diabolical shadows across the *vato*'s Satan-suave facial hair.

"You sure you don't want a soda?" he said to my amateur friend. "There's a market right around the block. Your scrawny *huero* can run down there."

He put on a smile that communicated to me something contrary to what it communicated to her. *Why, hello again!* it said to her.

"I said I'm not thirsty," she said.

His eyes lingered all over her. He pictured the flesh below the black leather jacket and the Sid Vicious T-shirt. His gaze was speculative, but he was picturing from memory, and not from a memory of amateur strip night at the Cave.

She'd given me no indication that her history with the connection went anything deeper than fully clothed.

"So," he said to her, "when this dude leaves, we'll party together. For old sakes."

"That's sweet. But I'm with this dude now."

The *vato* appraised me. "That true? You the dude she's with now?"

I shrugged my shoulders. You know how it is between dudes of the world. We don't like to admit any one woman has us tied down. I pictured Tommie heading to work that morning in her navy blue King Tut blazer. The sight of her averted my studied flat gaze from the *vato*'s stony eyes.

"Look." My stripper friend fanned a clutch of twenties and tens. "I have the money."

He motioned her closer. She went around the television, right up between the dealer's spread legs, and wedged into his lap.

The gray *vato* raised his eyebrows at me as though seeking my permission. "You could leave us alone for a minute?"

The girl looked back and shook her head in the negative. I never would have left them alone anyway. I had my reasons.

"Just joking around," said the *vato*. "Can't blame me for trying, can you?"

The three kitchen *vatos* passed around a laugh. It was like a smirk made audible.

This claim to be joking around was the *vato* being courteous. He could have stabbed me in the eye, and I would have had no grounds for complaint. The fact that I sat unmolested was testament of the dealer's affection for my stripper friend. For her sake, I was not treated to a curb job and dumped in some alley behind Peck Road. I'd received a courtesy pass.

Somewhere between her hands and his, the money vanished like in a magic trick. The amateur stripper popped up off the dealer's lap and landed on her feet at the backside of the TV, outside the dealer's reach.

"That's how it is," he said. "You get your drugs; you jump and bail."

I hadn't seen the drugs handed over any more clearly than I'd seen the money disappear. The dealer cut us off on our way to the front door. He tapped the stripper on her chest: "Don't let me hear you're strung out on this shit."

He placed a hand near me, palm forward: "Don't let me hear you got her strung out on this shit."

I spent a moment digesting that threat as a compliment.

"So get the fuck out of here," he said.

Back in the car, too stupid and enchanted with my own unfolding legend to recognize the dangers I'd just weathered, I wheeled the Ford toward the Garvey on-ramp. My amateur stripper friend reached down inside the front of her black jeans. She tugged out a piece of adhesive tape.

"He gave me two extra bags. He hid them in me. That's why he wanted you to go outside. So he could give me a separate stash."

She placed the two surprise balloons in with the balloons we'd planned for. She let her hand linger with the balloons in my jacket pocket. This girl really wanted to be my friend. How lonely she must be!

We found a place to park, not terribly far from the Canterbury, just to the west of the transgender prostitutes. The stripper touched my wrist as I turned off the Ford.

"Walk slow," she said. "Look bummed."

Together, the stripper and I passed the sex changelings. The hookers stopped their chatter and sized us up. Even to them, we appeared to need advice.

"Girl, you're not making that boy happy."

"You better spice him up, chick, or he'll be out here after us."

"Take a look, boyfriend. Take a long, hard look."

I don't deny it. I wouldn't have denied it then. I saw some appeal there. The mixed-race girls in particular had an exotic attraction—exotic beyond having been born with a penis. They drifted as a group with us, escorting our stroll to the Canterbury gate; then they drifted away again.

The Canterbury courtyard looked deserted. That was a relief.

"No smiles," warned my friend.

We stepped inside the courtyard, and Black Randy burst out from behind some failing bushes. Dead leaves littered his hair, like the remnants of some Greek hero's wreath.

"Basho, my dear!" He gripped the hem of my jacket. "I understand you have been on an expedition to El Monte. Is it true? Have you brought back some of that region's indigenous brown heroin?"

He stared into my eyes, rather obviously checking for pinned pupils.

"We got burned," I said.

Randy immediately suspected the girl of having double-crossed me. He grabbed the hem of her black leather and peered deep into her pupils. They were fat and open, clear signs of heroin deprivation.

Randy was disgusted: "You should have put me in the car to El Monte. I know how to handle those people. We'd all be high right now."

I felt terrible, as though I'd failed everyone. To look at the amateur stripper, you would assume she felt as bad as I did. That must be what they call method acting.

Randy tagged along toward the building, but our air of hopelessness was so complete and enervating that it overcame even his obsession. He drifted away. The transgender sirens were calling him.

Up in my apartment, Tommie was fine-tuning her makeup.

Rushing past in my heroin haste, I noticed a few things within the frame of the wife's vanity mirror. Set off by a sleeveless turtleneck lifted from the French new wave, her face confronted itself with ruthless objectivity. Brushes and pencils made deft, short work with pigments and blushes. Tommie's mirror image was serious about itself, and seriously slowed my push toward the kitchen.

The surviving photos make some sense of my living memories: Five, ten times a day—and no wonder—that face captured and stopped me, clammy and cold. Its allure was inescapable. To entirely resist was beyond my power. Drawn to a halt, paused a distance from the kitchen base of operations, feeling weak and susceptible to Tommie's force, I clamped down and crimped that surge of devotion.

I had a question for her: "How did Black Randy find out I went to El Monte? Only you and I knew."

"Did you go to El Monte? Is El Monte where you went? Maybe you left without telling me you were going anywhere. Maybe you were spotted driving off with a part-time hooker. Maybe certain presumptions were made around the building."

While Tommie and I had our discussion, the stripper opened all our balloons and combined their powder on a magazine cover on top of the kitchen table. She divided the mound into even thirds. These mounds broke Tommie's spell over me.

I had to ask: "Why three? It's me and you; that's two. Are we the types who save a mound for later?"

The stripper nodded toward Tommie. "What about her?"

"Tommie hasn't asked for anything."

"We're in this together," said the stripper, "aren't we?"

"Tommie doesn't need to get sucked into this kind of thing."

The stripper hunched her shoulders. "Whose decision is that?"

Still in a slip, Tommie walked with aimless intent over to the kitchen table. She had every opportunity to decline. While the amateur stripper cooked at the stove and loaded a syringe for herself, Tommie said something about the bands set to play the Whisky that night, she said something about the animist building manager coming around for the rent money, she said something about needing to be ready for King Tut at 9:00 a.m.

She said all that and more; I'm sure I didn't hear what all she said. But she certainly failed to say, "No, thank you, no heroin for me."

I assumed I would take half of Tommie's mound, as the husband's prerogative, but the stripper showed herself to be a stickler for even-handedness. She passed the rinsed syringe over to me and then sat on standby, like a first-world observer at a third-world election.

The stuff cooked up with a rich, medicinal smell, turning the water black—black like the pus from one of Satan's pimples, like a lanced boil on a cancerous rat's ball sack, like the juice from a suppurating sore on Black Randy's ass.

My fanciful imagery was no deterrent to Tommie. She tied off without any instruction and laid her arm bare on my thigh. I put it into her. This was her first time, first time that I knew of. The hit was almost immediate. That happy plume of blood squirted up into the chamber, just a shade darker and thicker than the dope itself. Tommie took it like a champ. I pumped the plunger in and booted it back out, drawing blood into the chamber, diluting the drug mixture until it was a purely red fluid.

This insertion, truly adept, felt imperfectly good and right. That cornball "giving her something better than me" cliché always clanged lame in my mind, and the government-sanctioned scare tactics hadn't exactly frightened me, but injecting the drug into Tommie felt sort of like what I'd imagined swinging would feel like—watching her with the other dude might be something you might wish you could take back, except you wanted to be sure you got off, too.

The patient didn't blanch, didn't flinch, didn't blink. The drug hit, and she sank into it, then lifted out, quite pleased.

"Thank you," she said.

While I did my allotment, Tommie touched up a portion of her makeup. The mirror image absorbed more of her attention than it had before she took the shot. That frost of objectivity melted away as she looked at herself, in love with what she saw.

"Honey, look," she said, extending a tube of lipstick to my stripper friend. "Try this shade."

Heroin had warmed Tommie, transforming "that part-time hooker" into "honey, look."

Feeling nothing near urgency, we headed off to the Whisky.

"Honey, look, sit here. Sit up here with us." Tommie pulled the stripper into the car's front seat. Tommie was in the middle; Honey, Look pressed a cheek against the passenger window.

I steered the Ford down toward Sunset and the Whisky. Tommie lit a cigarette, dragged deep, and handed the butt to me. She knew I'd want one right about then. I offered the stripper a beer after opening one for myself.

"That's okay." She let her head loll on her neck. "I don't want to cut the high."

Streetlights, car lights, stop lights, and police lights floated past on all sides.

"This stuff makes me feel cold-blooded," I said, behind the wheel. Lights slid across the windshield. A glow from Tommie lit up the rearview mirror. I saw invincibility at every angle around me.

"What do you mean *cold-blooded*?" asked the stripper.

It bothered me that I had to explain. Explaining cut my high. "I mean, anything can happen, and it's like it's happening to my advantage. I would come out ahead."

She thought that over, or maybe she was thinking about something else, which arrived at: "Careful, you're going to light your jacket with that cigarette."

Part Two

A Dangerhouse band was on the bill at the Whisky. Black Randy had greased the experience for us with VIP passes that entitled us to the private balcony.

I guided Tommie up the stairs. Every time she picked up a foot, you weren't sure if it would come back down again or just glide straight on up, lighter than air. I half expected her to float off and hover at the highest recesses of the Whisky.

"It's like you'd be watching the show like an angel," I said to the back of her heels. "An angel painted on the ceiling by Michelangelo." This romanticism was lost in a surge of feedback from the stage.

Tommie picked a chair in the first row of seats above the stage, right next to the backstage entrance. We settled in and fired up fresh cigarettes. Tommie put an arm along my slouched shoulders. She leaned over her seat back and threw up like a princess into the row of chairs behind her. She moved with grace and economy of effort. Anyone who noticed could not help but be impressed.

Between bands, Tommie was content to sit still and let the world come to her. The dope made me feel that I should move about and share myself.

I got the hand stamp from the suited doorman and floated across the Sunset Strip to the parking lot behind the Licorice Pizza record store. About twenty or thirty of us were out there. Drinking, smoking, and trading pills in the Licorice Pizza parking lot was what we did when we went to shows at the Whisky.

Jane and Margot from The Go-Go's were sitting on a curb back there, drinking sixteen-ounce cans of beer. Jane was also smoking. She smoked Virginia Slims that were about a foot long.

"Belinda is so selfish," said Margot, or maybe it was Jane. Belinda was their singer.

"She knows we need money for rehearsal rent."

"She blew 200 dollars on shoes at Frederick's."

Jane and Margot both lived at the Canterbury, as did Belinda. They'd mangled their first three chords down in the laundry room. The Go-Go's were pros now.

"Where is Belinda, anyway?" I wanted to be sure she was out of earshot before I ragged on her. This heroin stuff helped me to be cunning. Drunk, I would've just blurted out whatever I'd been thinking.

"See?" said Margot. "She's not even here."

"Have you noticed," I said, slyly, "that she's the only punk rocker we know who's fatter than Black Randy?"

Margot and Jane were both leery of wearing vertical stripes; so this remark met less approval than I had hoped for.

"That's not really true," said Jane.

"It really isn't," agreed Margot.

I needed to work on my social cunning. More heroin might help.

Four males I'd never seen in the Licorice Pizza parking lot—or anywhere—were competing to catch the attention of Jane and Margot.

They were guys who tried too hard. I considered advising them. Trying is overrated. But these newcomers were industrious, parking-lot social climbers. No one could have reasoned them out of concentrating their ambitions on the trash-filled Licorice Pizza Dumpster.

The Dumpster was one of the large blue ones, with tiny steel wheels on the bottom.

The four industrious dudes leaned their weight into the Dumpster. They rocked it back and forth. The Dumpster's wheels turned. The wheels screeched. The Dumpster moved, at first by inches. It picked up a slow, heavy momentum. Smoke wisped from the top.

A handful of parking lot regulars joined the four industrious newcomers, pushing on the Dumpster. I stayed where I was, of course, squatting with Margot and Jane.

The Dumpster bumped over the slump in the driveway that exited the Licorice Pizza parking lot onto San Vicente Boulevard. Flames lifted from the top of the container. Someone, maybe two of them, had fired up the trash. The rolling, smoking Dumpster merged onto the steep gradient of San Vicente below Sunset.

This was as good a time as any to walk back toward the Whisky.

I looked behind me. A two-ton inferno rolled down San Vicente Boulevard. The dudes who had been pushing ran along beside the rolling Dumpster, but dropped off one by one. They couldn't keep up with the larger, flaming thing they'd set in motion. Approaching traffic veered off to the right and to the left to avoid a fiery, head-on catastrophe.

Helicopters—news and police—would be arriving soon.

Back in the Whisky VIP section, Tommie accepted my kiss and threw up again. She was perfectly regal about it!

Critics say that narrative needs action and struggle in its characters. They say that an active character is a character that grows.

With the flaming Dumpster, I didn't act there. But my view of the Dumpster rolling down the street was just as close and clear as if I'd plotted its route myself. I'd been at hand to the business of it, and I had firsthand observations. On top of that, my hands were clean. That was my idea of a compelling character—someone who lets everyone else do the work, but basks in the fiery glow.

Later, we were home in the pull-down bed in time to catch a TV recap of the flaming Dumpster rolling down San Vicente. While the room slowly spun, I described the genesis of the event to Tommie. My pride swelled as if I had played a pivotal role.

The newscasters couldn't make sense of this juggernaut of burning filth, but I knew what it meant: a whole world of disruption and chaos was out there, waiting for me to take credit for it.

SCENE FOUR:
DUST RUN

Don't ask me how, but I owned a car; so I was driving down to Norwalk with Black Randy as my passenger. Norwalk is a town twenty-five miles southeast of Hollywood, renowned for its mental hospital. No one wants to be from Norwalk, and a sane person needs a compelling reason to go there. For Black Randy and me, the pull was angel dust.

Angel dust—PCP—is a drug that you can't really explain the appeal of. A few puffs or sniffs, and the PCP stuns every nerve ending in the body, sending back a distress message to the brain: "I am your body, and I am dead. I am your body, and I have died."

The feeling of sitting trapped in death fades after six to eight hours, unless the user goes crazy. The high also brings a breakdown in physical coordination and an inability to form words with the tongue.

Randy and I would go all the way to Norwalk chasing that experience.

Freeway traffic kept snaring us. Crawling semis hogged lanes and boxed in the family Ford. There was no way around the trucks, and they spat black air into our windshield. We were hot and grimy, and I had no money.

Randy received SSI welfare payments, which was something like being wealthy. So Randy was financing this Norwalk expedition.

"Open your mind to possibilities," he suggested. "Manifest the image of you driving to Norwalk and back without stopping at a gas station. Gas mileage is largely a function of driver skill."

Randy considered me slightly retarded. One reason for that was because I did not receive SSI—government subsidies for individuals who are ruled disabled due to mental instability.

I kept watch for the next gas station and took that off-ramp. I was smart enough to squeeze gas money out of Randy at the start of the journey rather than at the end.

After pumping the gas, I lingered in the cashier's shack. Impatience was one of Randy's strong suits. He was losing his mind in the car. I pink had a few dollars of Randy's change; so I bought an ice cream bar and three beers.

Back in the car, I cracked a beer and did not offer the others to Randy. He sat speechless with rage. Pleased, I started the car.

We had no map, and the directions we'd been given were abstract; so I drove aggressively. Forty minutes later, the Ford was overheating and we'd overshot Norwalk. I pulled into another gas station.

Randy demanded a justification for the stop.

"I'll go in and check our coordinates," I said.

The service area—unlike the Ford—was air-conditioned, a place made for loitering. My mission became vague. To be honest for a change, I had just wanted to be out of the car and away from Randy for a while. I'd smoked the last of my weed prior to our departure, and his bickering had entirely worn away that high.

Randy barged into the service area. Get a look at him. He walked as if his entire crotch area were one big rash—fists clenched; jaws clenched; eyes tight with indignity and irritation.

He zeroed in on the lady cashier. I'd judged her to be implacable and sedentary, and she proved me correct.

"We need the quickest way to Norwalk," shouted my passenger.

The cashier wasn't from around there. She took in Randy's facial sweat and drifting eyes. She took in my shaky cigarette hand and wan simper. She wasn't even from the same hemisphere. "You look for the Norwalk hospital? For the withdrawal."

The Norwalk mental hospital's drug dependency and alcoholism unit was widely praised. Randy and I intended to stay far away from there. We hadn't traveled twenty-five miles without a map to address mental health issues.

We left the gas station with no new information. I drove worse than ever. By the time I'd drained the second beer, the Ford had blundered into Norwalk, the city we'd been looking for. We remained lost.

"If suburbs were bodies of water," said Randy, trying to bring us back on the same team, "Norwalk would be the Dead Sea."

No one in Norwalk had a nice car. No one had a nice house. No one on the road had any reason to be in a hurry to go anywhere in Norwalk. The cars seemed to be stuck in demoralizing inertia. In Norwalk, the inhabitants didn't even know they could hope for a flow. It was just like Pomona, or West Covina, or Azusa, or any of the other incorporated housing tracts of my youth.

We were looking to pick up this girl I knew, a butch-light girl who was always in black jeans and a leather coat. She was like Joan Jett but without the brilliant career. She supported herself by rooming with her parents in Norwalk, and entering amateur strip contests at the Cave on Hollywood Boulevard.

Living at the Canterbury and socializing at The Masque, amateur-night strippers were the friends you'd make. They'd take you places you may have thought you'd left behind, like Norwalk, crimped-future places just like the ones you were so proud not to have become tied down in.

Randy read numbers off curbs until we hit the one we wanted. I parked the car in front of a house like all the rest.

"Let me go in for her," ordered Randy. "Her parents may have something in the medicine cabinet, something you kids don't know about."

That was Randy—the eternal optimist. But my stripper friend was the eternal realist; she'd been waiting close to the street and slid into the Ford before I had time to turn it off. The cured-hide smell of her jacket slid in with her.

"Any chance of a guy going in to use the bathroom?" asked Randy.

"Not really."

"I'm Randy. *Black* Randy."

"No chance at all."

From the backseat, she directed us toward the guy's house where we were buying PCP.

"What do people expect to make of their lives," asked Black Randy, "when they grow up in Norwalk?"

"I don't know what you mean."

"Exactly what I mean."

We navigated a warren of residential streets where I had to assume no one really wanted to be living. The trees appeared to be dying. How could trees live with that smog clinging to their leaves? You didn't see a single person walking on the sidewalks or standing on the front lawns, which is one thing that made sense about the place.

The girl sat forward, leaning against my seat back, scanning both sides of the street.

"Usually he's right around here," she said.

Randy made a great display of incredulity. "You don't know where the connection lives?"

She put a hand on my shoulder. "How's your wife doing?"

I tried to make up my mind how to answer that. The wife seemed to have more fun lately hanging out with Russ than with me; the two of them often sided against me in small matters. That alliance between wife and friend might be significant, or it might be a figment. Should I monitor indications of an intimacy between them that did not fully meet the eye? Make some inquiries? Be keenly observant, for a change, of Tommie's relations to me? But why? Either I would find that Russ and Tommie's chumminess meant nothing whatsoever, or I would be crushed with a heartbreak I might never scrape myself up from.

So I spieled about some reconfigured punk band in England or some other thing I no longer cared about. Randy didn't want to hear any of that.

"When we find the connection," he said, "if we find the connection, just shut up. I will do the talking. We'll all be better off for it."

"There he is," said the girl.

He wasn't exactly wearing a sign saying "I SELL PCP," but I could have picked him out. For starters, he was the only human out of doors. There was the black sunglasses. The no shirt. The beaded headband. The ratty black hair hanging past his neck. The no-belt jeans slipping off his hips. The scuffed, square-toe cowboy boots.

"Hippie," said Randy, but that wasn't exactly right.

I was pacing the dealer, with the slowing car. He looked over, resigned that trouble might be rolling beside him. He would be fine with the trouble.

I stopped the car.

"Pedro," called the stripper. "What's happening?"

Pedro, if that was his name, lifted his sunglasses and gave us all a look into his eyes.

"Dusted and disgusted," he said.

Clearly, the stuff was very strong.

"These are the people I was telling you about," said the stripper.

"That's enough out of you," said Randy.

The PCP connection leaned his crossed arms on Randy's open window. He took Randy's measure and carefully re-measured.

"Dusted and disgusted," he repeated, like a mantra.

"We're not here to rip you off," said Randy. "We need to go somewhere for a taste."

"It tastes like shit," said the guy. "You don't know that? What are you, a cop?"

Pedro made me laugh. I indicated Randy and me. "Look at us," I said. "If you saw us two hundred feet from a schoolyard, you'd call the principal to come out and save the kids. *Cops!*" I had to laugh again.

The connection slithered into the backseat with the amateur stripper. They locked into a kiss.

"Which way should we go?" I said, putting the car into gear.

I switched through three or four radio stations. The music was all crap. I shifted the transmission back to park. In the backseat, they were still kissing. I started to understand that my friend had a thing for Mexicans. "No, really," I pressed. "Which way do we go?"

The girl took her mouth off Pedro. He reacquainted himself with his surroundings.

"What are you guys into?" asked the dealer. "I never seen people who look like you."

"Have you looked at yourself?" said Randy. He said it as though he were withholding judgment.

"I look like I'm from around here, fairy goblin. You don't."

"That's why we need you," I said, always the peacemaker, "to show us where to go."

"Go straight for a while. Can you go straight for a while? Is that too hard for fairy goblins?"

He seemed to know the area. He directed me to make a few turns, then to pull over to a curb on the right. We parked along the side of a corner house, in the shade of two drooping maple trees. A cop car went by without slowing.

"I insist on sampling the goods," said Randy, which was absurd. PCP takes time to come on.

"What are we going to do?" This was my anxiety talking. "Sit at the curb and wait?"

Pedro was out of the car: "Okay, don't go goblin tripping. I'll be right back."

Pedro scuttled around to the front of the house and out of our sight. He had bells on his boots! I heard the jingle go silent.

Randy turned to the girl. "Does so-called Pedro live in that house?"

"You do the talking," she said.

I was glad I'd bought that extra beer with Randy's change, and that I'd saved it.

Another cop car went by. I opened the beer. The amateur stripper had a joint. When we were done smoking it, somehow we had two girls in the backseat. The one I knew, and her friend. I heard music, bells.

Pedro leaned his crossed arms on Randy's open window.

"Let's see the cash," said Pedro.

"Let's see the stash," countered Randy, but he forked over the bills.

A bindle appeared in the crook of Pedro's elbow. Randy plucked it, opened it, covered a fingernail with powder, and sniffed.

The LAPD had adopted a policy of shooting suspected PCP maniacs in the chest and also in the head. A single shot was believed to only enhance the duster's superhuman strength and rage.

Pedro didn't know the second girl, and he seemed smitten when my friend introduced him to her.

"Can't we go inside the house?" asked Randy. "We're conspicuous out here."

Now he's talking sense, I thought.

"You've torn your dress," answered Pedro.

"Look, we've got two girls. Why don't we all go into the backyard and relax?"

"Your face is a mess."

I had to suppose that Pedro didn't live at the house we were parked alongside. There may have been motion at the curtains of the house. We were being watched. I knew it. At least the car was in the shade.

Randy made an impatient gesture, but only I seemed to notice. "Why am I not coming on?"

The stripper and her friend cuddled in the backseat, ignoring the drama in front of them.

"Why am I not feeling the drugs?" asked Randy, as if the answer were obvious and odious.

Pedro leaned cross-armed in the open car window, his face set in an expression of mild surprise. "Maybe you should wait two minutes?"

A smog-sticky leaf landed on my windshield, with a wet splash, *like suicide.* Randy hadn't come on to the drug yet, but already I had a contact high.

"This shit is a burn." Randy felt personally betrayed. In retaliation, he sniffed a ludicrously big lump of powder.

"That's going to cost you," said the dealer.

He backed away, bells jingling, and disappeared into the dead sun of Norwalk.

SCENE FIVE: SLEEPOVERS

Sometimes, if you want to tell your actual story, as it really happened, you have to give up any notion of being the narrator who can look himself in the mirror and be pleased with what he sees. It's like your part in your personal history is engineered to not come off well. It starts to look like your role was to do your best to doom everything, as if everything hadn't been doomed from the start, in which case your fault is in not having done anything to lift the doom.

Later, if you survive a few of the decades ahead, maybe a person acquires some philosophic objectivity—or develops it. That's what adults do. They survey the mess and reach deep with something like "it is what it is," and everybody is off the hook. But if I'm off the hook, if it just was what it was, why would I bother with any of this?

Don't think I haven't noticed that this entire set of memories so far, with no indication of changing, recalls the author as unpleasant, grasping, an indulger, boorish and wishy-washy, selfish and afraid, a groundless snob, arrogant without achievement, a self-suckered chump.

Believe me, I get the picture.

What I'm saying here, now, is that even that character is pained to view himself in the story of Viva moving in with the wife and me, for a week or two, in our Canterbury single room, and then moving on.

The story starts with an evening dip.

We'd manned our King Tut posts at the county art museum for an endless day, herding people who looked down upon us through the sunlight of an unseasonably hot LA springtime. People of means, with places in the world at large and planned futures, a populace not like us, had paid by the thousands to gawk at Tut's golden artifacts. The cultured elite, covetous and gold-fevered, arrived in well-heeled hordes.

Our job was to control and enclose the masses, to funnel impatient crowds into progressively tighter waiting areas. Their worlds became smaller and more cramped, more like ours, at each next stage of the queue. Baiting the street entrance, Viva and Tommie lured the arrivals forward, welcoming eager museumgoers into a series of holding pens. My task was to bully and hector, using strict courtesy and unyielding politeness as flails, to pack these humans so tightly into the final roped enclosure that they all touched like livestock. The work was thankless, endless, and sweaty.

It was Viva, the wife, and me, all shift long.

Finally, we were in my car, driving back toward the Canterbury, trying to find something that wasn't infuriating on the radio. Boston. Journey. Seeger. Seething.

All four of the car windows were down. Viva and Tommie sprawled across the back bench seat, faces slack in the furnace-dry rush of wind. They'd ditched their blue Tut-attendant blazers and yanked their uniform white shirts from the waists of their navy slacks.

"Ladies don't sweat," said Viva. She used the drawl that announced she was making a two-part statement. "But I'm even sweating where I'm a lady."

"I wish the air-conditioning worked in this car," said Tommie.

"But it doesn't," I said. "The heat is just one more shit thing that none of us can do anything about. Like every other shit thing."

"Sentiments like this seem to be thematic with you," observed Tommie.

"We can go swimming," said Viva.

"Be logical," I said, unbendable and accusatory. "We don't know anyone who has a pool."

"That's right," Viva agreed. "We don't know anyone. So we'll be trespassing. And naked."

Even in its most general terms, Viva's plan sounded risky, but Tommie didn't wait for details. "Okay," she said. "Let's do it."

I yanked the windshield mirror around and framed Tommie in the view.

"Why not?" she said, eye to eye. "Tell me one good reason why not."

"I don't even know what we're talking about," I said.

"Skinny dipping," said Viva.

"All you ever want is to be naked with two girls at once," said Tommie. "Here's your chance."

That desire must have leaked out when I was drunk. I groped for a way to take it back, or to diffuse it in context.

"First we'll find a pool," said Viva. "Then Tommie and I will take off our clothes. If you don't like it, we can try something else."

"Tell me one good reason why you won't like it," said Tommie.

Following Viva's direction, I drove to West Hollywood and parked south of Sunset on one of the streets stacked with apartment complexes. We grouped on the sidewalk, selected a likely courtyard, and walked boldly in.

Like probably every apartment stack on the block, the residential units were arranged two high around a swimming pool at the courtyard center. A second-floor walkway with an iron railing overlooked the water. Anyone might be standing up there.

The pool was still and vacant; lights shimmered under the surface of its heated water. TV voices and dinner sounds came from open windows and sliding doors.

Viva dropped her Tut uniform in a heap of shadows beneath a set of stairs that serviced the upper tenants. She seemed taller when she was naked. The clothes had been holding her down. Glistening like a pink tuna, she dove into the water.

Tommie emerged naked from the stairwell's shadows. She was like a girl I hadn't seen before. She took a proud step toward the water. I tried to catch up on what I had been missing while living with her—the color gradations of the flesh, the interlocking contours, the resilience and flex. She flung herself into the depths after Viva.

Two water-beaded heads popped up in the bobbing blue. Wet eyes and wet teeth shone in the evening mood light. Water-treading limbs glimmered in and out of focus under the refracting surface.

Viva and Tommie laughed, at volume, loudly mocking my hesitation. I'd unbuttoned my shirt; I'd unbuckled my belt.

"This is a whole lot better," called Viva. "In here."

"It's one shit thing temporarily remedied," I countered, "in a whole world of shit things."

A few windows and glass doors slid shut. An air conditioner cranked on.

I stood on the pool lip, back to the patio lights, across the water from the shadows of the stairs. My shirt and my slacks were folded at my feet, neatly upon my socks and shoes. My boxer shorts remained in place as though I were a tease.

"C'mon," said Viva.

"Come in," urged Tommie.

I was worried about my penis. Swimming naked is easy for girls. They may battle body issues, but they don't contend with the intractable prick. My cock was always sprouting into erection when it needed to be still, or shrinking to nothing when heft was called for.

Still, there comes a time when you have to decide, *Do I keep the underwear on, or do I kick it to the side?*

The evening air on my chest puckered my nipples to nothing. My thumbs hooked the waistband of my underpants, and hesitated.

"The cops are already on the way," drawled Viva. "Jump in. They'll arrest you whether you do or not."

Tommie floated on her back, laughing—really happy laughter. Her nipples and her bush broke the surface. I dropped the shorts. I knew not to turn away. I faced the two girls head on and defeated the urge to look down and see how I was holding up.

I sliced into the water and came up laughing, just like Tommie—happy laughter. Where had that come from? My rigid conception of life as a preliminary hell cooled and became fluid. I laughed in Tommie's face; she laughed in mine. Viva burst up out of the water and laughed between us.

That was the trouble with Viva. She was smart enough to acknowledge that existence meant shit, misery, and hangovers. Then she tricked you into fun.

We stayed in the water until a gay couple came out from their ground-floor manager's unit and gently told us we'd overstayed our welcome. The girls dressed in a manner that flaunted how naked they had been and how naked they remained, insolently draping garments across exposed body parts.

They were a team—these two—and I was with me.

My dressing technique was furtive. Bent at the spine, frustrated in pulling my underwear up my wet legs, hopping off balance on a single foot, angry that I had stopped and had fun, I cursed myself for not being at home getting loaded.

Once we reconvened in the car, with the girls watching me, all aggravation drained away. We were clothed, but under those clothes lurked the sweet secret of being naked together.

We drove to the Canterbury, all relaxed, and Viva came up to the apartment for tacos and spent the night. It seemed natural. It wasn't like we hardly knew each other. We'd been on the same plane up to San Francisco to see the Sex Pistols, and we'd stayed at the same apartment in the Haight, the apartment where Sid Vicious OD'd after the final Pistols show.

Viva had been knocking from apartment to apartment at the Canterbury. Her essential belongings fit into a pair of mismatched satchels. She retrieved them from somewhere, we smoked weed, someone pulled the bed out from the wall, and we all slid under a sheet. The lights switched out in time for plenty of rest before the morning's commute to serve King Tut.

I couldn't sleep, and neither could Tommie. Her wide-awake fingers snaked up and down my body, squeezing my pulse.

A lot of sex took place on the left two-thirds of the bed that night. None of that sex touched Viva, although she couldn't possibly have been asleep, not with all the agitation inflicted on the bedsprings. She curled up on her own, keeping to the right-hand third of the mattress.

Eventually, panting and sweating, Tommie and I collapsed flat to the mattress and from there into sleep.

In the morning, Russ dropped by in his museum-ready blue blazer and white shirt to catch a ride to work.

"I can't find Viva," he said.

Viva emerged from the bathroom, dripping and undressed. She stood with her legs spread and toweled her hair.

"Russ," she exclaimed, "you're a mouth breather!" She went to find her pants.

The routine for the next week was this: the four of us carpooled to the museum in the morning and fraternized throughout the day. Driving home, we coordinated plans for the night. At the apartment, we'd switch out our clothes, take a preemptive dose of alcohol, and go out. We might see Viva across a club, or share a few drinks in an alley or parking lot. She would disappear, and the Ford would make its run back to the Canterbury without her.

Around bedtime, the wife and I would be in our room with the Murphy bed pulled out. Neither of us said a thing, but I wasn't the only one wondering. A knock on the door, we'd be careful not to answer too quickly, and there she stood, coy and smiling. Viva, sheepish, slid in under our sheets. Everyone would settle in, tugging the covers back and forth. It would be like: *Maybe this is the time when everything breaks loose.*

Tommie and I were having sex every night, intense bouts of it, spilling off the bed, wheel-barrowing across the floor, splaying on the mattress in positions graphic and acrobatic. Viva lay within range, so still that you couldn't even be sure she was a spectator.

In the mornings, during the evenings, all throughout the days, in short at all times outside of bed, Tommie and I were as remote from the sex as Viva would be while in the bed. Evidently, nothing was remarkable about all the screwing being done by two people on a mattress holding three, or we would have remarked on it.

Every night, without fail, Viva knocked at our door. At a minimum, her reappearances were cause for speculation. Tommie and I refrained from speculating out loud to one another. I never asked the wife if she desired to push an overture to include Viva. When not in the throes of vigorous coitus, we were shy people. We voiced none of the pertinent questions raised by the one empirical fact: Tommie was more turned on than she had ever been, in my experience.

Once toward the end, Tommie climbed on top of my erection and sprayed an orgasm like I'd never caught across my pelvis and thighs. Initially, I thought she'd pissed on me. Clearing up that misconception, wordlessly, lead to more confusion. Should I be embarrassed by this spurt of oily fluid? Or suitably awed?

The soak had clearly seeped over to the right-hand reaches of the bed. The three of us lay still, separate, rigid and silent on our backs, no touching from head to toe.

In April, we went as a unit to see David Bowie at the Forum, me, Tommie, and Viva. Viva had colored her hair scarlet to herald Bowie's visit.

I'd seen Bowie the first time five years earlier in Long Beach. Then, the tripping mass had all been freaks. Ambiguous oddballs of every conceivable gender had sung along to Ziggy Stardust's wonder tunes, a mellow and accepting mob of otherness. By 1978, the audience was crude, straight, and lame. The typical paying customer was tight-eyed and hostile in limited contact, ill prepared to meet anyone like Viva or Tommie.

We ran into complications in the parking lot. Apparently, these Bowie-come-latelies felt that no one beyond the Thin White Duke was entitled to electrified crimson hair. Lames and drabs from the outlying flatlands moved aside for Viva and Tommie, with me discretely bringing up the rear.

The moment we'd passed, opinions were voiced:

"This chick thinks she's David Bowie."

"David would never fuck you! You're a slut!"

Who were these tools? With their flared slacks and Frye boots—on the chicks and the dudes? They looked like the well-nourished scum who form sororities and fraternities. Of course they outnumbered us, twenty to three.

"I know who I am," said Viva, "and I know who you are—jealous cunts."

Tommie rewarded Viva's retort with a swipe of tongue across the mouth, in midstride, further confounding the pestering lames.

"She's a faggot!" taunted a spokesperson.

"Fuck you," I reasoned.

"The chicks are faggots, and you're a faggot, too."

A lifelong love of logic and the current blood alcohol level impelled me to stop and explain that girls do not qualify for the pejorative *faggot* and that we were all attending a performance by a male artist who occasionally wore a dress.

My failure to explain self-evident truths to obvious dolts developed into a circular argument, the kind that goes nowhere and might go there forever. Tommie and Viva doubled back to pull me out of it, but my need to illuminate where no light can shine had made us late for the concert's opening song.

As we pushed into the aisles, the band had started. Bowie's voice surged:

"Sometimes you get so lonely, sometimes you get nowhere."

We offended the only usher in our section—I can't imagine what the cause could have been. He refused to help locate our seats.

Viva negotiated: "Don't be a pussy," she insisted.

"Find it yourself," he shouted, "you fake, redhead bitch!"

"I've lived everywhere, I've left every place."

Viva lifted the hem of her dress above her hips and rotated her panties-free crotch at the usher's face. Her pubic hair had been stripped of color and dyed the same scarlet as above.

"I'm a real redhead," she claimed, "and you can kiss my ass."

"Stay with me, be my wife."

After the show, we skirted a series of altercations in the parking lot, and Tommie and Viva kissed off and on all the way home in the backseat of the Ford. With an effort, I coolly drove the car, staying cool until we hit the Murphy bed. Then the three of us were a steamy, blurred mass.

Both women were totally naked. The apartment door was shut and locked. I couldn't really be sure it was happening. Where had my clothes gone? Had someone helped me out of my pants, or had I just presumed I was invited and shed all garments in a single shrug? Tommie was breasts-deep between Viva's open thighs. I belly flopped onto the mattress and slid across. Tommie moved up and locked lip-to-lip with Viva. Their eyes opened and smiled at each other. Their eyes closed.

Their faces went taut, digging into some deep, inside place. Both of them knew where I was, right?

Somehow, my hips had swiveled my pelvis into a grinding pattern against Viva's pelvis. That contact unleashed a sudden, alarming dread: the girls might change their minds. I snuck my cock into Viva, fully prepared to yank out if either woman protested.

"Hey, hello, Allan MacDonell," said Viva. She sort of purred. "What took you so long?"

Before I knew my wad was pooling, it jacked, spat up, and overflowed. Viva's purr died off. I hadn't even moved around inside of her, and I slid out, deflated.

That immediate prematurity shamed me like I'd been caught in an underhanded act. All those nights of prolonged sex bouts, and now a pop upon insertion. I shrank within myself, rolled away from the two girls and wanted to be somewhere else.

Opportunities were all around to kiss, stroke, massage, lick, sit back, and admire. If I'd just known enough to relax and have a good time, to this day I could be telling a story that a compromised character such as myself would gladly linger over in the reliving. Instead, I can't even look at me, an inert, awkward, and retreating lump inserted between a pair of abruptly stalled and self-conscious girls.

That's the tragedy of sexual betrayal. Your intractable prick lets you down, destroying happy memories meant to warm a lifetime.

How was Tommie taking this ruined adventure? How would I know? It's not like I could look over and meet her eyes. Curled on my side in a contraction of regret on that mattress, within my internal collapse and throughout the world beyond, everything was all the same to me—nothing.

In the morning, we skipped the customary start-of-the-day banter, even once we were in the car, and drove to the museum and King Tut. After work, there was a party or a concert, drinking and doping, and then more drinking and doping in the suite of a band staying at the Tropicana Motel.

At home that night, the Murphy bed was a quiet place.

The next morning, just as the Ford was pulling out for the museum, Viva appeared, heels in hand. She changed into her attendant uniform in the backseat.

"Can you tell I'm still drunk?" She twisted her bra so it would sit right. "I was singing duets all night and doing shots. With Tom Waits, in his Tropicana cabana."

He'd rushed her back to the Canterbury in a prepaid cab. She made it to the car in time for work, but she never stayed over again.

SCENE SIX:
BLACK RANDY'S FAT TASTE

We were on the 5 Freeway out of Norwalk, heading north toward the blinding sun above Hollywood and home. Traffic was thick and moving at top speed. Something was not right. Black Randy rode shotgun, still and quiet. The stripper and her girlfriend sat holding hands, silent in the backseat.

I tried to smoke a regular cigarette and keep both hands on the wheel, pretty glad that I hadn't sniffed up a tester of the PCP. I didn't like what the drug seemed to be doing to Randy. A beer, for me, would have helped.

From the backseat, the amateur stripper gave great directions.

"What's wrong, Allan?" said her girlfriend. "Haven't you ever been on this freeway before?"

"Of course I've been on this freeway before." Just never in these circumstances.

Randy was not in control anymore. Angel dust had blasted him into an outside dimension. I knew that an outburst would come. It would arrive as if there had been no warning.

"You're doing great," said my stripper friend. "All you have to do is stay in this lane. It takes you all the way to the Highland Boulevard off-ramp."

She saw that I was under stress; she did what she could to make things easier. That's what I call a great girl.

We slid into the transition from Interstate 5 to the Hollywood Freeway. It's a tricky juncture. Last time I'd navigated it was moments after I'd convinced Tommie to give me a blowjob while we were driving. It had nearly been the death of us, but not quite. I warmed to this memory.

Randy rocketed over from the passenger seat and slammed across me. His face smashed into the driver's side window. The Ford swerved a lane to the left. Randy's trunk wedged between the steering wheel and me. Gravity pulled him down toward the floorboards.

I assumed he was joking, overplaying his toxic state, but he had knocked the wind out of me and aggravated the ribs I'd broken while seeing the Sex Pistols in San Francisco.

Randy's face burrowed into my lap. He howled like an abandoned dog, his howl muffled by the fabric of my pants.

"That is pretty funny," I admitted.

I elbowed him in the back of the neck, again and again. I had to keep my attention on the road and couldn't put as much force as I wanted into the blows. Still, I hit him hard enough and often enough. He would have decoded the message if he were capable of receiving it.

"If you kill me, you will pay," I said, squinting into the sun. "Sit up."

"He's trying to get up," said my amateur stripper friend. She leaned forward from the backseat, interested, like a kid with a magnifying glass on a hot day. "He doesn't know which direction is up."

Angel dust, if it's any good, reduces spatial reality to a thing of abstract theory. Randy was evidently wasted on superior dust.

He flailed a fist, punched me in the face, and clamped onto the steering wheel. He jerked the wheel from my two hands— only for a second or so.

Looking back, I realize that Randy was trying to get a grip on balance. The car pitched sideways. My stomach flipped. All of this could only have made things worse for Randy's equilibrium.

Again like a dog, he tried to vomit, convulsing and lurching with his face in my crotch.

"Can someone get him off me?"

The girls bellied across the seatback and grappled with Randy.

"I can't hold him."

"He's too slippery."

Finally, the girls latched onto one of his underarms each. They heaved in unison, pulled Randy off of me, and pinned him against the passenger door. This is all at seventy miles per hour.

"Oh my god," squealed my stripper's girlfriend. Rashly, she sniffed the fingers that had dug into Randy's armpit. She gacked. "Oh my god. Oh my god."

"You did what had to be done," I said.

The girls buttressed their weight against Randy, preventing his blackness from flopping upon me anew. They twisted their necks, keeping their noses as far from the action as possible.

"Did he shit himself?" asked the girlfriend.

Randy huffed like a runaway train wreck, but he failed to break away from the girls' restraining embrace. I was proud to know them. We eased off the freeway at Highland and coasted down Yucca across Cherokee. We found a parking spot close to the Canterbury. We were lucky people!

The stripper's friend leaped from the Ford. "Leave him in the car." She wiped her hands on a Kleenex from her jeans and threw the tissue in at Randy. "I won't touch him again."

I voiced reservations about leaving Randy unattended. He could do a lot of damage to the Ford's interior, just with his body being unconscious.

"Okay," conceded the girlfriend. "Make him crawl out onto the sidewalk, then lock up the car, and let's go."

The amateur stripper had a stronger sense of the code. She and I shouldered the chore of carrying our benefactor toward the Canterbury. The girlfriend supported us from a distance. She pinched her nose with delicate disgust.

Randy had developed profuse sweats. He may also have peed his pants. Angel dust can be like that. It is, generally speaking, a misnamed substance.

Moving Randy through the Canterbury lobby was tricky. The building manager had banned him from the premises. There was a perception that Randy enjoyed urinating in the elevator. To complicate matters, he made himself heavier than he needed to be, dragging his feet and dropping his pants over the final twenty yards. The stripper and I dumped him into the elevator, in with the piss stench.

We pushed the fourth-floor button and raced the lift up the stairs. The tomboy stripper and I arrived at the landing, and stood sucking in air. We had survived so much! She and I almost embraced. Behind us, her slow and aggrieved girlfriend was stomping up the stairs and would arrive shortly.

The elevator doors opened to reveal Randy pretzel twisted on the floor. His beady eyes stared out as through milk. He was some monstrous newborn, gazing in horror at a world the baby monster innately knew would be correct in rejecting him. The stripper and I each took a shallow breath. We grabbed an ankle and dragged Randy along the hallway carpet to my apartment. Thank god the wife was away. I opened all the windows and spread some newspapers on the floor, Sunday job ads that I had never made it through. We rolled Randy onto the newspapers. The girlfriend brought up the rear. We sat and watched Randy from as far away as we could in a single apartment.

"Do you hear that?" said the girlfriend.

Someone was trying the doorknob. A key turned in the lock. The building manager entered the apartment. This self-professed animist had stabbed an intruder dead in the lobby a week before the wife and I moved in. He looked angry, all the way up to his knit skullcap.

"Hey, it's good to see you," I said, like I was working a sales floor.

The animist pointed at Randy: "He's going to die. Get him out of here."

None of us had imagined Randy might die. It was an intriguing possibility. He fluttered his eyes and waved his paws.

"He ate a bad burrito," I said.

The manager was less than reassured, but he left.

Randy rolled onto his back. He had a few false starts, but sat up on the third try.

"Bad burrito," he said. "You are not a gracious man."

"I'm leaving," said the stripper's friend. "Now that he's talking."

"Can you close the windows?" asked Randy.

"You stink," said the stripper. She wasn't being mean about it. "And it's one hundred degrees in here."

The girlfriend went out to the hallway, and left the door open behind her. She and the stripper weren't so close after all.

"Really," said Randy, creeping on his belly toward the door, like a dog once more, "at this height, open portals are not safe."

Randy, I realized, had become suddenly afraid of open windows. He crawled as far away as possible from the four-story drop and pulled the packet of angel dust from his pocket. He tossed the bindle of drugs blindly and lurched to his feet.

He swayed against the far wall, about to make a pronouncement. He decided against speaking and bolted through the doorway. Something fierce was chasing him. I walked over from the couch, looked both ways down the empty hallway, and closed the door.

Randy had gone, but his sweat outline was imprinted on the newspaper on the floor. The amateur stripper and I sat still for a few minutes.

She and I moved to the windows that surveyed the courtyard. Leaning out from above, we watched Randy scuttle past the dirt-filled fountain, headed toward Cherokee. He walked with his legs held wide apart, as if protecting some wet, delicate, living thing shoved down into the crotch of his pants.

The tomboy and I pulled our heads inside the window and avoided each other's eyes. We had both marked the spot where Randy's packet of angel dust had come to rest, and our gazes went to it.

SCENE SEVEN:
BLANK FRANK PAYS HIS
RESPECTS

I t's an off Sunday night in 1978—no shows, no parties, no better place for the Canterbury contingent to be. Mooches milled around the dirt-choked courtyard fountain, vigilant for any acquaintance who might have purchased drinks.

Blank Frank stood apart, smoking. He kept to the shadows beside the iron gates that opened to Cherokee. Dusted in pancake powder, Blank's face glowed like a bored moon above the black leather of his coat.

I was headed to the pay phone at the Laundromat with Tommie. It was Mother's Day, and I was working up the nerve to give mine a call. I didn't know how that call would go. She might have questions: *Where was I living? What had I been doing?*

Did Frank owe me a cigarette? I slowed, put the brakes on Tommie.

Frank trained his eyes on a clump of Canterbury kids, as if his eyes could keep them away. "Hey," he said. "Do you guys want to take a walk?"

"Do you have another cigarette?" I said.

May is one of those warm months before the hot LA summer. It's cool enough after sunset to wear long sleeves, or even a light jacket. Nobody thinks you're trying to hide anything, such as marks on your arms.

Unless you're the arms of Blank Frank; Frank's every stylistic nuance was layered on to arouse suspicion.

He drew out his Marlboro pack, flipped the top, and extended a cigarette. It wasn't quite so deliberate as a ritual, but there was more to the gesture than met the eye. That's how it was with Blank Frank.

Blank Frank was a quiet guy who kept his apartment compulsively neat. He was almost alone in the Canterbury with that. Maybe he'd picked up the neatness during his stint in the Navy. People who live on boats learn to stow everything. Not that the Navy figured much in Frank's conversation, which was—as stated—limited.

I lit the proffered cigarette myself—it's how things were done.

He spoke again: "I need to see a queen who owes me a Thai stick."

Thai stick? It was an off night for Frank too.

Frank had played bass in the Plugz. If you have a copy of the Plugz first album today, you can probably find somebody to give you a hundred bucks for it. But this was only 1978, and already the Plugz had fired Frank for being undependable, or on drugs, or inept. It's a proud thing to be kicked out of a punk band on a proficiency clause.

Strolling south, tightlipped, the three of us did a pass through the young sexual mercenaries clustered outside the Gold Cup coffee shop at Las Palmas and Hollywood. The young mercenaries struck perfectly casual poses, and their eyes darted from car to car. Traffic always bunched up on that corner. Everyone out there, on both sides of the curb, seemed to know Frank.

Frank huddled just inside the door to the Gold Cup with some hustler dude and the Thai stick queen. They put on some little act with the cigarette machine.

Tommie and I waited outside, blending in and standing separate. Runaways and castaways lipped Marlboros and jostled for position on that tight corner. The few girls all looked like some variation of my friend the amateur stripper.

The wife stood out, I couldn't help but notice, and not just because she was lined up with Gold Cup girls. My view was colored, I admit, by all the times we'd been together naked and enraptured, and during the late nights and the mornings after that, but it would be a mistake to dismiss my observations due to bias. Her looks and style were original to her and standout superior—anywhere, any time. One glance, and you see this is a woman who stands her ground wherever she might set down. Every generation that makes a mark has a few who are the real thing, and I was looking at it. I knew it during the loaded now of then, and I see it in dry retrospect.

Frank rejoined us, his blankness slightly animated. Still, his face didn't move when he talked.

"C'mon," he said. "I know a place down the way."

We walked along the curb through the Las Palmas meat exchange. Sellers and buyers alike offered Blank cigarettes he hadn't even asked for. For a block or so, it was like walking with a star. Then we made a turn at the cruiser church on Selma. We took the sidewalk along its facade—three compatriots heading to get high.

Dudes for rent flexed and slouched on the church steps. They posed like higher-end trade than the kids working the cross traffic at the Cup. Frank was known on these stairs, known as unproven talent.

Cars idled at the church front, headlights on, all dark inside. Tommie was completely out of place here. The spotlight was on male, and the lighting, from a pair of bulbs high on the sacred wall, was most flattering on the top church step. John Rechy might have been presiding up there in his cuffed jeans and rolled T-shirt, leather jacket slung over his pumped muscles.

"Did you ever read *City of Night*?" I asked.

Frank thought about it. "I don't have time for magazines."

He led us into a garbage alley and went straight up to a sagging two-car parking garage—obviously deserted, obviously dilapidated, obviously never again opening its broad awning. Frank knocked on a side door.

"I don't know about this," I said to Tommie.

Weed was best smoked in alleys, not in abandoned structures. There's an added burglary charge if you're busted in a structure that's not your own. Plus, if someone wants to put a hand on you, it's difficult to flee from a confined space. Cops might drop by totally by chance. We'd be trapped there, inside four walls. Some grudge-bearing rival might come looking for Blank Frank. He was quiet, but who was I to presume he had no enemies?

Frank rapped a glass pane in the side door.

"Let's go," I said. "No one's here."

"There's a light inside." Frank pressed the door; it was flimsy, and the frame had been splintered in more than one spot. He popped the latch. "We're cool."

Frank held the door open. Tommie stepped forward. I wanted to hold back, but I needed to keep her in sight; so I followed.

"Jack crashes here," said Frank. "It's his mom's place."

I peered around in the murk. Was that a Deep Purple poster? A cat smell didn't seem current.

"And who's Jack?" I said.

The question hung for a while in the dust that we'd kicked up by walking in.

"I'm Jack." This kid, Jack, maybe seventeen, was collapsed in a plush chair. The chair frame, legs busted off, centered directly on a massive oil stain in the cement floor.

Jack's face was impossible to focus on. It was shifting and lumpy, red as a welt, like a sculpture in hamburger meat.

Blank Frank didn't betray any trouble looking into Jack's face. "Do you want to smoke some Thai stick?" he said.

"Can't," said Jack. His voice was like sludge, slurry and toxic. "Don't have any."

"What are you on?" said Frank.

"I took some, uh…"

It was painful to watch Jack's brain labor. Frank tried to help him out.

"Quaaludes?"

"Don't know."

"Dust?"

"Don't think so."

"Reds? Nembutal? Methadone?"

Jack's brain kept working toward it. *Working* is being used in a specialized way. Jack's brain worked all right. It worked like a tongue works, a tongue that has lost the mechanics of speech, a tongue working a wound in anesthetized gums. That behavior was a clue.

"Placidyls?" I said.

"You're right!" Jack's face coalesced for a moment. He might have been a regular-looking kid under different circumstances. "Placidyls. Maybe two."

"Wow," said Frank. He admired me. "How did you figure that out?"

"It's the anniversary," said Jack. Now that his brain had identified what it was mired in, thoughts and data crawled in the sludge.

"No it isn't," argued Frank. He crumbled Thai stick into a small pipe and handed it to Tommie.

"It's the seven-month anniversary," protested Jack.

"So, on the fourteenth of every month, you hold an anniversary party?"

"It's not a party. It's a wake." Jack had become sage. "And today's not the fourteenth. It's the fifteenth."

"You can't even keep the day straight. He was your brother, and you can't even keep the day straight."

"He took the dope on the fourteenth. It was the fifteenth by the time he died."

This was all news to me and Tommie. At Blank's urging, we passed the pipe back and forth. Tommie took a hit and held the smoke until she coughed. It was really Thai stick, and not regular weed soaked in formaldehyde or some other shit; so that was a relief. Tommie's coughing prevented her from passing the pipe.

"Hey, Jack." Frank indicated Tommie, hacking out of control. "What do you have to drink?"

This was a whole new subject. Jack's brain went to work again, numb but painful.

"In the house," he said.

"Oh, no," said Frank. "We'll just go get something at the store."

That was too late. Jack was on his feet, testing his sea legs, in motion. Faster than could have been anticipated, he was out the side door.

"You can stay here if you want," said Frank. "Or come with me and Jack."

Tommie silently pointed out what might be rat droppings.

Frank missed that. "Just don't let anyone in," he said, "unless it's me or Jack. Hookers from Sunset try to trick in here. They bring all kinds of problems."

Tommie and I locked in step with Frank as he moved after Jack. We crossed a square of dead lawn where they kept the trash cans and moved into the living room of a duplex proper.

A woman sat in a plush chair, perhaps the new chair that had replaced the busted one out in the garage. The woman was dark haired, hyper and subdued at once. She looked like she had learned to live holding her breath, for a long time.

Jack staggered in front of the woman in the chair, unsure if he was in greater danger of plunging on his face or flopping onto the back of his head. He and the woman seemed to have picked up an ongoing conversation.

"You don't know that," yelled Jack. "You don't know any of that. You don't know any of that."

"A mother knows. When you were a little boy. Coming through that door. With your brother. Your mother knew."

The living room was pleasant enough, what could be seen of it. These people didn't place much stock in lamps. A sofa and an empty plush chair were slanted to face a TV stand. The only thing missing from the stand was the TV. I'm guessing the glow from the absent TV screen had been counted on to provide the room's illumination.

Tommie was still coughing, intermittently, impossible to ignore.

"Sit down, sit down," said Jack's mother. She told us to call her by name, something like Rosemary. "Our family was raised better than to fight in front of guests. Sit!"

Tommie and I crowded into the most remote corner of the sofa. Frank attempted to make the common civilities: "Rosemary, these are my friends—"

Jack interrupted, angrily. "See, mother? Frank has friends. Real friends."

Tommie and I stared off at where the TV should be.

"My brother's friends shot him up and didn't bring him back."

"You don't know that, honey," said Rosemary.

"Why didn't they just tie a plastic bag over his face?"

"That's not how it happened," said Frank. "I told you already, a hundred times."

"You weren't there!" Jack revisited an anguish he'd stirred up at least a hundred times. "How do you know what happened?"

"What's happened has happened," said the mother. "Even Jesus died."

"They could have saved him. Frank, you know they could have saved him. They parked the car, and they ran."

Frank accentuated his blankness and his quiet; Jack's dead brother could not be so blank and quiet as Blank Frank. "There was nothing anyone could do."

All the fight surged out of Jack. Only his belief remained. Deflated, Jack sat on the empty TV stand: "If you'd been there, you would have saved him."

Frank leaned on the back of the empty plush chair. It was fine with me that the living room was dark. One of them, either Frank or Jack, was crying.

If there had been something Tommie or I could say, things might have been less awkward. Even Jack's mother saw how unfair the situation was, emotionally, on Tommie and me.

"Is your name Tommie?" said Jack's mother. "Come over here. I want to show you something."

The kid's mother switched on a table lamp next to her chair. Tommie got up, and I wasn't about to be left alone. The table lamp put a new accent on the shadows around Rosemary.

She pointed out the dead brother's high school portrait, in a chrome frame on the table under the lamp.

We couldn't make out the dead guy's features in the gloom. He wore a sport coat and a fat tie, and his hair covered his ears. He could be anyone we knew from high school.

"You could have been my son's friends. If he was here, you could be friends with him."

She was right. Even in the shadows, you could see he was a guy we would be in a car with, the kind of guy who would OD in that car, the guy we would leave in that car once we'd parked it somewhere distant enough not to be traced back to us.

"I think we might have met him once," said Tommie. Tommie had taken the mother's hands in her own.

The mother was glad somehow. *Glad* is another imperfect word. She was mostly pain under a smile. But she was touched, literally touched by Tommie, and touched that Frank had come over.

Rosemary pulled herself out of her chair and stood facing Jack. She left the room. Tommie and I sank back down on the sofa, watching Jack, who sat where the TV would be.

Jack's mother came back in.

"Maybe you never knew my son." She gave us big, plastic tumblers of flat soda. "You could have met him."

The soda was undrinkable. We sipped it. Frank polished off his tumbler so he wouldn't give any offense, so he wouldn't cause distress, so he would be the good guest. We said our goodbyes and were back out on Selma Ave.

A sense of duty distinguished Blank Frank from the rest of the friends who had failed to save the brother. Pancake makeup, needle-marked arms, selling sex, Blank Frank was a man who paid his respects. Was the sense of duty from having been in the Navy? Or did he go into the Navy because he had a sense of duty? The Navy didn't feature much in Blank's conversation, which was—as stated—limited.

We walked away together. Near the cruiser church, Frank split off from Tommie and me.

"Sometimes tricks pick me up because they just want to talk," he said. "And some tricks just want to not talk." Tommie and I were only a few blocks from the Canterbury. We had enough money to buy a small bottle. Coming out of the liquor store, I slipped the bottle under my shirt and pictured all my friends at the Canterbury who I was hiding it from. They were just kids, for the most part. Some were actual children.

A few might have known to hold Jack's mother's hand, but not many.

I was happy I'd met Tommie. I was happy I was with her. There were things, important things, I sensed, that she knew how to do.

Then again, we'd both been unable to make our Mother's Day calls.

SCENE EIGHT:
HOLLYWOOD AND HEAVENLY

I had stalled at the top of The Masque stairs, backing away from the descent in front of me.

I'd handled those steep cement steps a thousand times at least—wasted, wrecked, and ruined, spinning drunk in the dead of night. Here, in daylight, the blind corner at the bottom of the stairwell hid a fright I'd never sensed before.

The end of the world was waiting down there.

That might seem overly dramatic to someone who isn't me. Civilization at large, the streets, and parks, and apartment complexes, the continental alliances of nations with their complex global networks, none of that was in any danger of not carrying on. As for my own little universe? Its small end lurked behind that dark, concrete turn at the base of the stairs.

My amateur stripper friend clamped onto my wrist. I'd forgotten about her and her creaking, black leather jacket. I tried to smell the reassuring scent of cured hide, but my olfactory cells had been numbed out.

"Something feels creepy," the girl said.

The two of us wavered, suspended over the drop to The Masque. The amateur jerked my shoulder back, then forward; all sense of balance and security flew from me. I wanted to shove my friend away, or swing on her, but sudden motion—especially my own sudden motion—scared me.

Something had gone wrong.

About twenty minutes back, the amateur friend and I had sniffed prudent doses of Black Randy's jettisoned angel dust. We'd rashly left my apartment without giving the prudent doses time to process.

Right in the middle of crossing Hollywood Boulevard, our path to The Masque had morphed into something like a diabolical maze. Turning back and returning the way we'd come was incomprehensible. The way we'd come was uncharted territory. So we'd pushed forward, through confusion and disorientation. Why had we come to The Masque? What had we hoped to find here? All was lost in a low-hanging press of doom.

"Nothing is creepy," I assured my friend. "It's just the drugs."

We took a step down, and two more steps. The girl clung to me. The height was no good. Elevation was evil. I couldn't bring myself to descend further. Climbing back up? Unfathomable.

The amateur stripper let go of me.

"Holy Christ!" I grabbed the wall with both hands.

My friend reached into her jacket pocket and extracted the fold of angel dust. She made a motion to throw away the bindle. Her hand couldn't shake it loose.

I didn't want to, but I peeled one of my palms from the supporting wall. I plucked the drug packet from my friend's fingers and stashed it in my pants.

The amateur stripper squinted at me. She saw for the first time that I was an idiot.

Two or three seconds passed.

I was back on the sofa in my apartment. The wife was there, standing in heels and underwear, pulling a dress down over her head. I recognized her right away; so I concluded the drugs had peaked. I watched her lips move. I watched her body move. It took a while to factor in Tommie's relation to me, and what she was saying.

She had phone messages. Did that mean I'd been away?

A secretary at A&M records had called—Lindsay. The secretary's boss had called later—Chuck. The boss was intrigued by the marketing scam I'd plagiarized from Black Randy. A little later, said Tommie, The Dickies' management had rung up to verify that an executive team from the record company would convene the following afternoon to meet and discuss—at the Canterbury.

"They wouldn't dare," I said, "come here. They don't know what they're getting into."

"Neither did we," said Tommie. "I need to straighten this mess up."

Time played a sleight-of-hand and hid a stretch from me.

A group of us, seven or eight Canterbury residents, paraded down Hollywood Boulevard. I was in step with the wife and Viva, and with Michael Schmuck and a few more girls—Cow Woman among them, and maybe Jane Drano or Belinda.

I was in sync, that is, until we halted at the coin-operated photo booth outside of J.J. Newberry's five and dime store. My wife and my friends, my parade mates, had been headed to the photo booth all along.

I moved on down the sidewalk, shying away from having my picture taken, and stood facing J. J. Newberry's display window. Appearing casual, I searched my pockets, extensively, for a match to light my cigarette. I knew exactly where my matches were.

It had become midnight. My mind was clearing up in spots, and I spotted this bum ten yards distant, toddling close to the curb. He locked on me, on my isolation, and he altered his course so he staggered directly toward me. The bum walked holding his wallet open in front of him.

Up close, the bum's wallet was bursting with greenbacks. He had nothing smaller than a ten in there.

The bum asked me some pointless questions, like where to catch the bus to the mission, or directions to a blood bank open at this hour, dumb queries that made no sense to me.

"Look, I couldn't care less about any of this," I said.

Persistent, the bum came up with another ridiculous question that I knew nothing about, waving his open wallet under my face.

Although hunched over, and making himself small, and dressed in ill-fitting discards, the bum was clean, I noticed, with no dirt impacted in the crevices of his skin, with hands a person could eat off of, with a rash-free scalp line, and with the compact, yet muscular torso of a weekend touch-football linebacker.

His questions, I see in hindsight, were intended to distract me from these physical incongruities.

To put me off my guard, the bum should have asked about something that fascinated me. Such as: *Why are you so sad? What makes you special?*

"Where's the alley I can lie down in?" said the bum, aggressive about it. He lunged at me. I had to sidestep or his wallet would have hit me in the gut.

"Look," I said. "You're a nice guy, and so am I. But you can't be sure of anyone else out here. Put that cash away before some creep snatches it out of your hands."

The bum gave me an odd, disappointed look. He had misread me. I had let him down.

I fled the fake bum, like I would flee an undercover cop and his hidden crew of arresting officers.

The wife and friends had squeezed into the photo booth for a group shot. I squirmed in among them. Lights flashed; I winced. No one else seemed to be harmed by the flashing lights.

A few minutes later, a strip of photos popped out of a slot.

My friends clustered around the strip, gabbing and laughing.

Michael Schmuck's voice pierced out from the jabbering mass. "Allan MacDonell!" he said. "Look at that face!"

I stood behind Tommie, with a view over her shoulder. I invested one hopeful second focusing on the picture strip. There I was, my face, out of place, looking in the wrong direction, pensive and startled while everyone else mugged in unison. My pictures never came out in a flattering light. I always wanted to look better than I did.

"Look at that face," repeated Michael Schmuck. "Allan MacDonell!"

He spoke as if he were enchanted, harboring a crush. I suspected an ironic subtext. My mind was still sluggish with PCP, but I knew my face value when I'd seen it.

I wandered off from the group, on my own, relinquishing the protection of the herd, beyond touch, out of context, where I belong.

"Allan!"

"Allan, wait!"

Tommie and Viva split off from everyone else and danced toward me, waltzing and swaying among the sidewalk stars along the derelict Walk of Fame. They floated like hopscotch ballerinas, childlike, gleeful, pretending to taunt me.

The wife and Viva were a 1:00-in-the-morning vision in their thrift-store summer dresses and glamour heels. All of Hollywood Boulevard was free to look upon them and rejoice. The bums, and kooks, and freaks aligned with me—we gazed drunken and rapt as this pair of anointed street nymphs sailed from star to star.

I followed Tommie's and Viva's swirling vintage hems back toward the Canterbury. The PCP lingered in my system, but I knew I was a witness to grace, and innocence, and sex appeal, and light-heartedness, and fearlessness. I had touched them, both of them, even if I had blown it.

It was later, abruptly closer to daybreak. Tommie and Viva and I had gone for a drive. I know we had, because I was parking my car on Gower south of Santa Monica Boulevard with Tommie and Viva in the front seat beside me.

We squeezed through the side gate to the Hollywood Forever cemetery. Jayne Mansfield was in there, and Tyrone Power.

Arms linked, three abreast, we slogged over the deep, wet grass, weaving among tombstones and grave markers. My shoes were waterlogged and ruined. All you heard was the croaking of the frogs that lived in the pond at the center of the park.

Falling behind, I dropped flat on my back on the wet grass and let my clothes soak it in. The stars above, I knew they were light years away, but don't tell me that they weren't also in reach. I held two handfuls of stars, directing their heat and electrical currents down my arms to a storage chamber near my heart. I released the stars and let them go about their business.

I propped myself on my elbows. Tommie and Viva danced among the graves, leaping like hopscotch ballet girls from nameplate to nameplate, landing on one foot and kicking down the other.

My mind was calm, my body shivering and dew-soaked. My mind knew everything. The stars were in orbit, the planets were in orbit, and I fit in that orbit. The drugs had spun out of me, like they always did.

An abiding and breathable peace soaked through my clothes, drenched my hair, entered every pore—like a thick, pre-dawn fog exhaled by all the friendly dead below us. Silhouetted in the waning night's light, Tommie, Viva, and I stood and stretched on the dew-wet lawns.

Life was going to be great with Tommie. We were going to be okay. We would do things and have things like normal people do—we would take road trips and stay in hotels and pay by credit card.

I would be in my right mind for my meeting with the record company people. When the record company people finished and left, my correct brain would remain behind. My right mind would be with me for the rest of my years, from here on out, until the end of time, the first day of which was only a sunrise away.

SCENE NINE:
LESSONS FROM BEVIE LEVY'S
PROSTITUTE SISTER

A heavy, middle-aged lady, around thirty, in bustier and denim flares expanded out from the middle of Russ's sofa, unfurling like she was some large guest of honor and not a provisionally tolerated intruder. For us, thirty might as well have been fifty.

Some parasites didn't fit the Canterbury misfit mystique, but you couldn't throw them out. They knew somebody, or they carried an extenuating weight, or both.

This woman was Bevie Levy's older sister from her father's previous marriage.

"She's a prostitute," whispered Belinda. "And a terrible heroin addict." Two years or so ahead, Belinda will be nominated for a Grammy, but as she left Russ's apartment, and I arrived, her band hadn't yet decided on its name. Bevie Levy's sister scandalized and impressed Belinda. "She's been in jail. She just got out."

I walked in past the middle-aged hooker on the sofa, went into Russ's kitchen, said hello, and injected three Talwin. Talwin are prescription pills that give a crap high preceded by a fairly rich rush; so when you shoot them up, you concentrate on making that rush feeling linger, and you will look with disgust upon anything or anyone that distracts you from it.

The prostitute's boyfriend, Aussie, large and loutish, had been hanging around the Canterbury for a couple of days, maybe for a week. He wore big cuffs on his denim jeans and a wife beater under a leather jacket with the collar up. The look was a crooked cross between a ted and a skinhead, but lacking the sophistication of the ted or the menace of the skinhead. It's like he had been art directed for a scam modeling school.

He cornered me in Russ's apartment.

"I could tell you kinky tales," the Aussie lout said. "Tales that will shock; tales that will delight. Tales that will engorge you with envy."

He was the fat old prostitute's boyfriend. These engorging tales would involve her.

"You're cutting my high," I said.

A wet voice rasped in: "Good highs don't cut. You need a better high."

The butt-in was the heroin-addicted prostitute, fresh out of jail. She was meaty and experienced, and her voice box had been cured in cigarettes and god knows what else.

"I have the best connection in the city," she said. "He owes me for going down for him."

I wasn't quite sure what she meant by going down.

"Why are we waiting around here?" I said.

She put on a crop-waist jacket that had both fur and feathers to recommend it, and we squeezed into my car. It was just the two of us in there, and the jacket. The space felt cramped.

Her Aussie boyfriend banged on my car window. "Oy, mate. Let us in."

Half of this engorging couple was enough, and I waved him away. The brave brush-off is not usually within my bag of tricks. I'd been emboldened by drugs and my need for more of them.

The prostitute and I drove toward West Hollywood to cop from the manager of the seventies most influential mime-rock band. I can't remember its name.

"Jail is like a free detox," said the prostitute sister. "I went in on purpose, you know? I was really needing a detox."

"So you're giving up all this fun?"

She laughed with a gooey rasp. Humid breath reached my side of the car. "Don't be stupid."

I opened one of the beers I'd shifted from Russ's place. Fatty shouldn't have called me stupid. There was no chance of me sharing that beer with her now. I couldn't feel the Talwin anymore.

Her hand came in for a landing, but didn't quite touch down on my thigh. "You aren't very experienced, are you? Detox is where you go when your habit is too heavy. You come out clean of your tolerance, and you can feel a high again."

She seemed to be adopting a mentoring role with me. All I really wanted from her was driving directions and that her connection would be home and fully stocked.

"Detox is where you meet your best friends," she said.

"I don't want to meet any more people," I said.

"We're just alike," she said.

"I've made too many friends already."

"Me too, doll. That's why I do what I do. Trick."

The prostitute was about to explain the logistics of tricking and regale me with career high points. She smelled like broth.

More specifically, like vegetable soup from a can—with a hint of bacon.

"I worry about Russ," I said to divert her. "He keeps taking those Talwin pills."

"He could do a little more sharing," she agreed.

"I think those pills are poison," I countered. "I don't know the word. But the more of them you take, the high is more like withdrawal than it is a high. It's like they're…I don't know the word."

"Toxic?"

"*Poison.* I'm really worried about him."

"He should do more sharing."

The Talwin crash and alcohol mush were undermining my stony reserve. I wanted to keep to myself, but the swirl of booze and synthetic morphine was twisting my emotions inside out. I choked back an urge to confide. It was absurd, I knew, but the prospect of revealing myself to this woman welled up irresistible and repulsive. A desire for intimacy, to share life's bonding history, flicked my gag reflex. I physically retched while forcing my mind to swallow puked up bites of sour autobiography.

We reached West Hollywood, and not a moment too soon. Another few blocks of traffic, and I would have been telling her the secrets of my childhood, about my father telling me I was stupid and the kid in junior high who severed the brake lines on his dad's Buick and the continuation school kids in Alhambra who smoked out a wino with angel dust and, when he decided he was dead and wanted to stay that way, gave him a lift to the train tracks.

I managed not to talk about any of that.

Bevy's prostitute sister and I parked across from a gated security building south of Mayfair market, just below Santa

Monica Boulevard. She shrugged out of her feather fur jacket, opting to go in wearing the sheer, sleeveless bustier. Her upper arms were red with extensive marbling, like Spam.

I stopped short, leaving the sidewalk as a clear zone between us. The prostitute sister leaned on the security building's public door buzzer. The door razzed, and the bulky pro moved forward. Someone seemed to be expecting her. I committed to crossing the sidewalk. I puked a little, into a planter, and felt much relieved. My secrets were safe with me.

I followed the prostitute's insolent hams into a stale elevator and wondered what that smell was. Going up, I pinpointed the odor as coming from her. A new element had been added to her broth fragrance, but I couldn't quite distinguish the makeup of the scent. The rising elevator stopped, its doors opened, and I was happy to put this investigation on hold.

A couple of seemingly random turns in a deserted hallway brought us to a door that had been left ajar. She opened without knocking and led me into an apartment where all the drapes were drawn. The lights were down.

Four reclining beard-and-sideburns dudes in their early thirties sized us up. They were all too cool to grunt, let alone get up from their sofas and armchairs.

They were playing an Eagles album. It wasn't on the radio; it was on the turntable. They all had the costume of Laurel Canyon outlaws, and they gave me those glowering looks meant to signify I was a punk kid who they couldn't be bothered to front off. It didn't work. Many people scare me. These people did not scare me. In my world, you can't play the Eagles and be intimidating at the same time.

My angel dust acquaintances from Alhambra, the two girls and two dudes who'd taken the wino to meet his train, they'd driven around for about a year basking in their notoriety, making people nervous wherever they parked. One of the angel dudes owned a van, the Dodge version of the Ford Econoline. He liked to drive it fast and reckless, and only a pussy wears a seatbelt. Naturally, deservedly perhaps, they'd sped that van into a light pole face first, with that windshield like a breakable movie screen—four dead upon arrival, and the light pole needed work.

The mime-rock band manager took our money and said he was driving to Silver Lake to make the connect. So the band manager wasn't the connect. He only knew the connect. Silver Lake was back beyond where we'd driven from.

"Come back," he ordered. "In about an hour."

The prostitute plopped on a sofa.

"We'll wait." She unfurled.

The Laurel Canyon outlaw who'd been sitting on the sofa moved across the room and swirled a kitchen chair around. He squatted like a cowpoke, leaning forward on the chair back.

I just wanted my money back and the chance to start anew elsewhere. Sadly, my drugged boldness had worn off before I'd had an opportunity to speak up. Lassitude was the name of my game, and it allowed the prostitute to pull me down onto the sofa beside her.

The band manager left to make the Silver Lake run, and the prostitute sister let the three other dudes believe that I was her boyfriend, seemingly to forestall anyone coming on to her.

Maybe she owed some blowjobs. Who can know what relationships exist among any four acquaintances in a room? Her body touched my clothes all down my flank. It was as if her sweat were crossing through the fabric between us and settling directly upon my skin.

Part Two

The Laurel Canyon scofflaws ran out of Eagles albums and turned on the TV to some late-night rock concert show. Dave Mason was playing. The three dudes in their early thirties talked about Mason as if they'd all worked with him. One of the dudes might have been an actor, a baby-faced version of Gary Busey, from Iowa or something, all corn-fed and athletic.

"Davey's on the needle. Isn't it true that Davey's on the needle?"

They kept fingering their noses and sniffing obnoxiously, as if they were doing mounds of coke. They'd done no coke since my arrival. The lethargy was palpable.

Hours passed, two. Everybody slept in shifts, but I did not. The prostitute offered to stay awake and watch over me.

"I want to go get a beer," I said.

"You can't," said the actor.

For an instant, I thought he meant that he would stop me if I tried to leave.

"It's past two a.m.," he said. "Cutoff time."

To calm myself, I cataloged objects within arm's reach that would make effective improvised weapons.

The band manager came back. Many aging hours had passed, but he seemed refreshed and younger than when he'd left. He tossed our balloons to Bevie's sister and clapped his hands. I snapped my balloons from the prostitute's wet palm before her sausage fingers could close.

She may have shaken off her habit in jail, but the jones came back on her heavy. She tried to corner the band manager with her bulk. "You have to let us get off here. You took so fucking long."

The mime-rock band manager was shifty from years of music industry experience. "This stuff is too potent. I won't be responsible to bring you two around."

I didn't want to get high there. I'd had enough of these people.

The corn-fed Gary Busey rushed to tie off. He cooked it and jabbed in the needle. Like for a screen test, he sighed and heaved his eyes in an overstatement of ecstasy. That move sealed it: He was an actor, and a bad one. He didn't pretend to puke, and that was an ill omen for the potency of the drug.

The night air was cool and damp and made me feel better just to be in it.

The car faltered. It wasn't going to start.

Bevie's sister worried. "He wouldn't let us get off at the crib. We've been beat."

The car was just kidding. It started up.

"But he wouldn't dare beat us," she said. "We know where he lives."

She directed me to take a back route, climbing Kings Road into the hills above Sunset and swerving onto a remote residential extension of Hollywood Boulevard.

I put the radio on an oldies station, hoping for something from The Standells or even the Stones for Christ's sake.

Bevie's prostitute sister changed the station. She landed it on "New Kid in Town" by the Eagles.

"Johnny-come-lately, the new kid in town. Everybody loves you; so don't let them down." The prostitute hummed along. "Johnny-come-lately, the new kid in town. Will she still love you when you're not around?"

I made a mental note to broadcast her musical preference upon my return to the Canterbury. The prostitute's shunning would be absolute.

She pawed my shoulder. "Anywhere along here, I can have a john stop and give him a blowjob. This is a safe stretch of road. Nothing bad ever happened here."

I kept driving and diverted myself with thoughts of other people I didn't want near me, people I'd known and didn't know anymore, all people who never would have found their way into the Canterbury. I named the ones I had harmed, and the ones who had harmed me. I wasn't always sure which were which.

A whole mob of them crowded into the car, reproaching me, pushing me face-first toward Bevie's prattling sister. Finishing the ride east, under the Hollywood Boulevard bright lights, went on forever—it's still going on now. Repeating, interchangeable blocks of flash and neon took me nowhere. Me, and these passengers with their accusations and their insults, we never arrive anywhere.

I took the first parking spot I saw, about a quarter mile from the Canterbury. Bevie Levy's prostitute sister stuck with me for fifty yards walking down Cherokee, but she'd winded herself with all the talking. She lagged behind at the courtyard gate, and I ditched her at the lobby elevator.

Back at the apartment, Russ and Tommie had been calling jails, hospitals, and morgues, looking for me. They didn't seem all that happy to see me walk in alive, intact, and free.

"Where's Bevie's sister?" said Russ.

"She's in the building. She's looking for a place to shoot up."

Russ was out of our business pretty quickly after that.

When we were alone, Tommie said, "I can just get strung out along with you. And I can be a prostitute and buy both our drugs. How does that sound?"

For a moment, I didn't know she was testing me, and I failed.

I considered her offer.

She cried tears that sought no comfort from me.

"Some days," she said. "I'm usually okay with everything, but some days...."

I fingered the two balloons of heroin, the drugs that I had endured so much to score. *Now I will suffer this little bit more, from the wife, then I will be high.*

"Some days, when you're off wherever you go looking for whatever you're looking for, I wonder if you even think of me. Do you picture me waiting back here all alone? Or maybe you do see me as I...."

She faded off, and was about to say what she'd left unsaid, but I filled in: "I think about you all the time."

"You do? The other night, I guess you were out thinking about me somewhere, and I thought, *What if when he comes back, and he's sitting there on the couch, all high—thinking about me, I guess—what if I go up on the roof and throw myself off? How long before he notices?*"

Could anybody be unhappy enough to kill herself on my account? I had no significance to me. My presence, my thoughts, my affections, they meant nothing as far as I was concerned; how could they matter so deeply to her? She was real. She was a person who counted to other people. Was I missing a hidden message here? What, really, was eating her?

I promised myself: *I will come back to these questions later, to give them the full and sympathetic consideration they deserve. For now, my mind is on the heroin, anticipating the packaged relief.*

Bevie Levy's sister and Russ appeared at the apartment door. They wanted me to hand over those last two doses. From their faces—anxious, earnest, duplicitous—I knew there would be no point in me taking this dope except for the bitter pleasure of knowing that I had guessed right all along.

It was a burn.

SCENE TEN:
THE FIRST FUCK-UP OF THE
REST OF MY LIFE

I woke up in my Canterbury apartment with an hour and a half to prepare for the arrival of the record company executives.

If A&M bought into the promotional plan I'd stolen from Black Randy, I could make money, enough to buy heroin for every weekend and one or two days during the week. Exotic travel, such as to New York, might also be involved. Tommie and I could move into a better apartment, maybe a duplex. Living at the Canterbury was dragging her down. She deserved a better life, and A&M Records might provide it for her.

I was anxious about the meeting, with reason.

Tommie came from the kitchen, moving in tidy-up mode. "You need to look authentic," she said, "but not like a guy who has a problem."

She gazed at a collection of crushed Rainier Ale tins. "We don't have anything for A&M to drink."

The wife was acting nervous, and nervous activity makes me nervous. When I want to be still and feel calm assurance deep within, and someone is trying to put my mess in order all around me, that distraction irritates my nerves.

I decided to go down to Russ's place and have two preparatory beers. The A&M meeting was important to me as an individual, and to Tommie and me as a couple. Two beers seemed like the optimum amount of verbal lubricant for smooth talking—without spitting or slurring. I was thinking tall cans.

Russ was game. We strolled to the liquor store at the corner of Las Palmas and Yucca, where the transgender hookers would pop up once dark came. I loitered at the magazine rack, flipping through *Hustler* and *Penthouse*. My browsing was furtive and freighted with weird echoes of guilt and betrayal. Intuitively, the store's counterman turned his scrutiny to keep me under close surveillance. Russ slid four tall cans of Rainier Ale into his Ramones leather jacket.

We bought a pack of Marlboros. To exercise my discipline, I didn't open the cigarettes until we were seated back at Russ's kitchen table, overlooking the courtyard, and popping the tab on a Rainier. We lit up. I ran through my presentation, the A&M pitch, but it bored me. I preferred to rehearse the lifestyle I was about to adopt. Famous people would be my friends. Famous women would suggest threeways with Tommie and me. The good life was falling right into place.

Somewhere between the first tin of ale and the second, I was in the bathroom of the abandoned apartment next door to Russ's place, with Russ and Hellin Killer. We were hiding from our friends.

A spoon and Black Randy's discarded angel dust were set out on the lid of the toilet. I hadn't noticed taking the angel dust from my pocket.

"Are you sure it's okay to shoot this stuff?" said Hellin.

Hellin was one of The Plungers. She had a moony face and a maudlin disposition. Her laugh was the loudest thing about her. You don't think of maudlin people as being big laughers. The disposition is revealed in what they laugh about.

Real light never touched any of the Canterbury's bathrooms. Each one had a single opaque window over the tub, a window too small to squeeze your body through. If forced, the window would open on an airshaft. And across the airshaft would be the open window to some like-minded neighbor's bathroom.

Russ, Hellin, and I were embarrassed to be doing what we were doing. William Burroughs, Iggy Pop, Lou Reed, even Sid Vicious, none of your leading junkies had ever admitted to shooting up angel dust. Russ silently unwrapped a syringe from a sock. Wordlessly, I opened the packet of white powder. Without discussing it, we knew we didn't want anyone to hear what we were up to.

A clatter came from the bathroom across the airshaft. Someone clumsy had dropped a toilet seat. Piss splashed—a dude, or a hell of a woman. Water ran, small water in a sink. Our man was a hand washer. There was something else. Humming. The guy was singing, to himself, in a low voice. Singing Fleetwood Mac. His tone was furtive, and for good reason. Our groupthink at the Canterbury rejected as stale sellout hypocrisy the privilege, the excess, and the prettiness flouted by Fleetwood Mac—although privilege, excess, and prettiness all alighted upon my scheming dreams for a lifestyle upgrade.

"Go your own way," sang the guy across the airshaft. "You can go your own way."

"It's like he's singing in secret," I said. He'd forgotten about potential lurkers on the other side of the airshaft.

"In secret shame," said Hellin.

"Go your own way," sang our neighbor. "You can go your own way."

Russ drew water up through the needle into the barrel of the syringe. We only had one syringe, and we'd shared it for a week or two. A tight, round collar of dried blood had collected at the base of the barrel, down at the tip of where the plunger pushes the solution. It's inevitable that a bottom scab forms in a syringe after many shared uses. There's no fear or shame in a clot of blood, at least there was no HIV fear of it in 1978, and less shame than being caught humming a song by Fleetwood Mac.

Russ drew a water/angel dust solution up through the needle. The collar of coagulated blood broke loose from the base of the syringe and rose in the solution. It was like a nugget of scab, and it floated in the middle of the syringe, at the five-cc mark.

"Do you see that?" I said.

Ladies first, her arm tied off with a rubber strip, Hellin accepted the syringe from Russ.

"The scab?" She pierced her skin with the point and registered almost immediately. Blood plumed in, and the scab was out of sight and out of mind in her shot's crimson load.

Hellin finished and passed over the needle. Russ drew water into the rig and rinsed the chamber. He prepared his shot.

"The scab is still there," I said.

The fleck of dried blood hovered again at the five-cc mark. Black blood squirted in from Russ's vein, and the scab faded from view.

"Go your own way," sang the neighbor. "Don't go away."

Hellin's face had trouble I'd never seen in it before.

She said: "Hey, doesn't that old lady with the burns live in this apartment?"

A few ancient, broken characters had been at home tottering in the Canterbury halls when our invasion of youth and vitality had first swept through: an ancient ventriloquist whose wig moved whenever he tried to speak through his ancient little dog's wheezing snout; a stooped Navy vet who juiced big once a month and claimed to have survived the Japanese attack on Pearl Harbor; and an old lady with burn scars up and down her arms.

Russ's teeth clamped down on the belt around his arm. "That old lady died," he said.

"Are you sure she died?" said Hellin. "Were you at the hospital when it happened?"

"She didn't die in the hospital." Russ finished injecting and yanked the prick from his elbow crook. Success! "She died right there, in her room."

This news rocked Hellin. She and Russ peeked out the bathroom door into the studio apartment. The old lady hadn't owned much, and it had all been ransacked. Mary the Rat and Margot were both wearing dresses they'd salvaged from the estate.

Russ handed me my shot. The collar of dried blood floated free in the chamber. For all I knew, the A&M suits were in the elevator right now. Russ tried to figure out what had just hit him.

"Such a lovely place," came the airshaft serenade, "such a lovely place."

Afraid of being left hunched over a dead lady's toilet seat all on my own, I popped the tip of the needle into my vein and took the plunge.

Imagine being the misguided adventurer who shoots angel dust just to see where the rush will lead. Go ahead. Three of you are crowded around a dead woman's toilet in an apartment none of you has legal access to.

You put the rig away, and you know this trip isn't one you'll want to take a second time. The air doesn't make sense. How can you be expected to have any use for that stuff? What evil elements and polluted particles might be hidden in it?

Up and down become arbitrary and interchangeable. You wake up shambling onscreen during a showing of *Night of the Living Dead*. The movie's almost over, and you're still trying to figure out, *Am I a zombie? Or am I one of the traumatized and pursued townspeople?*

"I'm late," I said. "To my apartment."

"What is he talking about?" asked Russ.

Hellin Killer had no idea, and who could blame her? She'd injected first, and the PCP had corroded further along in her nervous system.

"A&M Records," I explained.

The company's fact-finding executives had surely arrived to interview me. Their quest for knowledge wouldn't wait forever.

Hellin's full moon face opened, and a shocking, flat laugh blurted out: "What happened to the old lady who lived here?"

"She died," said Russ.

"Yes, we all know. What happened to her then?" Hellin's disturbing flat laugh erupted once more, and her face clamped shut.

My legs had no confidence in themselves. Working on faith, they walked me through the dead woman's furnished single and into the Canterbury public hallway.

Russ followed after me. Hellin could find her own way out of the bathroom.

Once in the hall, I ducked to avoid something moving in the air and dropped flat to the floor. The disturbance passed close by above me, real or imagined, and a sudden and absolute fear of heights came on. I didn't dare stand up. My full height was too high for safety.

The wife would accept no excuse for missing my meeting with the A&M executives. True, I was unable to walk, but that could be overcome. Inch by inch, on hands and knees, I crawled to the stairwell.

The atmosphere weighed heavy on my shoulders. All the way up to the top of the stratosphere, the shaft of air directly above me condensed, solidified, and bore down upon me. My elbows locked, and I was afraid to lift my hand from the carpet. Surely, the force of gravity would slam my face into the threadbare burgundy rug and straight on through the floor.

My apartment was one short flight above. That short flight was in a frightening direction—skyward.

My hands maneuvered up the face of the stair without breaking contact with the surface.

A Vietnamese refugee woman passed to the left, two children in single file behind her, loaded with grocery bags. This family had seen every atrocity, presumably, during the years our country was carpet bombing theirs. Mom diverted the attention of her children from me and hurried them past.

I caught sight of myself as if through the view of a passerby. Here I was, twenty-two years old, the age of a grown man, squirming on the stairs like a monstrous infant. What would Russ think? Embarrassed, I looked over toward my left, hoping to verify I was out of his sightline.

Right beside me, Russ crept on his hands and knees. His face had the concentration of a dog being forced to walk backward. He planed his palm up the vertical surface of the steps, mimicking my hands. His shoulders quivered under the relentless crush of the atmosphere.

Russ's struggle brought the reality of the situation down upon me: the pressing distress was not, after all, merely an effect of the drugs. It was the boot of the universe blotting out all life in its rapid descent. We would be squashed like bugs.

Defying all odds and hazards, I crested the stairwell and kneeled at the door to my apartment.

Russ caught up with me. We looked at the closed door as if it were the first of its kind we had ever encountered. "You knock," I said.

My dusted friend tried to lift a hand off the carpet. "Stuck," he said.

I leaned forward and thumped my head on the door, quietly once—*thunk*—then harder, with volume. *Thunk.*

Tommie opened the door and looked down. I didn't like her grim, humorless aspect. She stepped back.

"Look who's here," she said.

We had company. Behind the wife, one Dickie and three A&M adults sat on the sofa. Chuck and Lindsay were playing it cool, seated at opposite ends.

Tommie's expression could not have been charming them. Our guests deserved a better effort.

I crawled in, advanced to the center of the rug and curled into a fetal ball. My notes on the proposed marketing campaign were out of reach, and incomplete. Perhaps I could wing it. Black Randy had winged it.

Scraps of Randy's fan club spiel came to me. Eyes closed, I muttered by rote. Eventually, I became aware that our visitors had stepped over me as they walked out. Chuck, in fact, had trucked across my prone body.

I rolled onto my back. Russ groaned, curled under a chair like a dying baby. Tommie stood looking down at us. Her lips squeezed out a smile that was too tight for sympathy or patience or playfulness.

"I don't understand how this can be fun for you," she said.

"Fun?" I said. Here was the lasting disappointment of the morning. The woman I had wed did not understand me, not at all. "What does any of this have to do with fun?"

SCENE ELEVEN:
COTTON FEVER

My knowing head was hanging upside down inside a toilet bowl on an unseasonably warm August night. My smart mouth heaved what might be the last gasps of my life into rusty porcelain. I'd done a stupid intravenous thing.

Viva had taken over a vacant Canterbury apartment, two floors down. I'd spent the early evening among her guests at a dinner party, smoking cigarettes, drinking gin, and eating potato soup pureed from Dumpster-recovered produce.

I'd been first to arrive, alone. Wet and pink from the shower, Viva had been selecting her party costume. Nothing satisfied her. She couldn't even pick a pair of panties.

It was unnecessary to inform Viva that I had been shooting up phenobarbital prior to dropping by. No one needed to be told I was that lame.

Over dessert—shoplifted Tootsie Pops—I seemed to be arguing with Michael Schmuck about something that meant very little to me. For a moment there, Schmuck and

I looked to be actually coming to an agreement. In fact, we were competing to make the same point. Suddenly, I was very cold.

I retreated upstairs, to our place, where Tommie and I lived, to put on a sweater. About halfway up the stairwell, it felt like a cutting mix of ground glass had been sprinkled into the joints of my arms and legs. That's not all—metal shavings had been dusted between the bones of my spine and shoulders.

Physical pain like this had never afflicted me, before or since. To describe it beggars exaggeration and hyperbole. I was too sick to cry.

No one was home at my place. The lack of witness was cold comfort. The Arctic winds of Los Angeles breezed in through our open apartment windows. Freezing and hurting, I knew it was ninety degrees outside, but the breeze felt like icicles shredding my skin. Hobbled, I shut the windows, shivering, aching, and sucking for breath.

Keen-minded, I suspected that this discomfort had originated in those Phenobarbital injections, and in the gin. Vomit, I deduced, was on my horizon. My wise move was to collapse on the bathroom floor.

A small window above the bathtub was open into an airshaft. Across the shaft was the bathroom window of the apartment shared by Belinda from The Go-Go's and another yellow-haired girl who had no real sympathies for me.

I retched. Pain shot its bolts, overriding every nerve ending. I bit back a howl. Belinda and her unsympathetic roommate might hear a howl and would surely mock me. I pictured three girls standing, looking down at me, sharing two beers and one cigarette, and mimicking my agony as I squirmed at their feet like a worm in the sun.

I could no more stand and close that bathtub window than I could fly up the chimney of the fireplace of the apartment I did not have.

A groan eked out. A loud one erupted; three or four more followed. The sounds came as if some large, wounded animal had sprawled out inside of me to give birth and was struggling to break free. The beast's pain was loud and clear.

Females laughed in an apartment not too far away.

Tommie had not come back from working on art, or decorating, or her job.

I suffered like a dog—crawled off alone, curled in upon its belly and biting its own flesh to rearrange the pain. The cold departed in about half an elapsed instant. My body temperature rose alarmingly. Sweat dripped off me in a septic rain. My genitals shrank up, evaporated, leaving no indication that they would ever be back.

The rest of the world, the living portion of it, was completely absent from me, doing the things that people in a living world do, every person alive doing these things without me. With each shallow, hurried breath, I felt a boot to the ribs.

The time has come to make up with God.

What hole had that thought slithered out of? God was for dopes. His existence or conception, notions of His mercy and wrath were ordinarily absent from my thoughts. This was a sign. I had arrived at an extraordinary moment.

Sickness, alcohol poisoning, acute contraindications to prescription and outlaw medications. None of these were strangers to me, but this agony was new. Dying might be more than a theory after all.

"Jesus, fuck. What have I done?"

Three blonde witches cackled with nasty glee. Humiliation would hound me beyond my grave.

Death, the great inevitable mystery, had a pulse, an antirhythm to my heartbeat, and it throbbed no further distant than the thickness of the bathroom linoleum. I envisioned vast nothing below that yellowed skin of flooring. I felt the bottom opening to swallow what had been me.

After I'd crossed through, would I know what happened on the other side? There would be no more me. Would I gain knowledge about where I wasn't going?

Dying was like arguing with Michael Schmuck, with both of us trapped inside my skull.

What were the chances that some supreme being was listening, hearing my mind from under the floor, from beyond the walls? I assured this attentive and unlikely presence that my painful, and pointless, and premature demise was nobody's fault but mine. Full and absolute responsibility belonged to me.

That busted, dim moment of reflection wasn't much in terms of reconciliation with any basic conception of mortality. It was the best I could do, and it exhausted my last shred of effort. I had nothing left except to twist on the floor and wonder: At what notch will life ratchet out of my racked body?

Tommie came home, looked at me, walked out of the room, and came back crying. She tried water to my lips, washcloth to the forehead, a teary kiss to close my eyelids. She sat on the toilet and watched.

What did I fail to see in Tommie's eyes as she observed me maybe dying? Surely, she was hoping for something, pulling for some outcome.

My throat and jaw were beyond making meaningful sounds—and Tommie wasn't saying anything to explain herself. She didn't go for help, didn't bring in other witnesses. It was between her and me, whatever was happening.

Part Two

For the next few hours there on the bathroom floor, I pictured myself being better off in a hospital. But there would have been police.

At dawn, I was able to drink water and straighten out my limbs enough to lie on the bed. Tommie placed towels under my body to soak up what was left of my sweat. Soon, I would form words.

"You didn't die," said Tommie, beside me with the sunrise, the rebirth, the renewal, the starting it all over again, beside me and also far off someplace else. "Not this time."

PART THREE: THE PRO-CHOICE LAMENT

"Don't ever let him know."
—Girl A's word to the wise

SCENE ONE: FOREPLAY

One dusty August afternoon in 1978 the wife and I braved a rain of ignominy from the apartments stacked around the Canterbury Arms courtyard and moved out. We pushed three linked shopping carts—our amassed fortunes—from the lobby toward Cherokee. Trash and verbal bombs spilled out from open windows. A new contingent of malcontents had moved into the building's spare closets and abandoned flats. This younger sub-generation needed slapping into shape, but who could be bothered?

Tommie had enrolled in trade school. She believed that landing a job as a production artist would not be life's worst fate. One afternoon in late July, as Tommie carried her work portfolio into the Canterbury courtyard, headed home from class, three white-lipped girls who had misappropriated her style accosted her. The white-lipped girls derided my wife as a student and as an old person—two awful insults. These listless upstarts might have placed hands on Tommie's portfolio, except for the physical intervention of Hellin Killer, and Blank Frank, and Rock Bottom.

We couldn't really call the sullen copycats *fresh* meat. They were like week-old sandwiches. Pushing your shopping cart toward a new horizon, you didn't mind leaving the whole stale wad behind. It was easy not to take the rain of hostility any more personally than you'd take the August heat beating down.

"Even the fucking sun," I said, closing the Ford's trunk on the last of our possessions, "is fucking with me."

A misled landlord rented us a two-bedroom apartment in a sixteen-unit building a few miles south of Hollywood Boulevard, near Melrose. Russ moved into the second bedroom. We were still in Hollywood, and we were still in walking distance from two liquor stores. But we didn't have gauntlets of hooker dudes and spare change moochers between those liquor stores and us.

It seemed like a prime time for life to give me a fresh break. My unemployment checks had dried up, and I'd been hired to create charts from market research questionnaires. No thinking was required.

I passed three or more months cramped behind a desk contemplating sex with any woman who happened to lodge in my mind. Once or twice each day, Tommie rolled around in these contemplations.

Sometime before Thanksgiving, the wife and I reclined mostly naked on a mattress on the floor of our bedroom, taking stock. We had the door closed to keep Russ and his guests at bay. The wife and I smoked street weed. Seeds popped and burned holes in our sheet. I like to think that we were also drinking wine, to add that sparkle of sophistication.

"You and me, Tommie," I said, "we can talk about anything, right? With what we've been through, I feel that I don't need to hide what I'm thinking, like if I had thoughts that kept coming into my mind?"

The wife took the joint out of my fingers. We discovered I could not meet her eyes. My wily sightline brought a deep sigh from the wife, followed by a deep hit on the joint.

"What, really, is wrong with you?" she asked, trotting out what sounded like a running theme. Her eyes—I snuck a look—were earnest, quizzical, and plainly exasperated.

What *was* my problem?

Coincidentally, just that day at work I had been deep-thinking about my struggle. I seemed to have pinpointed the pressing crux of an ongoing dilemma. My problem was no more or less than the long list of women I had no chance of having sex with. A reasonable, grownup man would have guarded this self-diagnosis from a wife. A reasonable and grownup man might also be lounging upon a bed instead of on the floor. After moments of mute reflection, I coughed, and my failing blurted out: "The only thing that's wrong with me, really, is I haven't been with enough women…like, sexually speaking."

The wife refocused on me, calculating and speculating. Evidently, I'd given her something to ponder. Her calm evaluation wasn't the exact reaction I might have expected. She kept her eyes open and tight, tight on me.

To avoid the evaluation in her gaze, I looked at the wife, really looked at her. Her body was supple and relaxed, sure of itself. I saw why I had fallen for her, but that didn't explain why we were married, not at our age, with no children to have forced the issue.

Our wedding had come on something less than a dare. Back in Pomona, hardly more than a year back, I'd walked out of a liquor store carrying two sixteen-ounce cans of malt liquor and a Slim Jim meat stick. I ran into Michael Ortega.

Michael had started a band with our friend Larry. They'd been rehearsing, and they had eight songs. They were having a party in two weeks to unveil the eight songs. Michael told me all this as if such developments were a constant in his life. Then he'd said, "So, what are you up to?"

I had nothing. So I dug: "Me and Tommie are getting married."

"No shit. When's that happening?"

"Tuesday. You want to come? You can drive and be our witness."

I took my two sixteen-ounce malt liquors and my meat stick home and told Tommie about the plan. Don't ask me why, but she accepted the proposal, which was a big step toward what brought us to our bedroom floor in Hollywood and me putting out wheedling feelers.

Tommie's silence unnerved me.

"You've probably been with more women than I have," I said. She'd revealed a few details to me, about her explorations. I'd bulked out those details through a number of observations, adding suppositions based on those observations. My twenty-two-year-old's experience was so limited. My ignorance was so vast.

On the floor-supported mattress, I asked: "Do you know what I mean?"

"Tell me," she said, flat, mild, and curious.

I drained off the last of the wine. Well, let me try and dig my way out of it:

"Women, everywhere I go, they have an unfair advantage over me. In a store, at the doughnut shop, on a job interview—I can't even look a girl in the eye. I want them, and it's wrong of me to want them. Because I'm married, married to you. Women have a power over me because I can't talk and be normal. They come on to me, and I don't know how to behave. They see my mixed feelings as weakness. They think less of me."

The wife remained noncommittal and silent. Really, my audience was me. It's as if I'd sketched out this presentation off and on for months on end, maybe even staged a dress rehearsal, but this was the naked-truth command-performance premiere. I invested emotion in my theme. My voice thickened.

"It's like I'm walking through a world that I don't know. It's like the human exchange has a whole depth and side that is hidden from me. I can't be part of the other people. I'm excluded."

I was buying it. Tears brimmed over and dripped out, from my eyes.

The wife smiled. She displayed compassion for me. She didn't share my problem—picking up girls came to her as naturally as eating a jelly doughnut—still, she empathized.

"You poor fucker," she said… "You mean thing."

For a few seconds, it looked like she might cry, but no. That was laughter, unrestrained, merciless, right in my face. I'd seen it before, but not for about a year, not since I'd been popping beer bottles in a prospective boss's shower stall.

And then, because the wine was working and the weed wasn't bad, and because we were in our vigorous twenties, and there was nothing further to say that would not have been increasingly ludicrous, the wife drew me to her, and we made some version of floor-level love and passed out.

In the morning, upon awakening, I said an earnest prayer that the wife had forgotten the previous evening's ungainly and thinly cloaked plea for sexual adventurism. I opened my eyes. Tommie watched me in a calculating way. Her knowing smirk said that she remembered my beggarly ploy, perhaps with greater precision than I recalled myself. We didn't mention it.

Day upon day, I drove to the boiler-room office on Sunset near Fairfax and passed as employable. Intuitively, I refused all invitations from my coworkers to take drink or drugs. Those people didn't need to see the real me.

I come home, I go to work, a weekend rolls around, Christmas is weeks away, and the real me, my actual buffer-free self, showed up at a house party in the apartment of Don Bolles from the Germs and Pat Delaney from the Deadbeats.

Pat and Don had vacated their shared Canterbury single, among the last residents to leave, and taken tenancy of half a collapsing duplex south of Santa Monica Boulevard, on Gower. Their new place was across the street from Hollywood Forever Cemetery, a fabled resting place fallen into neglect and disrepair.

Russ parked the Ford along the cemetery wall, a few car lengths down from the decrepit residence where we were expected. Santa in the form of a piñata sat smashed on the porch. Don and Pat's get-together was a holiday party. *Slash* was sponsoring the seasonal celebration, which meant the magazine had supplied three half-gallons of vodka. People who my working routine had crowded out, including a cross section of Canterbury alumni, had crowded into the place. My nerves recoiled at being in the presence of former allies.

I'd wondered, *Will anyone try to recreate that long-lost energy and camaraderie of 1977?* But even in late 1978, time refused to go backward.

I filled a water glass from a vodka jug and hid the bottle behind a sofa. Naturally, that calmed me, but for how long?

I scoped out the setting: a teddy bear hung by the neck from a living room ceiling fixture. A syringe poked into teddy's fingerless arm. The light had gone out behind the bear's button eyes. Standing directly below the hanged rag doll, Michael Schmuck cast puppy glances up at the dead teddy, as if it were some twisting, moth-eaten version of mistletoe.

There was a vague sense between us that I owed Michael Schmuck an apology. I was disinclined to ask him for specifics. The Christmas season is hard enough without unwrapping a lot of pointed details better left packed away.

I made a cut for the hidden bottle. "Kickboy" Claude Bessy, one-half of the *Slash* brain trust that had refused to pay me for writing, placed the heel of his hand on my chest.

"Ah, the Basho Macko," said Claude, mocking my dust-balled penname. "The defector. The defective. The defecator. Your life, it is so much richer since you left us? With the trivial *Slash* gone, you have accomplished the much more important work…certainly. Have you not had enough vodka?"

I took a pull of vodka that would have been reckless if the liquid were water.

"From your attitude, Kick Face, tell me if I am wrong, I sense an implied suggestion that I am guilty of having deserted *Slash*." I put my non-vodka hand lightly on Claude's throat. "To the contrary, the truth is that *Slash* betrayed me and, beyond me, *Slash* has betrayed the ethos, the ethics, and the aesthetics of the entire punk scene. Money sins are the least of the *Slash* crimes, a tally of infamy I shall now enumerate for you."

My conscious self stepped aside, freeing my unspeakable outrage to articulate on automatic. Out of nowhere, I realized that something had happened to sour my stomach.

"Comrade Basho," asked Kickboy, "where did you go?"

He had a point. I'd come back, seconds ago, but I'd been gone, and not just wandering off in my mind. I reviewed the very recent past, and I learned I'd walked away from Claude and jaywalked across Gower with Russ and Greg and jumped the Hollywood Forever cemetery wall. Something had happened in there to disturb me, but not right away.

At first, in a shared celebration of life, Russ, and Greg, and I had toppled tombstones and scattered fake flowers from graves. We'd captured toads at the edge of the reflection pond. Then I'd been slighted. Russ had brought along pills to shoot up, but only enough for him and Greg.

Russ ate the wife's potato tacos. He had a room in our apartment. Surely, he should have split his high with me. The rejection, the marginalization, was intense.

Back at the party, Kickboy turned his back and stepped away.

People looked strange. I felt estranged. Hilarity broke out from the kitchen and from the bathroom. Did anyone remember I was there?

I slipped out the backdoor with a clutch of canned beer. The side yard was overrun and downtrodden. Sinking back against the stucco, I looked up, as if toward the stars, and saw the walls of Hollywood Forever Cemetery. Russ and Greg were within the confines still, mainlining bliss among a bunch of stiffs.

Would somebody—anybody—inside Don and Pat's house pause to realize I was gone? Would even the wife miss me? If only Viva would come back. She'd sent a postcard from New York City to Tommie, without mentioning me. Her absence was a looming presence all over town, especially at Pat and Don's.

So I was squatting in the weeds, staring up at where the stars must be, unable to see beyond my own orbiting inanity.

The position suited me. The only reason that I did not recline there unto eternity is the wife appeared around the corner of the house, looking for me, arm linked to arm with a young pixie sophisticate who shall be known only as Girl A.

Girl A held her profile high. She'd been a Canterbury original, on The Masque front line; she'd joined a band. The world would soon know her name, and some of them would never forget it. Her face smiled at me. I felt something like an exotic blend of drugs and happiness.

Maybe the wife had swallowed my line about needing to expand my sexual parameters. Who can say? It's not like I would dare to walk over to her place today and ask. Whatever her motives or sympathies, she'd taken my divulgence as the opportunity to snag Girl A and lure her out to the murky side yard, where she'd presumed I would be moping.

Girl A smoked one of those long, skinny cigarettes you couldn't even pull a hit off of. These flammable gimmicks were marketed to whimsical girls at the end of the seventies. You might as well not even be smoking. You might as well be waving a magic wand with a glowing coal on the end.

Girl A said, "I always think Allan is the one who's going to be really famous."

The three of us shared a pretense of having retreated outside to smoke weed. Beyond that small conspiracy, there must have been a negotiation, at the very least an exchange of driving instructions.

None of the logistics remained with me as I opened my eyes and filled into myself naked, kneeling on the floor mattress of home, melded into a three-way kiss. My gaze drifted down from the two mouths swabbing mine. The wife and Girl A were naked as well.

Three mouths melding as one was something I had not anticipated to be so natural.

Girl A stared at Tommie with open, impressed appraisal. "You should find someone to take pictures of your body," she said.

Girl A's nipples popped up translucent and pink. My chest quivered from the force of my heartbeat. The wife put her hand to my bouncing ribs.

"Are you going to be okay?"

I'm pretty sure I was okay. I came at least once, shooting off inside of Tommie, instead of pulling out and spraying on her skin, our customary stab at contraception, and I lived to glimpse Girl A pulling up her panties like a bunny covering its tail and hopping away.

The next day felt pretty good, all things considered. Girl A was somewhere else, but had left behind perfume on our sheets like a promise to return. The hangover was bearable by the mid-afternoon. I looked forward to making an early evening of it, with two tall boys and a dime bag and a head full of skin-toned recollections.

Around dusk, Tommie left the apartment to catch her ride to a Women's Building printmaking workshop. *I feel okay,* I thought, *on my own, awaiting her return.*

A sharp knock on the door crashed my optimism, but a single thought revived it: *Maybe that's Girl A dropping by!*

I calmed myself and rushed to welcome this unexpected delight.

Don Bolles and Claude "Kickboy Face" Bessy stood upon my threshold. They'd snapped the lock on the outer screen door and held it open behind them. Claude struck a cross-armed pose like I'd seen on a lot of television cops: "I'm here as the impartial witness," he said. "Nothing beyond."

Kickboy, older than the rest of us by something approaching a decade, had slipped into a Founding Father role, like a punk elder arbitrating a tribal dispute.

Don's eyes, as usual, seemed too big and active for their sockets. He was a habitual mutterer, chronically nattering in a semi-private pidgin. His lips twitched and crawled if he was muttering or not.

"Hey," I said. "What's happening?"

Don's mouth pulled a grimace. He said, "How's it going?"

I shrugged, intending to communicate utter indifference, and Don accused me of having stolen a valuable chunk of his record collection during his party the night before. Don was hurt; Claude was peeved. I suddenly realized Claude's absolute dislike for me. How had he so masterfully hidden his acrimony? And why?

Amusement seeped into my voice: "You can come in. Look for your records."

"We don't need to," said Don. "We got everything back. The Highland Records guy hadn't put anything out for sale yet. He said it was you."

"The Highland Records guy said what was me?"

"You brought the records in."

"I've never been to Highland Records."

"We showed him a picture."

"A picture of what?"

"A picture of you. He identified you."

Don and Kickboy met eyes and nodded. Their story was plausible; they were both buying it.

"There are no pictures of me."

"That's not cool," pronounced Kickboy, impartial, but sneering. "How does it feel to always be the worm in the apple?"

They glared at me. I smiled, and they doubled down on the glare. Did Don and the impartial witness intend to menace me? Enchanted by the hazy erotic events of the previous night, I'd been lifted to a place beyond detecting threat. But I detected something shifty.

"Wait," I said, "you guys have been watching my apartment. You waited to knock until Tommie was gone. You're afraid of her."

Passively, I wondered why Don and his witness were not asking the obvious questions. Russ, I couldn't help but notice, was nowhere to be found. There had been no sign of him or his mainlining friend Greg since Don and Pat's party. These two were junkies, known thieves, prime suspects. Russ had a hole on the inside of his left elbow, a live scab the size of a half dollar, where he squeezed in all the things he stole. It was not my place to point out all that.

The silence was something like awkward. If Don and Claude would go away, I could shut the door, get high, and set myself loose in reliving the night before.

"I have an alibi." I pictured Girl A, my alibi. I smirked to think of her, a smirk open to interpretation. "I won't tell you what it is."

Don and Claude moved inside the screen door, forward into the apartment, and crowded me.

Girl A could have stepped up and freed me from so much troublesome scrutiny, but she hadn't come home with us to spare me trouble.

SCENE TWO:
THE NIGHT SID VICIOUS DIED

The fog had caught me while I was blacked out. I came back into my body as a solitary pedestrian, in my trench coat, tromping along what I took to be Santa Monica Boulevard. I judged the time to be an hour before or after midnight.

Mist shrouded the traffic lights. Green, yellow, red; the colors flashed fuzzy one after another. A street sign came clear in the soup, clear enough that I put a read on my coordinates. I'd listed far to the east, all the way out to Vermont Avenue.

How had I drifted beyond Western? What trouble had I been in out there?

I don't have those answers, never will, but I can pinpoint the date: February 2, 1979. It was the night Sid Vicious died. I'd be twenty-three in twenty-four days.

I went through my pockets for clues to where I'd been and what I'd done there. I came up with a wad of cash. A clutch of twenties and tens; it added up. My last clear location was the New Masque, an aboveground, rectangular warehouse that the old Masque had moved into, a few miles west, where Santa Monica crossed Vine. The wife and I had arrived there around ten, in our Ford. I remembered vividly that 200 dollars had not been in my possession.

Black Randy had once assured me, "A sin you don't remember is a sin you didn't commit." There might be exceptions to that rule.

How to explain the money? I slipped a hand around the trench coat and down the back of my pants. Everything seemed intact.

I made good time walking back to the New Masque, or maybe I hitched a ride in the fog or jumped on a bus. The guy at the door didn't accost me for an entrance fee, verifying that I had been in already. I squelched an impulse to ask if he'd seen me leave. When? With anyone?

My people, ones I'd known for the past year or more, and interlopers who wanted to be among my people, crowded the floor space.

The wife hadn't noticed my absence. There was no reason to mention how far I'd ventured, or to bring up the mysterious financial windfall. The general conversation was right where I'd left it.

We'd all heard that Sid Vicious was dead. The sexiest Sex Pistol, their atrocious bass player, had heroin-croaked himself in New York, which was three hours ahead. The news had spread out to LA before the time difference had even caught up. Things hadn't gone right for Sid since his girlfriend showed up knifed to death in his hotel bathroom.

New Masque girls were crying, as if Sid had meant something personal, as if they'd carried his child, or given him a disease and regretted not having made it up to him. The topic exhausted itself, but people kept talking it up.

One second, I was in the girls bathroom mashing mouths with Margot from The Go-Go's; the next second, the last band of the night was on.

God alone remembers who the band was. The crowd, that part of it not in mourning for Sid Vicious, swirled in appreciation at the front of the stage. One particular blonde, slender, very sure of herself, swirled around the wife.

The band refused an encore, or ran out of songs, or got their plug pulled. In the relative silence, the swirling blonde invited the wife to an after party at Joan Jett's place. There was an indication that something beyond drinks and chatter might be served.

I accepted, on behalf of both of us.

"Oh, wait," said the blonde. "Who's he?"

We were at Joan Jett's place, below Sunset from the Whisky. Probably I'd driven there. I had the car keys. The kitchen was a magnet to me, specifically the refrigerator. Three of us were in the kitchen. The other two were strangers to me, and I refrained from meeting them. Joan and the blonde who'd recruited Tommie were in the living room, on a sofa, with the bulk of the guests, numbering perhaps ten in total. The refrigerator, I calculated, contained no more than twelve bottles of beer. Until those numbers greatly improved, I could not picture myself leaving the kitchen.

The wife moved back and forth between the living room and the kitchen, freely.

"Why don't you come out of the kitchen?" she said.

"You know what I'm doing."

"So does everyone else. Your drinking makes Girl A a little sick."

This was sobering. "A little sick? When did she tell you that?"

Tommie, it is revealed, had spent a day at Girl A's parents' house—while I worked—and met her mom. The wife had lunched in Girl A's bedroom. That news made me anxious to leave Joan Jett's. The wife and I needed to discuss private matters in private.

"We already discussed it," she said. "On the drive here."

I had no memory of any conversation.

"I'm not having that discussion again," she said.

"We'll talk about that on the way home," I said.

I opened Joan Jett's refrigerator and extracted beers, one by one, inserting them into the pockets and lining of my trench coat, wedging them under my armpits.

Something in my face convinced the other people in the kitchen to mind their own business, until I had turned my back. Comments were directed at me as I yanked Tommie from the party, but I had a six-pack secured in my coat; so who really had the last word?

I spotted the Ford in the upper parking lot behind the Licorice Pizza record store, kitty corner from Joan Jett's place.

Exene and John Doe from X were milling in the lower parking lot. X was positioned as a big-deal band at that time, a view hundreds hold to this day. A guy I'd nicknamed Noodle, his girlfriend, and a Rainbow DJ named Sondra stood around John and Exene. Sondra had been part of the Germs circle, but was in temporary exile for being a loudmouth. Noodle had been very helpful to me at one time, allowing Tommie and me to stay in his Culver City apartment during our transition from Pomona to Venice. That was way back, before the name Noodle had stuck. He was in a bulky sweater phase. He would wear a bulky sweater, then chew on a sleeve and gaze down at his shoes. In my judgment, Noodle was someone who should have been finished with all that. He'd started balding, and he was older, beyond twenty-five.

I struck up a bit of conversation with Exene, just enough to determine there wasn't a bottle or drug among the lot of them. I leaned toward continuing on home, and the wife rushed me along. John Doe was wearing black leather rock star pants. The wife understood that if she didn't remove me, I'd comment at length on those pants.

I had trouble locating my car keys. I knew which pocket they were in, but beer bottles were in the way. The wife stood against the car, her gaze abstracted and general.

Her eyes took a specific focus, and I followed it.

Down in the lower parking lot, where we'd been less than three minutes ago, Exene had picked a fight with three bulky, hairy dudes who had nothing to do with us, Valley mopes who'd come out to Hollywood with their dates to zoo view the freaks of the Sunset Strip.

In fact, I realized, Exene had been debating these hairy bulks while I was down there conversing. I had heard a man shout, over and over, "Shut your hole! You skank bitch! Shut your hole!"

I'd dismissed that background demand as something senseless that had no relevance to me or to anyone I might be speaking to. From a distance, the dynamics of the exchange came clear.

Shoulders hunched, Exene lunged and clawed at the trio of antagonists. She had found the rhythm of rebuttal: "Fuck you! Fuck you! Fuck you!"

John Doe stepped up to reinforce his wife's honor. Whether or not he knew it, stepping forward meant he had agreed to fight the loudest of the three hairy, bulky dudes. Belying the macho cow-skin jeans, John Doe fought poorly. He flopped to the blacktop and curled like a big, black-leather-clad fetus, shifting on the ground while the most aggrieved of the three bulky dudes lobbed kicks into his midsection. The bulky dudes' dates laughed.

Exene stood over her man, screeching into the face of his assailant, further energizing the attack. Noodle wavered off to the side. He chewed on the sleeve of his oversize sweater and gazed down at his shoe tips. His legs crossed as if he needed a pee.

I took in the whole picture.

"I have never been so irritated in all my life," I told the wife.

"That's an exaggeration."

I'm not brave now, even less so then. I was simply annoyed beyond control. Every single person down there was in the wrong. I walked toward the beating of John Doe, intending to directly express my displeasure. I unloaded beers from my trench coat as I approached the fracas, depositing bottles one-by-one on parked cars, on an overturned trashcan, atop a low brick wall.

Kicking John Doe must have lost its challenge. The burly dude spread his arms and bellowed to the sky: "Who's next?"

Other than the burly dude's two burly friends, everybody was either a girl or Noodle.

"I guess I'm next," I said. I was casual about it. I sipped from a bottle of beer in my right hand.

The burly dude charged me. I clocked Tommie, watching from the car, more exasperated than amused. She motioned as though she were returning to Joan Jett's party.

The charging dude was half a foot shorter than me; his head was down. I shot out my left arm and deflected him with the palm of my hand to the top of his head, which was greasy. He passed off to the side. I envisioned a bull diverted by a sly matador. Tommie had taken a seat on the Ford.

Burly man regrouped; I shrugged a shoulder and smiled in an overture of friendliness. Rejecting my charisma, he charged again, this time with his face up. My palm caught him on the forehead. His head bent back, but not much. That neck was thick, and hairy, where it melded into the shoulders. My jab kept him far enough away that his fists couldn't reach me, but the impact bounced me a foot and a half backward, and further enraged my opponent. Probably drunk, he failed to realize that I had eight months of karate training behind me, about six years previously, but still.

My angry attacker made a few more lunges with the same results: He couldn't charge close enough to hit me or grab me, and I kept lurching backward. His friends and their dates lost interest and loaded back into their cars. They had two Trans-Ams, one behind the other, pointed toward the driveway onto San Vicente. My beer was either half full or half empty, depending on your worldview.

I tilted the bottle above my nose and realized something. The burly dude's lunges had backed me up to a fifteen-foot drop from the parking lot to an access alley below. The assailant stamped his feet, ready to bull forward again. I wavered on the ledge above the access alley. The fall would hurt. I sat down on the blacktop to think things over. The burly dude stopped midcharge, suspecting a trick. I had no trick.

I had put myself in an exact replicate of John Doe's collapsed disadvantage. It was a matter of moments before burly would recognize his advantage and stave in my ribs with relentless kicks. I saw the puzzle piecing together in his swinish eyes.

Sondra, the Rainbow DJ, pieced the puzzle together, too.

Sondra and I had history. In the early weeks of the Canterbury invasion I'd consoled her as we'd walked along Hollywood Boulevard a little after 2:00 a.m. A night earlier, she had passed out, and her friends had used Magic Markers to draw dicks on her face. In the morning, they'd allowed her to hitchhike home while dick faced.

"Those aren't your friends," I had counseled. "Fuck those people."

We jaywalked across Las Palmas, and I stumbled over a parked police car, landing facedown on the hood. The cops wanted to see some ID; all I had was my name on a bottle of painkillers I'd been prescribed after my ribs were broken at the Sex Pistols show in San Francisco. The cops had kept the pills and released me into Sondra's custody.

Here she was, seizing the opportunity to act as my guardian once again, on the night Sid Vicious died. Sondra stepped forward and bellowed straight into my burly antagonist's face: "Leave us alone! Leave us alone!"

Her volume shocked the assailant. It brought him almost to his senses. He looked around. He was alone. His friends regarded him from inside the Trans-Ams. Car horns honked, and voices assailed him: "Hurry up and come on!"

I unfolded to my feet and dusted off my trench coat. My attacker climbed in behind the wheel of the second Trans-Am. Two or three inches of beer remained in my bottle. I had come out ahead.

The lead Trans-Am paused at the turn onto San Vicente; its signal light flashed. My burly attacker put the second Trans-Am into gear. Exene stepped up to his open driver's window and screeched in at him. I couldn't quite make out the words.

Something she said must have struck a nerve. The driver flung open the door of the second Trans-Am, neglecting to put his vehicle in park, and charged out. The driverless car shot forward and rear-ended the lead Trans-Am. Taillights and headlights snapped.

I followed my trail of purloined beers toward Tommie and our Ford. The burly dude, embarrassed, deflated, mocked now by his own camp, returned to the driver's seat of the second Trans-Am.

I could not comprehend how exasperating and completely unnecessary this entire spectacle had been. The two Trans-Ams moved toward San Vicente. They were incomprehensible to me.

I drained the last sip from my beer and lofted my bottle in the direction of the departing cars. The bottle flew in a perfect, beautiful arc, spiraling as it passed over the lengths of both vehicles, from behind, and shattered square in the middle of the lead Trans-Am's windshield.

What a toss! I felt like the quarterback who's just fought from behind and won the Super Bowl! This bottle throw was a moment of perfection to be cherished for a lifetime. An entire stadium of stunned and exalted observers should have been there, screaming witness, but it was just Tommie and me.

"Did you see that?" I said.

"I need to get up in the morning," she said.

I piloted my car from the parking lot, watching in the rearview as Exene and Noodle aided John Doe to his feet. His soiled leather pants were one more demonstration that punk rock had failed me.

I hammered down Willoughby at a reckless rate. We hit a bump. The passenger door flew open. Tommie grabbed something, not me, and saved herself from being cast out from the Ford. That door had been stuck shut for months, a potential death trap. It had worried me. The car door flapped open, and life had one less problem, one less closed avenue to escape. Count that as a victory.

Tommie didn't see the sprung door the same way I did. There was no use trying to talk her out of this mood. We went to bed, on the floor, without exchanging much of substance.

Waiting for sleep, I pictured the arc of the bottle I'd thrown toward the Trans-Ams, followed by the satisfying smash. Not even Tommie's ominous quiet could diminish this high point. The happiness pendulum was swinging back our way. Wasn't Girl A another sign of incoming pleasure and abundance? I breathed deep and faked a swell of optimism.

On our bedroom floor, I flipped over, facing Tommie, thrashing for a comfortable position. Maybe that flash of utter satisfaction, when the beer bottle shattered, was how the soul of dead Sid Vicious would feel all the time, from here on out through eternity.

No, scratch that. Fire, brimstone, silent scorn; these and worse were all waiting for me to close my eyes.

SCENE THREE:
ONE NIGHT OF MEMORIES
BEYOND RECALL

I slid out from behind my boiler room desk, snuck down the fire stairs, bolted myself into the lobby phone booth, and rang Girl A at her parent's house in Woodland Hills.

"This is the most fulfilling part of my workday," I said, and she laughed.

My goal on any given call was for Girl A to find me funny. She seemed amused. She laughed about whether vertical or horizontal stripes best flatter pudgy girls. She laughed about the barbaric rudiments of her surgeon father's craft. She laughed about tripping on Christmas-morning acid as a fourteen-year-old glitter girl.

Girl A's easy phone-line laughs were a blanket promise. The easy laughs smoothed over the rasp of betrayal. We set up a one-on-one date, going out without Tommie.

The evening started out well enough, with a phone call to tell Tommie I would be joining the people where I worked for drinks.

"What happened to your plan?" she asked. "To not let them see you loaded?"

"I don't think you have anything to worry about there."

Girl A had band rehearsal, with the band that would let the world know her full name; so I circled the Ford around her band's Hollywood Boulevard practice space until I wheeled onto the block and she stood under a street light, ready to go— wearing fat sunglasses, thick lipstick, and a butchered sixties party dress. None of her band mates were in sight, which suited me. She tossed her pointlessly long cigarette into the gutter, stepped off the curb, and into the car. Her scent made talk from me impossible, but my gloating, idiotic face said all I had to say.

She lit another of her triple-length cigarettes.

"Did you put any thought into where we'll go?" she said.

"Of course I have. I'm a big thinker."

In my mind, we needed somewhere we wouldn't see anyone we knew. I didn't want passing acquaintances or deep, dear friends cutting the intoxication of our isolation.

"Some place fabulous and daring?" she said.

I looked at the cigarette smoke spilling from her crimson lips and pictured her sitting on just such a place.

We went to Soul'd Out, an R&B music venue set up like a supper club, except it didn't serve food. On Sunset near Wilcox, in the heart of Hollywood's eternal skids, Soul'd Out catered to the petty hustler who might sell a burn bag on the stroll from the parking lot to the club—and to the women drawn to him. I'd been to Soul'd Out once before, with Tommie, but little chance existed of us returning.

Forcing my eyes off Girl A, I parked the Ford in a spot behind a dark instant-printing shop. I'd taken to sporting a floppy cap, like reggae hood Jimmy Cliff in *The Harder They*

Come. I poised my head at a rakish angle, and Girl A reached up to adjust my hat. She raised her mouth close to mine. Our mouths held in abeyance. I tasted what I was not tasting. Then she stepped back, locked my cold-cocked eyes, and took visible pride in her handiwork.

The longsuffering Soul'd Out doorman—African American, forever hip, fronting age thirty, carrying more like fifty—hadn't been prepared to greet someone like me with my rhythm-crippled strut, or Girl A with her subtle, sweet waddle, both of us with our paste-white mugs.

Looking away, ignoring us, our host pulled back an unnecessary velvet rope, and we passed inside.

Crystal, white, and mirror dominated Soul'd Out's interior elements. Tables covered with crystal-trimmed cloth, each sporting its unique mirrored centerpiece, were ranked across the white-parquet floor. A tight square was left clear for dancing in front of a low stage. Girl A and I sat—the only customers—at a table in the middle of the floor. A nine-piece combo in white platform shoes and snowy jumpsuits played music that wasn't far astray from the greatest hits of Earth, Wind & Fire. As far as their bored, black faces were concerned, they were performing for no audience whatsoever, but they played funky and loud. Girl A and I moved our mouths close and cozy to talk.

"You're so lucky that Tommie is the way she is," said Girl A. "What made you get married? Was she pregnant?"

"What way do you think Tommie is?" I said. I watched Girl A's lips siphon off her second cocktail.

"Well, she's almost gay and not at all jealous," Girl A said. "For starters."

I tallied the financial impact of our cocktails and asked a loitering waitress for the bill. The damage arrived just before

I went broke. Girl A made no pretense of offering to share the tab. I'd taken her to be a more fun type of girl. Viva would have split it.

We cleared out of Soul'd Out and stood on Sunset looking up and down the Strip: Nothing but motels for blocks and blocks either way. "Where do we go?" I said.

Girl A put a hand on my heart. A pulse shot into my cock. "We could drive," she said.

While I backed out the car, the radio played "Lotta Love," a lightweight lullaby. A hippie lady from the generation ahead of us warbled about needing a lotta love to get through the night and make things right and craving relatin' and not to be kept waitin' in solitude. The lyrics, I felt, were poignant to the arrangement Girl A and I were embarking upon.

"This song makes my skin crawl," said Girl A. She switched off the radio, decisively. That settled that, but it didn't help pick a destination.

"My place isn't wholly available," I pointed out. "The wife lives there, too, after all."

"I have a bedroom in Woodland Hills. Mom and Dad are probably up waiting for me to come home."

"No sense in driving all the way out there."

We took a cruise to the backseat of my car, parked on Las Palmas, facing the Musso & Frank Grill across Hollywood Boulevard.

Framed in the Ford's windshield, a staggering parade of foot traffic crossed Las Palmas in front of us. I blocked out the bums, and hippies, and panhandlers, and dope sellers, and muggers, and pickpockets, and narcs, and also the lowlifes.

I paid attention to the prostitutes. Hard-legged power hookers, ethereal ladies-of-the-night, common streetwalkers, runaway waifs on the cash chain, cowboy dudes, drag queens, and glam-frocked transgender entrepreneurs—one hundred blends of sex for sale passed in front of the Ford. None of the presenting professionals approached the curb appeal of Girl A, in the car with me, or—I paused to give due credit—of the wife back home, where I would repose later.

I counted myself among the world's luckiest men. Still, my satisfaction seemed incomplete.

"I want us to drink martinis at Musso's," whispered Girl A, snuggling along my ribcage. "Won't that be fun?"

Musso & Frank's logo curved neon red in the Ford's windshield glass. The Canterbury, condemned now and evacuated, and the original Masque alley were mere blocks from the car. Over the past year of lit-up nights, I'd been drunk in and kicked out of every bar for a mile around, but never Musso's. F. Scott Fitzgerald and William Faulkner had pickled there. The place was legendary. Its cheapest drink cost more than a six-pack and a Sherm.

"Let's drink at Musso's next Tuesday," I said. My mind designated Tuesdays as our date night.

"*Mmmmm.*" Girl A snuggled in tighter and lit another of her foot-long cigarettes. I counted the minutes while it burned down, expecting each passing moment to be the one in which my mind snapped. Finally, she pinched out the butt.

As sane as I've ever been, I moved my mouth to her lips. All hands were on deck. I chewed on the taste of Girl A's lipstick and palmed her thighs. Her stockings stopped short, and her legs parted for my grasp. We slid off the seat, and she steered me by my cock toward the floor of the car. I sank into a perfumed cloud of warm spun sugar. We came up for a moment; the windows had fogged like cotton candy.

A knock, metallic and impatient, rattled the glass at my head. The knock struck again.

"If that's Michael Schmuck," I said, "I will beat him half to death."

"You'll both come in your pants."

Girl A cleared a space in the window fog with her palm. My hand burrowed to a center of warmth between her legs. A big cop face pressed up to the glass. I extracted my hand, subtly shifted my erection, and cranked open the window.

Two cops stood out there, one a lady. Upon request, we handed our drivers' licenses to the lady cop. The male partner covered her from behind, one hand at all times on his pistol grip.

"Do you know how many serial killers are out here victimizing this neighborhood tonight?" asked the lady cop, wanting us to not answer. "By parking here, you're asking to be raped and murdered. Working this section of boulevard is dangerous for me. Looking out for lost swingers like you only makes it harder." She handed back our ID cards: "Take your party elsewhere."

Under the watchful eye of the LAPD, I walked Girl A to her car, next to the Hollywood practice space. Shivering from cold, she hurried into the driver's seat. "It's not like we'll never see each other again," she said, and slammed the door.

I returned to my Ford and moped unto pure abstraction until I was home in the apartment with the quiet wife. She was drawing but wouldn't let me see what. I smoked another joint and could almost picture her sketching out our future, shading a whole new line and form of fun into the composition.

*   *   *

BACK AT WORK, I pivoted out from behind my desk. Girl A and I had talked Wednesday and Thursday. I bolted myself into the lobby phone booth. This would be our second call today, Friday. She picked up on the first ring.

"Is it really you?" she said.

A world of promise streamed through the line.

"I talked to Tommie," I said, although I had not. "We both think you should drive."

"But if I drive, we might all die."

"This is true," I admitted, "but if I drive, we'll all end up maimed and broken, but alive for the rest of our lives. What would you rather be: dead? Or alive, and maimed, and broken, and old?"

She laughed. She was charmed. She was fascinated. She was enchanted.

"I'll pick you guys up at nine," she said. "We'll hang out."

She rang off, but her voice went with me back upstairs. We remained together through the day and early evening until I pulled the door to her car's backseat closed behind me and matched the sound of her with the face of her. She and Tommie pecked a little kiss up front.

10:00 p.m. brought us to the relocated Masque. Code violations and permit restrictions had shifted the venue to an airy warehouse on Santa Monica Boulevard near Vine. This Friday was the last night before cops shut down the clubhouse for good.

I was watching for it closely, but our grand entrance—the wife striding in with fake suede tights and real lizard salvaged pumps; Girl A teetering on needlepoint heels, flaunting a lingerie set as outer garments under a patchy fur—somehow slid away from me.

*   *   *

I'M ON MY OWN out in the oil-stained concrete parking lot. I'm in a circle of hostile new kids; four penis-necked cutouts with uniform buzz cuts and bomber jackets. They're in a band—the Red Faction or China Army. Hundreds of these clench-jawed idealists had showed up uninvited and slapped anarchist stickers onto their guitars. Who can keep track of their hardcore political masquerades? Swarms of kids, nineteen or twenty years old and not a scrap of originality in their entire style, were mocking the twenty-two-year-old innovators, calling us grandma and grandpa.

The guys ringing me were tall, and lean, and pinched in the face; they'd probably played junior varsity high school basketball. They pushed me, goaded me, elbowed me. This is what happens when a person, an innocent—me—is too happy with himself. Some cluster of bitter tools full of testosterone and envy takes on the job of bursting my bubble.

"Who do you think you are?" Shove.

This was all so rudimentary. Of course I had an answer.

"I think I'm nobody. You get that? Nobody. Try being nobody."

One of them knocked the Jimmy Cliff flop hat off my head.

I squatted to pick up my cap. While I was down there, with my guard lowered, would have been a prime time to attack me. These guys looked at each other to determine which one would strike first. They failed to coordinate the assault, and I was back on my feet.

"What makes you special?" Shove.

"Like I said," I explained, "I'm nobody; and nobody is special; so that makes me special. Get it?"

I functioned on an elevation well beyond their understanding. What was I supposed to do, lower myself to take blockheads seriously? This punk thing had started because we—we being me and the other people who started it—thought we were pretty great. Our feelings of greatness were purely unsubstantiated. No one had required anyone else to submit proof of greatness. We had imagination. We had belief. We had faith and goodwill. We didn't have callow prigs setting requirements and demanding some standard of achievement.

"What makes me so special is self-evident," I explained, as if I were Black Randy talking to stupid people. "If I weren't so special, why would I act the way I do?"

They had their rebuttal: "We don't like you."

These guys caromed me from one to the other, but they had no real idea of fun. Any one of them could have dropped me with two punches. But it took all four to brave their amusement.

I dug in. I would stand my ground, whatever that ground might be. I would grin and endure my teeth being kicked in, if that's what it took, to prove my point, to exercise the fundamental principle, to defend a stack of values and beliefs that I could not be bothered to put into words and that might well be pointless and wrong and not exist. Being pointless and wrong and nonexistent made digging in all the more necessary in my mind.

Let me assure you, I was very drunk and had perhaps swallowed pills and sniffed a crystalline powder. If my blood had been strictly pristine, none of this principle business would have applied. But I was on fire, and the moderation switch was fried out.

No one had actually hit me yet. Once struck, I might go so far as to sacrifice my life to my ineffable code. My opponents couldn't help but see that depth of commitment. Day to day, I am mostly superficial, almost all pretense and straw bravado, but an underlying, genuinely insane and volatile love of my own conception of personal dignity sometimes shows up. In that way, I am like anybody else who is worth knowing. That's what made the cutouts hesitate.

Still, they would conclude soon enough that four driven dullards always beat one inspired egotist, and they would do just that. Nothing I could possibly say might switch them to my side.

Even if words could diffuse their hostility, fuck those words.

"You're poseurs," I said. "Fucking twat poseurs."

They wouldn't have been more stunned if I'd pissed in their mouths. The truth can knock the gas out of anybody, but that pause wouldn't last.

"Allan, come on, leave them alone."

"Allan, get out of there."

It was Girl A and the wife, arriving to derail my martyrdom. Look at these women, my rescuers, my scolders: The wife strode in reptilian pumps; Girl A elevated on needlepoints. One lady took me by each arm, undulating at my hipbones, hamming up the sensual aspects, disarming and infuriating anyone with an antipathy toward me.

"We're going home now," announced Girl A, pulling me away, basically humping my leg. "To home and to bed!"

The four penis-neck cutouts liked me even less. What could they do?

"Jealous twats," I called, being led backward to Girl A's car. The Red Chinese, or whatever they were calling themselves, stared in hurt disbelief. I grabbed my crotch. "Your hardcore anarchy's swinging! Right here!"

*   *   *

DURING THE QUIET MORNING after, you'll remember very little of the night before. You'll come to on the bedroom floor, alone, unclothed. The headache will be unbelievable and typical.

You'll listen, extending your hearing out into the apartment at large, tracking for Girl A. Detecting nothing and no one, you'll pull on pants and venture into the shared living room.

Your wife will be sitting silent and still on the couch, staring blankly at you, smoking one of Girl A's pointlessly long cigarettes. Your wife does not typically smoke. An ashtray crowded with skinny butts and a mauled cigarette pack will be on the sofa cushion beside her, just in case you had any notion of sitting there.

You will not know how to begin.

"For starters," the wife will say, "I came into the bedroom... again and again...from two until four in the morning, hoping every time that it would be over, and there you were...locked in."

She'll stop talking, and she won't quite cry. Standing in front of her, you'll manage to put her out of your mind for a few moments.

Your sole memory, a five-second clip, is of the other woman curling around you, beneath you, tight to you, laughing, and saying, "I'm not Tommie."

Was that woman's delivery irritated? Exasperated? Titillated? You'll never find out.

The wife won't sit at the breakfast table with you; she won't stray from your sight line either. She deserves answers, explanations, an abject apology, and solemn promises. A morning beer is essential, but out of the question.

You search where your memories should be. You come up with no further vague recollections of your hours with Girl A. You don't know if you came, or had more than one hard-on or any erection at all. Was there oral? A rubber?

You have no picture of arriving at the apartment or of shedding clothes.

Later, in a week or two, you'll realize that you have no idea what had caused the wife to leave the bedroom. Had she tried to play along? Was she awkward and in the way? Did you tell her to clear out?

At the empty breakfast table, you feel these questions about the wife somewhere, below the hangover, under the disappointment and bewilderment. The wife's grievances aren't your most pressing lament; they do increase the pressure on your most pressing lament.

Having no Girl A images to pull out and cherish makes you gypped and angry and sad. That's the worst of it.

The circle of cutouts hating you in The Masque parking lot is perfectly recalled.

You look around the breakfast table. You fix on the coffee pot, percolating and ignored on the stove. Russ comes out of his room and turns off the burner. Even he, the junkie, the thief, can look at you with contempt.

The wife and your friend don't understand. You have been gypped, and you have no one to take that anger and sadness to.

It's the last time Girl A will be at your house. It's the day she refuses to accept your calls. Her surgeon father will come on the line and suggest you find someone else to phone.

In the wife's eyes, you raise a blank.

Three decades on, you want to contact the other person, the partner, your wife, and tell her that she is a portion of your greatest regret. But you're something like a coward and a psychic, and you anticipate her reaction.

The only question that could matter to her at this point is the same one she must have been asking herself that morning: Wouldn't it have been better to let the cutouts beat your head into The Masque's oil-stained parking lot?

SCENE FOUR:
THE FOOD CHAIN

The number four lane on the 101 is no place to dissect a bad feeling. There's no turning around; there's no slowing down. We'd been on the freeway for half an hour, heading north into the deep Valley for a house party I never wanted to attend. I drained a beer bottle, placed it into the bottom of a wet paper sack, and withdrew one of the few full bottles that remained. The car would soon run out of alcohol. I'd been happy enough on the floor at home, before the wife and Russ prodded me into the car, my car.

Russ had promised a great party. He'd been staying with us for a few weeks, back in his old room, between habits. "Everyone you know will be there," he'd said.

"I don't know anyone anymore." I shifted my position on the floor, turning my back to all upright human beings.

My whole world had fallen off the face of the earth. I hardly left the apartment, except to go to work and to buy weed from the dick hustlers on Santa Monica Boulevard. Concerts and clubs were out. Hordes of fans had overrun the punk shows. A fan is one thing I could never allow myself to abide.

"My social skills are rusty," I insisted, at home on the floor. Not that home offered any unadulterated sanctuary.

Tommie looked down, checking the seams in her stockings, and we saw eye-to-eye for a moment. I caught a smile, for me, mine alone. "They'll give you drinks," she said. The sad, mocking uplift of her lips hinted at something I wanted. Affection? Reconciliation? "Free drinks," she said.

I could argue for buying our own and staying home; I considered whipping up my brainpower. Tommie squinted into a mirror and slashed a streak of makeup on either cheek. The effect—angry and impulsive—pleased her, and that pleasure remained on her face once it turned toward me. All of my logic and reasonable discourse counted for nothing against that effect.

We piled into the front seat of my car, Russ at the wheel. I preferred to avoid the responsibility of driving, like any responsibility, but more so. I can really only imagine I'm on my way to somewhere good if I have a drink in my hands during the drive there. A steering wheel can get in the way.

Russ and the wife beamed into the windshield with high expectations. Forced beams, I sensed. Before, when I'd met her, Tommie had been naturally optimistic. At the moment, rolling on the freeway, I couldn't imagine what she might be looking forward to. Maybe Russ was picturing good things ahead of us, good things he could steal. Second thoughts plagued me. Thoughts had been plaguing me since that last night with Girl A. The Coors and the Smirnoff failed to wash them away.

I had not officially been invited to this party, not personally— neither had Russ or Tommie. Long, long ago, before the Canterbury, a year ago perhaps, the dandy hosting this party had been the random victim of a brick that I had needed to throw through the nearest car windshield. The nearest car had been a station wagon owned by the party host's mother. This incident of vehicular vandalism, if I knew anything of the world's ways, had not gone forgotten.

Our car eased down a freeway off-ramp. My anxiety pitched forward. We were entering one of the most affluent recesses of the Valley. My bladder throbbed.

Kickboy Face and tonight's party host had sweated Russ about my brick through the mother's windshield on the night of the infraction. Russ had told me about the grilling, but not all of it. By what he left out, I knew he'd fingered me as the brick thrower.

Our deep Valley trouble started at the driveway to the party house. Its steepness challenged the Ford. The driveway wrapped around a hill like a piercing spiral twisting up into the bottom of the house, which seemed to be perched upon the tip of an immense corkscrew pointed toward the sky. The dwelling itself was a transparent structure of flashing reflections and color bursts.

A ribbon of shiny, parked cars curved up around the driveway beyond where we could see. Russ found a spot on a side street, and we tramped up the winding incline. Who among our friends owned all these new and European vehicles?

"This is like walking up to a theme park from the remote parking lot," observed Tommie. Once in a while, her childlike optimism still popped up. "It's like Magic Mountain," she said, "and the roller coasters are at the top."

"I like the idea of roller coasters better than I like actual roller coasters," I said.

Above us, the party home came into view. Lights. Opulence. The dulcet sounds of Burt Bacharach.

I pissed on the side of a multivehicle garage, gazing through exterior walls of the main house as if into an aquarium full of exotic, glamorous, and grotesque specimens. A blink later, I stood in a celestial foyer, checking to make sure I'd put away my cock. Light fixtures every bit as massive as the pipes from the Mormon Tabernacle organ dangled ten feet above my head.

"These people know how to live," said some silly pimple kid notable for his yellow, rooster hair and blocky, two-tone shoes. He stood on his tiptoes, ambushed me with a kiss on the lips, and scurried into the crush.

Russ looked puzzled. "When did you make up with Michael Schmuck?"

The rooster blond—Michael Schmuck!—squeezed between a pair of Diane Arbus twins dressed in matching asylum gowns. One of the twins dropped a paper plate.

A Hispanic woman in skirt and apron snatched up the plate as it hit the carpet.

I studied familiar-looking faces reflected in a wall covering of mirrors and gold veins. A hilltop house with 360-degree views, a sunken living room, and uniformed maid service: Who could have guessed we had entered the family home of a Masque original? Using all my resources, I was able to pick out my lost-looking face, the wife, Russ.

A smattering of young sophisticates asked me, "How's it going?" They seemed to know me. Trying to come up with their names, I walked into a picture window separating an indoor conversation pit from an open-air deck. The face pain cleared, and embarrassment flushed in; somehow, people who knew my name were functioning perfectly well on either side of that plate glass.

A girl with professional-quality yellow stars dyed into her green buzz cut stepped up to me and said hello. In approaching me, she had stepped out of the anonymous party context, into the personal context. Still, I couldn't place her. In these conditions I didn't know anybody.

"What are you on, Allan?" She laughed. "Do you have more?"

I was mildly OD'd on spun. Russ and Tommie were adjusting better than I was, but neither was flowing with ease or festivity.

Alley mates—entire bands perhaps—who we'd taken as being at one with us were exposed in this house as originating in a richer world, a world we'd experienced while we were kids in cut-rate neighborhoods and cheaper schools as inapproachable, unwelcoming, rigidly segregated, at times openly hostile.

The wife and Russ, and I, following a common impulse, took refuge in the pantry, a room bigger than our kitchen and living room combined. We stood in awe of the foodstuffs, luxury sustenance for months. At home, hunger was always only an hour or two away. Our marveling at the pantry's delicious surplus gave rise to a suspicion of betrayal, to disillusionment and—most demoralizing of all—to envy.

Slumming money kids had fooled us. Their excursions into low Hollywood, into desolate downtown blocks and into flop-pad excess had all been the dabbling of vacationers, like we had been—but worse. Now these not-quite friends had chosen to reveal their privilege and resources. Against our wills, we wished we could be one among them and not stuck with our shoddy selves.

Unable to bear the company of one another's judgment, we shambled back into the party proper.

Kickboy Bessy stood unfazed, like a fixture, accessorizing a floor-to-ceiling flagstone fireplace. The *Slash* editor drank from an actual glass. He had upwardly assimilated without falter. Disregarding his standing threat to brain me, I sidled up to the entrepreneurial anarchist.

"Hey, Claude, have I ever told you how much I admire you?"

Claude took a peeved breath. "Surely not, Basho. Admiration is an attitude never associated with you."

I put on a contrite face. "May I tell you, then, why I admire you?"

The cofounder of *Slash* hooded his eyelids. His pursed lips crafted some terrible and true summation of my character, but elected to hold it back and be mild.

"Try to enjoy yourself, Basho. Or go ahead and be the expected asshole."

"Where'd you get the drink?" I asked.

He nodded to the juncture of a panoramic window and a wall of steel and mountain rock. A full bar was being actively replenished by a little man in a vest and bowtie. One problem: stairs, and optical illusions of stairs, and a vast, multilevel, densely populated living room spread out between where I stood and where the alcohol was dispensed.

Kickboy resumed his stand in front of the fireplace. He had the wrought iron aplomb of a lawn jockey, and I wanted some of that solidity.

I mapped out my path to the bar and took tentative steps. I heard my name and felt a tug on my sleeve. Rooster top Michael Schmuck held out a glass. He expected me to fetch a refill!

I turned away and laughed in amused contempt. Anticipating a drink, I relaxed. I was starting to feel like myself. I was about to feel better than everyone else. Then I was amazed to spot Girl A fitting snugly on a wraparound sofa in the sunken living room. The entire house tilted—no one else seemed aware of it—and rotated on the tip of the corkscrew.

Part Three

Girl A was in touchy-feely conversation with a pair of rockabilly players who were making a career of being from Kentucky. Girl A tapped the ash from a ridiculous cigarette and sipped effervescence from a cocktail glass. Delighted, glowing, giggling with open-mouthed aplomb, how could she so cruelly disregard my existence and the feelings that crowded in with it?

Shaky in my legs, I aborted the alcohol mission and ended up back in the pantry, staring at the shelves of plenty, sick to my stomach. Within what might have been moments, Tommie joined me there. We seemed to be not speaking, and she looked pale beneath the war paint. If we had been speaking, I would not have needed to ask to know that she had seen Girl A, too.

"Find Russ and wait here," I said.

I strode, perhaps it looked as though I were fleeing, through the voluminous crystal foyer and out the open front door. The party at my back, I paused on the landing and contemplated the drop to street level. If there had been a clean jump to the road below, I might have leaped to it. I hiked down the quarter-mile driveway, stumbling, picking up speed. The descent's momentum pushed me sprinting into traffic.

The Ford was easy to find; it was domestic and old.

I peered back up at the house. It might as well have been a flaming meteor pinned one hundred yards above the Valley floor, for all the connection it had with my life. The fiery windows were crowded with bright winners. They'd come down off their hill to enrich their sparkling prospects at the fabled punk rock career trough. They'd leeched away what could profit them along the low boulevards and left the rest. Tommie and Russ and I were among the leavings, snubbed in the blind alleyways.

I wheeled the car around and reversed it into the corkscrew driveway. I spiraled backward and upward past ranks of new and European vehicles. The Ford's rear tires skidded to a stop on the foyer landing. I popped the trunk and walked into the house.

Russ and Tommie instinctively understood my plan. We'd honed our organizational skills beyond intuition while whisking crowds through the King Tut exhibit. We plucked a group of ragged allies from the luxury setting, calling out people who were our kind of people: You take our kind of people out of the alley; they drag the alley along with them.

A relay line of ten stalwart urchins stretched from the pantry's trove to the Ford, transferring edible treasures hand-to-hand to the car's trunk. Canned hams, a prime rib, gallons of milk, tubs of butter, cookies, bacon, eggs, an entire fucking goose.

Kickboy Claude stepped out of the house and clocked the operation.

"Here to give us a hand?" said Tommie. She might have been taunting; she might have been sincere. Her husband no longer knew for sure.

Claude turned back and rejoined the party. He wasn't needed. We had a Go-Go in that relay lineup, Sheri the Penguin, Tony the Hustler, a kid named Howie from the Blessed, and two Germs. Virgin olive oil, bags of apples, tins of pears, banana bunches, pasta, balsamic, super-soft toilet paper, and a brand new mop. The trunk filled.

We—Russ, Tommie, and I—made plans with our accomplices for a shared feast. Everyone knew it would never happen.

I pointed the car down the hill and let it glide.

SCENE FIVE: ABORTION

We were adults now. It was 1979, and we did the things twenty-three-year-old adults did. We got pregnant.

Tommie spilled the baby news in the bedroom, alone. We were never far from the floor, and our mattress, and that's where I dropped, speechless.

Who was this woman kneeling beside me? I recognized her as the wife who'd resumed having sex with me. Her face was clean of makeup; she'd scrubbed it very recently. Red rimmed and glassy, the eyes stared straight into me. At first glance, before she'd said anything, I'd taken the red to mean she was stoned. She opened her mouth, and out popped this new secret that proved how wrong I could be. Pregnant! What else was she hiding from me?

"Don't worry," she said. "I know we can't have it."

Talk about relief. Arguing for an abortion might have made me look like a creep. Beyond that consideration, my mind split off, leaving any dislodged emotions on their own to lash themselves down.

Tommie and I smoked some weed and rested our heads on separate pillows. *Life is mysterious and complicated and full of sudden changeups!* That was the deepest meditation I was prepared to allot for my wife's pregnancy.

This is how we did it: The threesome with Girl A planted an embryo. In front of company, I'd been too bashful to pull out of Tommie.

I fired up that hash pipe again, in a hurry. A few minutes of stoned reflection, and I suspected that the wife had chosen termination not because she'd calculated what was best for us, but because of what she knew about me, because of the mess *me* made out of us.

Now would have been a good time to say something to Tommie, so long as I said nothing of every single thing that I was thinking.

If it had been a found puppy, or a kitten, she would have put up more of a fight to keep it. I gave her a hit of weed, took two. She was quiet. She'd been silent all the while I was quiet; now she was even quieter than silent.

There were details to be arranged; someone needed to be responsible for Tommie's transportation to and from the procedure. I learned about how none of that was handled.

A week or two after the pregnancy news, stuck in pre-noon smog along the outer limits of the Valley's vast traffic grid, a thought crossed my mind: *That whole abortion business has been dispatched with very smoothly.* So smoothly that I couldn't quite pinpoint when the voidance had occurred.

Three of us were in my car, and I was driving. Black Randy droned color commentary from the passenger seat. Lizard Breath, a Hollywood High heiress, was squeezed in the front seat between Randy and me. Lizard Breath's grandfather had been famous in newspapers and on the radio—a gossip-slinging moralist, shrewd, jingoistic, rich, and feared.

Liz pressed my way, trying to put space between her and the mottled flab that spilled out where Randy's sweaty shirttail failed to reach the waistband of his slacks. Lizard Breath wore tight, elasticized clothes, and she had extra cleavage to work around in them. Her hair curled into ringlets that seemed to bounce up from her bare shoulders. The face, you could tell, had been cherubic as a baby, but we were the same age now. She looked like a girl who belonged in a car between Black Randy and me. Which isn't to say Liz didn't attract appraising glances everywhere she appeared.

I turned my eyes back to the road. Irritated at the lack of urgency in the van ahead of me, I slugged the car's horn. The chrome horn ring popped off the wheel and sprang up into my face.

None of us laughed at the inadvertent slapstick. We were focused, serious, on an expedition.

"It's a clinic," said Randy. He was bickering with Lizard Breath. His instructional tone made clear that she had trouble grasping rudimentary concepts. "A clinic's business is to make people well."

"Hollywood has clinics," pointed out Lizard Breath. "Why drive all the way to hell?"

"My insurance card doesn't work in Hollywood." The state had issued Randy some sort of benefits ID to supplement the welfare payments he received for being clinically incapable of supporting himself.

"The problem is you've already burned through every clinic in Hollywood," said Lizard Breath.

"Practice your cough," demanded Randy.

Lizard Breath ripped a raspy hack of phlegm. She sounded like tuberculosis. The plan was to send in Liz to wheedle a prescription for opiate-rich Citra Forte cough syrup. We would split the bottle three ways, as a chaser to whatever pain pills Randy could hustle with his imaginary spinal and soft-tissue issues.

Lizard Breath had heard enough about the plan. She wanted to talk. The night before, these guys she was tricking had cut abscesses out of one trick's arm with a razor blade.

The images were fresh and graphic in her depiction, and I am queasy about bloody things.

"I held the lump like this." Lizard Breath pulled my chin so I would pay attention. She illustrated the pincer function of her fingers on the inside of my right arm. "They sliced in here, and the lump started to slide. So I had to press below and squeeze the mass back up and out through the incision. It was very interesting."

My left arm had a scabby area that wasn't going away and was maybe oozing a drop or two. I'd rather picture the arm gone than ask Randy or Liz for a diagnosis.

"Shoot a Tuinal and miss, and you have an instant abscess," said Randy.

I'd shot Tuinals. Injecting the pills gives a strong initial rush, but you can't shoot Tuinals without messing the vein. The problem with injecting Tuinals is you hit on the first one, harmlessly squeezing off the load within the walls of the blood vessel. Then you're stoned on Tuinals. Being stoned on Tuinals, you think it's a good idea to shoot more Tuinal. But your eye-hand coordination is obliterated. Finding the vein becomes more miss than hit. Some portion of the Tuinal load is always deposited into the muscle, or fat, or whatever cells surround the blood vessels. I'd once counted up twelve needle pokes for three successful injections of Tuinal.

I signaled for a turn.

Even nerve tissue might be affected by a Tuinal miss, according to Black Randy's data. "So, when you shoot Tuinal, you're practically guaranteed an abscess," he said, "putting you at the mercy of some street surgeon's razorblade triage."

Numbness spread out from the ground zero in my left arm, the spot where I stuck most of my spikes. I pulled the steaming Ford into the clinic's parking lot.

The two junkies and I occupied remote corners of the clinic's waiting area. We were impatient for Lizard to go in and work her lung charm. The three of us intended to seem as though we did not know one another. That way, the nurses and orderlies wouldn't jump to the conclusion that a trio of conniving drug addicts had invaded their facility. We were the only three people in the lobby. Still, I played the role, sticking my nose into magazine after stale magazine.

After a few hours, Lizard was called in to see a doctor. What seemed like half a day later, she came out, clutching a prescription sheet.

"What did he give you?" hissed Randy.

"Cherry-flavored NyQuil."

This sounded odd to me. "Isn't that shit over the counter?"

"What the fuck is this doctor's problem?" said Randy.

"She's a black bitch," replied Lizard.

Randy's eyes went all beady. "My prostate has been bothering me."

He rushed the admissions counter and whipped through paperwork. He forgot all about our necessity to seem unaffiliated and fidgeted in the chair next to me.

A grin of sweet expectation exposed his tar-ridged baby teeth. "Tell them you need your prostate checked," he advised me.

"I'm fine."

"So am I. Don't you want a black woman's finger up your ass?"

I tried to work up some enthusiasm for that scenario, out of affection and respect for Randy. Then I went ahead and minded my own business.

The door to the examination rooms opened. A male nurse stepped out and scanned the waiting area. He didn't like what he saw and rechecked his clipboard. "Jon Morris?" he called. That was Randy's real name, but the nurse sensed an alias. His voice had the slur of a skeptic. I held back an impulse to applaud him for it.

Randy scurried through the examination door. Lizard Breath curled up in a chair across from me, and we plowed into old magazines until Randy reappeared. He seemed dejected.

"She wouldn't finger you?"

"I have diabetes," he said. "She took a blood test. It's serious. I could die."

The drive back to Hollywood was somber. We stopped at a pharmacy, entering like three doomed outpatients, and picked up the cherry syrup. Lizard and I split the one bunk bottle. Randy, due to the diabetes, passed. The juice was nothing like the real stuff. It gave a slight sugar rush, not quite as fizzy as a bottle of strawberry soda.

The car made it to my apartment building, but was overheating. Randy and Lizard came upstairs to wait while the motor cooled. We were exhausted. It had been a ten-hour day of all work and no payoff. We sprawled out and tried to imagine a scenario that would salvage our efforts.

Tommie came home. I'd lost my job without qualifying for an unemployment check. You could say I'd walked off the line, stepped away from making a gainful contribution.

Tommie dropped a bag of groceries on the kitchen counter and didn't say hello or seem pleased to see us. I followed her into the bathroom. She locked the door behind us. Wherever three or more drug addicts have congregated, two people locking themselves in a bathroom raises a red flag.

The empty and flat look on Tommie's face raised something red in my stomach, redder than all that cherry cough syrup.

Tommie hadn't been at work for the entire day. She'd left early and stopped at a clinic in Hollywood.

"For the abortion."

At the abortion clinic, Tommie met a Mexican woman in the waiting area.

The woman had five children in her home, and she loved them. The doctor had insisted that her health would not survive another birth.

The sad mother looked to Tommie to agree that she was doing right. Her husband would never have condoned it.

"She did the right thing," I said. "Of course she did."

Tommie had to use the toilet.

"I hid a beer in the refrigerator," she said. "Can you find it for me?"

She didn't look like she wanted a drink, but I left her alone, to go find her a beer.

Out in the living room, Randy said, "What's going on?"

"Tommie's upset."

"She's sticking it to you because we're here."

I lowered my voice. "She's upset because she had an abortion today."

Randy receded, seemingly softened. "I see," he said.

I went to the kitchen and scavenged that beer. It was stuck in an egg carton.

Tommie had come out of the bathroom. Randy seemed to be consoling her. He was speaking softly; his head was bowed. I moved closer with half a beer.

"I have diabetes," Randy said to Tommie. "Are you sure they didn't give you any meds?"

SCENE SIX:
THERAPY

A week or a month after the start of our baby was ended, Tommie visited a counselor at a community mental health center. Nothing fancy. Nothing with a price tag. We never discussed the wife's needs or plans for therapy. I only found out because Casey Cola tried to kill herself.

Casey Cola was a super fan. She was super devoted to Germs singer Darby Crash, and she turned her Kabuki mask of superiority upon all lesser devotees. Casey Cola took a shot at suicide on an arbitrary weeknight.

The wife, Russ, and I were at Greg's loft apartment in the Villa Elaine on Vine. The Villa Elaine had been down-market and transient since before we were born; it had a steel-screened entrance squeezing into a so-called community courtyard. We were drinking in the sanctuary of Greg's kitchen, doing whatever crap drug we had, making plans for an evening that might never come through. Casey Cola lived in the loft apartment next door.

Casey Cola's mom was rich, what we called rich. She owned a house in Hancock Park, in a neighborhood with no iron bars on windows and no apartment blocks. Casey Cola's mom's house had a guesthouse, a guesthouse that was better appointed than most of the places where the rest of us lived.

A phone company collector once called me, trying to trace Casey Cola.

"This can't possibly be a real person's name," the operator had said, over and over.

"Oh, Casey Cola is very much a real person," I had assured her. "And the phone company has very little chance of ever seeing that thirteen hundred dollars."

Casey was pounding on Greg's front door at the Villa Elaine. At first we played at pretending not to be at home. Russ was a Mau Mau now, along with Greg. Greg played guitar; Russ held the bass. Being a Mau Mau had turned Russ into an object of obsession to a certain type of girl—the super fan type.

Since becoming a Mau Mau, Russ had gone out with Casey Cola. In a way, she had been something like Russ's girlfriend. He'd had a few of these girlfriend impersonators. One of them had been sent by her mother to see a shrink. The shrink had told the girl that if she kept seeing Russ, she might as well load a gun and shoot herself in the head. At least, that's Russ's version of what the girl had confided to him.

The shrink's tale was retold over drinks at Greg's kitchen table on this arbitrary weeknight, with escalating hilarity, as Casey Cola bashed at Greg's locked front door. "She should just *load a gun*," Greg yelled, "*and shoot herself in the head!*"

Eventually, Casey left the door alone. Moments later, loud music rumbled through the adjoining wall from the loft apartment where Casey lived. After four or five of Casey's songs, we heard sirens mixed in with the music, far off at first. The sirens moved closer, higher and louder in the mix. It sounded like an ambulance, and a fire truck, and two police cars had assembled directly at the Vine Street gate to the Villa Elaine. The sirens wound down and cut out; punk rock played on, unaccompanied, next door.

"My favorite part of this song is when they blow the guitar solo," said Greg. "It's coming up."

We all listened for the guitar solo to blow.

Booted footfalls sounded through the wall connecting to Casey's apartment, stomping across the hardwood living room, up Casey's stairs. I pictured strapping rescuers cramming into Casey's bed loft and bathroom. The music stopped next door.

"This is the kind of situation where authorities in uniforms go around knocking on doors and asking questions," said Russ. Intuitively, and silently, Russ, Greg, Tommie, and I left Greg's place through the backdoor.

The four of us snuck single file along a trash-access path that emptied into the street. Voices made us pause beneath Casey Cola's open bathroom window. Her druggy whine came down clear and plaintive, telling her rescuers tales of us.

"I'm so nice to them. I feed them. I do everything for them. I bought them drinks. And they won't let me in."

This is the funniest thing we have ever heard. We plaster hands across each other's mouths to stuff back laughter. We shake and quiver and fall to our knees in spasms of partially contained hilarity.

Of course, not everyone sees humor the same way. The emergency responders, for instance, took Casey Cola seriously.

"What are their names?" said the responders, softly but firmly. "Who are the people who pushed you to this?"

These men had sympathy and a sensitive toiletside manner. We opted to scamper out onto Vine Street. Skirting the vehicles with the flashing lights, we located the Ford. Russ slid into the driver's seat, out of habit, which was a strong factor in all we did.

"Do we know where we're going?" asked Tommie.

By this time, moving into 1979, punk rock is all over the town. We had the option of concerts, bars, and a house party, all catering to people who looked like our crowd had looked in 1977.

The concerts and bars had filled up with people who didn't seem to realize who we were—not even those of us who were in the Mau Mau's—so as the ambulance doors closed on Casey Cola in our rearview mirrors, we headed for the house party.

"The drinks will be free," said Russ.

"Maybe they'll have food," said Greg.

We all laughed. *Food!* How absurd.

It was one of those situations where the directions were vague and the destination outside our known orbits. Paying no attention to any of those difficulties, we pulled up at the curb of a sleek single-family residence that looked like it had been assembled out of a groovy house kit.

The people who lived there would come into their own during the eighties. They were art directed and ambitious in ways that we were not. These were careerists with concrete agendas for self-advancement.

The hostess asked Tommie, "Who are you with?"

Tommie pointed to Russ and to me. "I'm with them."

"I mean, you are with an agency?"

We tried to mingle. We made a real effort, but people asked, "What do you do?" The question reminded me of the truth about us. Some of us went through medicine cabinets and bedroom bureaus looking for intoxicants and valuables, is what we did. So I blame our behavior that weeknight on social anxiety.

Tommie and I tagged along with Russ as he casually and thoroughly ransacked coats piled on a guest room sofa. Pushing ahead, I moved through a closed door at the back of the house. A command came from inside the room:

"Don't turn on the light."

I knew that voice. Tommie and Russ slipped past me into what shaped up in the gloom to be an in-house office.

"Come in, Basho, come in," said the voice. "Don't look over here."

I shut the door behind me. We all three moved toward the unseen voice. Russ switched on a desk lamp, and we said hello to Black Randy, whose jeans and underpants were bunched at his ankles.

Randy was squatting over an open desk drawer. He grunted in satisfied completion, selected a piece of correspondence from the desktop, wiped his ass, and dropped the soiled paper into the open drawer. In a coordinated motion, he bumped the drawer shut and pulled up his pants, restoring himself to decency.

"None of you seem surprised," he said.

We knew the legend: The Black Randy story included a chapter in which he'd smeared his own feces on a welfare caseworker's cubicle to ensure that a qualification interview ended with a payout.

"My guess," surmised Tommie, "is that the bitch at the door asked you what you do."

"Let me show you what else I can do," said Randy.

He sat in the desk chair and punched the phone into life. Randy was a performer by nature. He truly was best inspired in front of an audience. If Russ, Tommie, and I hadn't ventured into that home office, shitting in the desk drawer might have been disruption enough for him.

"Operator! I need the police. Hurry! A child's life is in danger." Randy was prepared to hold, but the response came before Russ had even finished inventorying the contents of the desk's right-hand drawers.

"Officer! Officer! Please hurry! She's only six, seven at the oldest. This is just too young, too young to be raped. Oh, please help! They hear me. They know I'm in here. Yes, I know where I am." He gave the telephone officer an address—rushed, urgent, but accurate. "I must go! I need to be safe. I'm only afraid because they were showing off the guns while they were shooting up."

Randy broke the connection. "I estimate we have four to six minutes in which to calmly leave the premises," he said.

Randy rode in the back of the Ford, with Tommie upfront and me at the wheel. Russ drove off with Greg in the car of two girls who might want to be Mau Mau super fans.

In that middle ground between where the party was and where Tommie and I lived, I ran into half an hour of being lost, which gave Randy time to apologize to Tommie for hitting her up for drugs on the day of her abortion.

"That was a terrible day for all of us," Randy said. "And I only made it worse. Next week, I'm coming into possession of a thousand Dilaudid pills. I will make it up to you."

"Dilaudid means nothing to me," said Tommie. "Allan's the one who wants Dilaudid."

"I may take a little nap," said Randy.

The Ford found its way home, and Randy wouldn't wake up. His sleep was deep. He gave off an unhealthy sheen in the car's overhead light.

"Is this what a diabetic coma looks like?" I asked Tommie.

"I don't really care," she said.

Leaving Randy unattended in the car was a risk, but the hour was late, and I had no motivation to drag him inside. If Black Randy passed through a diabetic coma into death, doing it in the car rather than in the house would eliminate one cumbersome step in body removal.

Back in the apartment, safe on the floor mattress, I made a move for the wife.

"Do you know where I went yesterday?" said Tommie. The room, with my effort, stopped swaying. I tried to remember where I'd been yesterday, what I'd been doing instead of looking for a job.

"You went to work," I said.

"I went to the mental health center."

This was sobering. Did she judge me to be incapable of making my own appointment?

"I'm okay now," I said. "Things were rough there for a little while."

"I went for myself."

I took some time to mull this over, which is what I think she wanted me to do.

"What did they tell you?" For instance, had they advised her to load bullets into a gun and shoot it into her head?

"They listened," said Tommie. "They're trained counselors; so they make eye contact and nod their heads about every half minute. They passed across a box of tissues. And when I ran out of things to say, they talked me around."

"They talked you around?"

"They told me things like what a guy tells his girlfriend when he plans to dump her, but not yet."

Tommie waited. She wanted me to ask: *What are those things that a guy tells his girlfriend to postpone dumping her for a more convenient time?* I guessed that specific answers to that question would be hurtful to me.

"The counselors listened," I said, "but didn't seem to feel it?"

She looked at me as though I were one of those counselors, and I had just interrupted her.

"I walked to the bus stop," she said. "Then I had an afterthought, and I went back. The center had closed for lunch, but I knew the way; so I just walked through the lobby into where the offices are. They didn't hear me, and they couldn't see me, but I heard them."

Tommie had stood unseen behind a corkboard partition papered with fliers promoting harm prevention and temporary safe housing.

Back on the home floor, she imitated a male counselor imitating her voice, mocking a distressed tone that I recognized all too well: "'I went in there again and again…from two until four.'"

She looked for a place to spit. "They told me to trust them, that I was speaking in confidence." Tommie switched up her voice, mimicking her laments being mimicked by a woman: "'I went in there again and again…hoping it would be over.'"

The wife stopped short of making direct accusations, but her teary eyes blamed her humiliation on me.

"They couldn't stop laughing," she said. "Even if they'd seen me, they would have kept laughing."

"I think we can afford a bed frame," I said. "People sell them used. We can lift our mattress off the floor."

"Do you really think that would help?" she said.

Lifting the bed was a start, but healing professionals had used us for comic relief. To the trained eye, the wife and I were funny—in the same vein that Casey Cola was funny to us.

In the morning, I volunteered to drive Tommie to work. She didn't want me to, even after we were in the car.

"You really don't have to do this," she said.

"We want to do this," said Black Randy, wide awake in the backseat.

I parked the Ford on a side street, with a clear view of the social services center. The center would open for business in a quarter hour. Civil servants straggled in, reporting for life-saving duty. A big, lumbering guy in jacket and tie unlocked the street door.

"Is that one of them?" I said.

"Really," Tommie said, "this is completely unnecessary."

"If you don't answer yes or no," I said, "we'll assume the dude is a yes."

"There's one," said Tommie. She'd fingered the culprit before Randy or I had a chance to spot him. "The preppy asshole in the brown corduroy jacket and the shitty brown loafers."

Randy produced a pair of yellow dishwashing gloves and began working his left hand into one of them.

"Hey," said Tommie, "did you take those from my kitchen?"

"Maintain vigilance, my dear," said Randy. "Did corduroy man offend alone, or did he have an accomplice?"

"That bitch, right there." Tommie's eyes fixed on a blonde with her hair in a sensible bun, dragging a cart of case files through the center's parking lot toward a side door.

Randy worked his right hand into the second yellow glove.

"You shouldn't put on the gloves until you're inside," I said.

Randy scoffed. "Who's done this before? You?"

"Yellow gloves will give it away."

"Some fuckwad might figure out what the gloves portend once I'm inside," said Randy. "By then, it will be too late."

Randy stepped out of the car. He was wearing a jacket he didn't care if he never saw again. He carried a ziplocked baggie of his own shit in each pocket.

"You can wait around if you want," he said, "but I'll find my way home."

He ambled toward the mental health clinic.

"This really wasn't necessary," said Tommie.

I watched Randy knock on the clinic's door and step inside. I started the car and we drove away.

SCENE SEVEN:
GIRL A'S SECRET SHOW

I'd taken the car and the wife up to Hollywood Boulevard to dig through dusty crates in old bookstores. Until the eighties showed up, the Boulevard and its side streets boasted the densest concentration of booksellers anywhere in the English-speaking world, outside of London, England.

You could find rare collectibles, exotic private printings, basic trade editions, and mounds of bunk titles people had cleared out before moving back to somewhere else.

Side by side with every bookstore was a crumbling dive bar. Now that we no longer lived in the Boulevard's rooming-house grid, the wife and I could adopt a sociologist's rosy glow as we sat at a stained counter lined with boilermaker-swilling pensioners. We savored a quick, short beer while someone like Sarah Vaughan sang sweet anguish on the buzzing jukebox. I drank down Tommie's moody profile in the bar's shady light.

None of these people, boozing, blabbing, brawling, lost in their minds, noticed or suspected that such a treasure breathed in their midst, jewel quality and precious, smiling freely—smiling at nothing and at everything, I suppose.

I refused the bartender's offer to bum a cigarette off me, and the welcome went out of the atmosphere. We moved back out into the sun, looking for the next bookstore.

We found Rock Bottom and Blank Frank outside the Spotlight bar on Selma and Ivar. Dudes would piss right at the bar at the Spotlight; they'd rape each other in the back room. This is not hyperbole. Rock Bottom had on his creaky leather bomber jacket and black wraparound shades. With his spiked green hair, he looked like a Halloween punk rocker—like some Valley kid who had dressed up in clichés.

The thing is, Rock Bottom had originated the clichés. The look was his. All you needed to do was lift those wraparound shades and glance into his eyes. Crazy people on the street—the kind who made erratic, jolting moves that scared normal people—would cross eyes with Rock and straighten right up. Rock Bottom owned that feral nihilist shtick, legitimately. In a just world, he would have owned a piece from all the kids who had followed along with it.

Blank Frank was understated—pale makeup, kitchen-sink bleach job, classic black Ray-Ban sunglasses, tight, thrift-store gigolo suit.

"What have you been doing?" I asked, mostly so they wouldn't ask first. The question always stumped me.

Rock filled us in: They'd started a band, or revived a defunct group, or had plans to do both. Until the music paid off, Frank was hustling, and Rock Bottom was dealing PCP.

They tagged along with the wife and me, trolling for shoplifting opportunities, but soon gave that up. Shop owners were blocking their doors at the sight of us.

"Do you guys want to get high?" said Rock.

"Sure," I said. Some people, not our people, might have asked, "High on what?"

Rock and Blank had holed up in a furnished single in a residency hotel on Wilcox, north of the Boulevard, about six blocks of sex shops and pimp boutiques away. People we passed on the walk over gave us plenty of indication that the location was dicey: Hippies, hoods, hookers, and moochers—not a sign of gainful employment among the lot of them.

"Keep your eyes on your wallet," advised Blank.

We stood with our backs to the brick as we waited to be buzzed into the building where Blank and Rock lived. Rock lifted his shades, eager to repel any incursion from the indigenous street population. No confrontation came, and the door rattled. Disappointed, Rock put the sunglasses back in place and led us up the stairs to their abode.

The room's one window overlooked Pla-Boy liquors on Yucca. You could sit there looking down for half an hour and see more opportunistic street crime than on any three *Starsky and Hutch* reruns. Blank Frank turned on the TV; the picture was fuzzy and drifted up and out of frame. There was no record player, and a short stack of records. That Velvet Underground album with the peeling banana was naturally the top record. The Damned's *Damned, Damned, Damned* and something by Johnny Thunders were right behind it.

"I'm going to double dip a Sherman," said Rock. "No charge."

Rock had an instinct for pampering his guests.

He stuck one end of a dark-wrapped, filter-free Sherman cigarette into an ink bottle filled with dark fluid. Rock touched his lips to the end of the cigarette and gingerly sucked fluid up through the tobacco. He held the cigarette sideways, capped each end with a finger, and let the chemicals soak in. He repeated the process, creating the "double dipped" effect.

"I hope you have some time to give to this high," said Blank Frank. "Like all day."

"Like the rest of your life," said Rock. He fired up the Sherman and passed it over.

We lost track of time, but events—such as the arrival of Rock's girlfriend with a grievance aimed at the Pla-Boy cashier, followed by three guys who believed Frank had shorted them on a deal for two pistols—alerted the wife and me that a wide world of book shopping needed us outside the furnished single.

Driving back home, at the wheel of the moving car, I realized that all my life I had been a steel marble rolling in a pinball game.

"I feel just like that!" yelled Tommie.

This pinball existence was funny and liberating. Tommie laughed, and beamed, and punched my shoulders and chest.

"You're really here," she shouted. She punched me again. "You're solid!"

I had her scout out the road ahead. Together, we looked beyond the windshield and coordinated the progress of the car through the pinball landscape.

Usually, PCP, angel dust, whatever the dealer calls it, is no fun. The high is defined by three hours of clutching the floor and wondering why you ever took this poison again.

But Tommie and I shared the reality on this trip, and the drug had peeled back the dead skin from our lives, like tearing the covering off an orange, exposing the sweet, messy segments within, juicy wedges adhering to and bleeding into one another. I was pleased to park the car correctly in our designated spot, click off the ignition, and pocket the key. Home. Safety. Together.

Part Three

The absurdity of existence, the vast and intricate strings of coincidence that had lead to animal consciousness, the bogus pillars carved of emotion and memory that support human personality like an unstable platform over oily waters—these truths were obvious, and amusing, and united Tommie and me in a cozy pod of shared epiphany.

Russ had moved out; Rick Wilder had given him a bed and a closet at the Mau Mau compound. Our apartment seemed spacious and private. The wife and I wandered around the place as if it were all ours, from kitchen, to living room, and on into both bedrooms and bathrooms.

A druggy chick from the wife's new job had forwarded a tester bindle from a cocaine-dealing boyfriend. Tommie and I sniffed that up, right out in the open, without closing any bedroom or bathroom doors.

Cocaine powder was dripping into my throat when Lizard Breath, the Hollywood High heiress, rang at the front door. She called for us to open up.

"Shhh…" said Tommie.

"She's really not so bad," I said.

Lizard was with Rick Wilder and Russ. A trick had kicked them out of his van at Arthur J's coffee shop, and they'd walked down from Santa Monica and Highland. Bottles clanked inside a paper bag. They'd brought enough booze to declare a party.

"Jesus was just another john," sang Rick. He was the Mau Mau's singer, and the world was his rehearsal space. "If he had the money, he would have bought him some."

In the standard chaos of arrival, Liz pulled the wife and me into the bathroom. She locked the door and slid out a fresh bottle of opium-based cough syrup that the Mau Mau's were apparently unaware of.

"I owe this to you," Lizard said. "For all the driving we went through. Think of it as a make-up high."

I cracked the prescription seal and upended the juice. This kind of reparation never happened. I looked Liz over.

If I were Tommie, I would have been wary of Lizard Breath's gesture. Hard drugs are the most precious gift a girl can give a man. If Lizard Breath had owned a house, or an apartment, or even an attached garage, I would have been welcome to move straight in.

The wife, Liz, and I came out of the bathroom; Russ and Rick were mixing vodka drinks in the kitchen.

"What were you all doing in there?" said Rick. "Making out?"

Their idea was to go to Club 88. Girl A's band was scheduled to play, a secret insiders show.

Club 88 was a piano dive trying to turn into a new wave nightclub. The address was way west on Pico Boulevard, out past Century City, family land where people had careers and mortgages, territory we rarely visited. But the 1970s were closing out, and everything was due to turn a new leaf—Club 88 as a punk bar, me and my friends as far-ranging party patrons.

The five of us fit into my car and rolled toward the Century City skyline.

I was in the backseat, holding Tommie under an arm. Lizard Breath kept watch from the edge of the seat. It had been a blessed sort of a day—three free highs, the angel dust, the coke, and the opiate elixir. There was some magic left in life yet. I let an arm hang out the window. I formed a fist, twisted my wrist; I took pleasure in the movement of muscle and sinew under my skin.

I hadn't shot up in weeks, and I was wearing short sleeves in defiance of all expectations. Short sleeves were a statement of rebellion, at this point. Being clean didn't feel so bad.

West LA was reached without incident, and Russ parked the car. We wandered toward Club 88, about half a block away, and stopped to stock up at a liquor store a few doors down.

I squatted with Lizard at the magazine rack. A misleading cover promise took me in, and I stole a useless skin mag. Out on the sidewalk, under the streetlamps, the photos turned out to be garbage. The magazine wasn't worth a jerk.

"You don't need that," said Lizard Breath, reading over my shoulder. She grabbed the book, threw it into an open car window, and pulled tight to me.

Inside Club 88, Rick Wilder refilled our drinks from a smuggled bottle of vodka. Two or three drinks later, Rick claimed the vodka was finished. So I hit him in the face.

Rick fought back, and our battle moved onto the pool table. We sprawled across the felt, throwing punches and wringing chokeholds. I tried to cram Rick's head into one of the table's side pockets. I might have done it if he could have stopped laughing and let me concentrate.

The Club 88 regulars chalked their cues redundantly and looked old and mystified. If the crowd had been spry, it would have beaten us to a pulp.

I came to understand that my wallet had gone missing. Rick and I stopped fighting.

The wallet was in none of my pockets. Tommie didn't have it, and neither did Rick. I checked the pockets in the pool table. All empty. The waitresses, the bartender, the manager of the place, they all had the same story: "Back up. No wallet has been turned in."

I wrote my phone number on scraps of paper towel and forced it on the Club 88 staff. I truly expected to be notified of good news. Despite the loss of my driver's license, cash, and immigration documents, my high remained perfect, inviolable.

It dawned on me I was hearing sound, a sort of music, and I recognized it. Girl A's band was playing.

A window had been cut into a wall behind the stage so the billiard players could watch the entertainers without interrupting their games. I gawked at Girl A, from behind. I was free to think this; I was free to imagine that. I tried to remember what she looked like naked, and she couldn't even see me.

Girl A's guitar snapped a string. The band stopped. They looked stuck up and lost. There was speculation that the show would not go on. But Michael Schmuck moved into the spotlight and restrung Girl A's instrument. The performance was saved.

I mooched a cocktail and poured it onto the chemical mix inside me. I have never felt that good since. Lizard Breath sidled up to me. Maybe she'd paid for the cocktail; her tongue took a proprietary swirl in my ear. My head jerked, and Lizard's tongue retreated, rebuffed. If ever again I alienated my affections from Tommie, it would not be for a tarnished-gilt heiress.

The day's highs were the kind that promise you they will last forever. I knew these forecasts were untrue. Tommie and I, on the other hand, we had gone beyond temporary union to *one*. Imperturbable, I left the enclave of the billiard room, scraped off Lizard Breath, and claimed a spot out front, in the general audience, leaning on a post facing the stage. When Girl A looked up from her fingers on the fretboard, she would see me. I had no fear of being trapped in her gaze.

A rockabilly poseur leaned against the opposite side of my post. A steady stream of fans stepped up and engaged him in conversation. Fans have never been high on my likes list, and Lizard Breath didn't endear herself to me by joining their ranks. She slithered through the lesser fans and attached herself to the rockabilly poseur. Their heads were close to mine, too close. I had no buffer from their shouted conversation.

"Are you still a thing with Girl A?" shouted Liz.

"I am, and I'm not," shouted the rockabilly poseur. "I do her when I have time, but I do whoever else I want to do, too."

They could do one another, all of them could. I found Tommie wearing a smirk—you know, a display of amused skepticism—watching Girl A's band from a back booth. I pulled her by the arm.

We blazed the shortest route outside. I stumbled in the rutted alleyway behind the club. My face tilted toward the black, empty sky. The heavens showed me nothing. The stars were there, surely. I couldn't see any. Infinite particles of urban blight were layered in-between the celestial bodies and me. But what did that matter?

Tommie was outside with me. I spun her around and pulled her face-to-face. We stood chest-to-chest. Our bodies pressed together, down to our knees. I tried to kiss her, but her lips were laughing. My mouth could not pin them down. Her teeth flashed. I looked up, into the sky. Now I could see stars shining up there, far away, but clearly piercing the dark.

I ran my hands under Tommie's shirt. I assayed her belt line. Her belly quivered with laughter. She was like Rick Wilder—hilarious in the face of my serious advances. The situation was urgent. I needed an orgasm, right there in the alley, with her, right away.

Lizard Breath, the rockabilly poseur, Girl A, what did they have that I would ever want? My high flipped. That caught me by surprise, and dropped me.

"Allan, you don't even have an erection!" Tommie laughed tenderly. She was my friend. She laughed as my tender friend. "You don't even have the beginnings of an erection."

I was crying, like a girl, like a lonely man who loved himself too hard. God on high, what will it take for me to be happy? My tears blotted out the pinpoints of light up there.

I was desperate to throw up. Nothing would come, not even a mouthful of bile. The wife stood beside me in this dark and deserted alley.

"What the fuck is wrong with you?" she said. "Why are you suddenly so sad?"

Here's what I admitted then, to myself: *The wife is unhappy. My emotional crashes are a betrayal to her. If I truly loved her, only she could make me feel so bad, so crushed.*

Here's what I did not admit then, to myself: *The baby, Tommie's accidental baby, is dead. Tommie is mourning that death. She will never share that mourning with me.*

In the following week, a call came from Club 88. They'd recovered the wallet I'd lost at Girl A's show. While Tommie worked, I drove to the bar and claimed my property. Nothing was missing, only cash.

I took the wallet home as a winning omen. When Tommie and I were settled in bed, in the dark on our elevated mattress, I took out the wallet and showed it to her. "*See?*" I said. "*This proves it! We're a really lucky couple!*"

"Let me sleep," she said. "Let me dream something lucky."

PART FOUR: THE BLACK ANGEL'S FIELD TRIP

"I came to myself within a dark wood where the straight way was lost."

SCENE ONE:
REST STOP

It was the last five hours of 1980. Black Randy and I were in a van being driven by some short, shaggy Woodland Hills fan, heading to San Francisco to score meth. Black Randy and the Metrosquad had played the Starwood the night before. The Starwood was located on Santa Monica Boulevard, across from where the Plunger Pit had been. Its owner, a cocaine-charged, Middle Eastern mobster, would figure prominently in the grisly Wonderland mass murder of 1981. The Starwood's unyielding management style applied to patrons and bands alike. Randy had booked the show a few months ahead, on the mistaken assumption that December 30 would be New Year's Eve. His negotiations to shift the date had been rebuffed with minor, felony-status violence.

Randy's disappointment at having performed one day off from the holiday was bitter. The shaggy kid driving the van and I felt no need to mention the mistake. On the plus side, the blackness was loaded with cash: He'd collected a Mafioso's ransom for playing the Starwood, and then he'd stiffed his band.

We'd left the oasis of Los Angeles in the early evening. The shaggy kid drove and Randy took the front passenger seat. I tossed around in the back of the van. The van's backseats had been torn out and not bolted back in.

"I didn't have time," said the shaggy fan, jerking the steering wheel. I slammed against exposed iron and steel. "Fuck it; I didn't feel like it anyway," continued Randy's fan. "I didn't know someone else was riding along."

"Come, come, there will be bathtub drugs and bathroom orgasms enough for everyone," said Randy, half interested in smoothing things over. The skin encasing his skull was sweating.

During the encore of the Metrosquad's show the night before, a new wave hairdresser had sheared Randy's locks onstage with a pair of power clippers.

Bald Black Randy looked like Mr. Clean, like a sallow, simpering, droopy-breasted Mr. Clean, a Mr. Clean who had the eyes of a tweaking owl. Something about the back of his head bothered me. I popped another Coors from the two-case supply that Randy had loaded in and fell over again. The drawbacks of having no seats in the back of the van were becoming clearer to me.

A few hours into our odyssey, we rolled into the rural desert night, and an impenetrable fog blanketed the four-lane blacktop. The strip was straight, like a runway, with extra helpings of wasteland stretching out to nowhere on either side, a nowhere that we could not begin to see in all that thick fog.

The shaggy kid's van had a magical tape deck that played any song in the world, provided it was by Blowfly, or the Mentors or it was that "Eat the Yellow Snow" crime by Frank Zappa. Additionally, Randy had a lot to say, and he said it competing with the music. I lost most of the narration in the road sounds coming up through the van's floor. Occasionally, Randy would turn backward in his seat and fix me with his owl orbs.

"Darby," slurred Randy, "was a sensitive soul." About three weeks earlier, Germs singer Darby Crash had killed himself with a deliberate heroin overdose. The death had been big news among us.

"Basho!" Randy referred to me by one of my dead *Slash* pen names. "You also, like Darby, are a sensitive soul...don't take that as a compliment."

"I don't."

"You, sensitive soul you, have your wife, your very lovely soul mate wife, and sensitive soul Darby had soul mate Casey Cola."

Darby had shot up Casey Cola with a lesser dose moments before self-inflicting his lethal injection. Casey had come out of her nod next to the Germ's cold body, which made her the failed partner of a half-successful suicide pact.

I had something pithy to say about Casey Cola's suicidal shortcomings, but I kept it to myself. "You really can't compare Casey Cola and Tommie," I said.

Bald Randy urged the shaggy driver to increase the van's speed. He threw an empty Coors can out the window and turned back to me:

"What did Tommie say about you running off to Sodom by the Bay? Did she try to stop you? No. Doesn't that bother you? You're sensitive. That should bother you."

"No, it shouldn't."

Without work, the apartment had been playing tricks on me. A week before Christmas, I started drinking in the morning and yanked down all Tommie's custom-created holiday decorations for lunch. It was the second year in a row

I'd pulled that stunt. Then I'd gone out and squandered every dollar I didn't have at the closest bar. When I'd come home, more lucid than I'd wanted to be, the wife had removed all her paintings and drawings and photographs from the walls, again. Had we talked about anything specific that mattered to us since then? I could almost remember something—

Randy butted in: "Who's doing her while you're away?"

"Yeah," echoed the shaggy kid. "Who's she doing while you're gone?"

The shaggy kid had never met Tommie and hardly knew me; the first I'd seen of him was when I'd climbed into his van. He was a fan, a fan of Randy and the Mentors, but a fan nonetheless. This fan would pay for his presumption; I was sensitive about things like presumption.

"Tommie won't do anything I'm not doing," I said.

"Then you should be very worried." Randy cackled, holding his mouth open and letting his head loll like a baby bird yawing for a worm. "I promise you a descent into the softest, most cancerous underbelly of the Tenderloin. We will make a study of North Beach's filthiest peep shows. The sperm on the floor will pull the shoes off your feet..."

"I've bought you two rolls of quarters, one for each fist. By the time you're five dollars in, you will have a view of human depravity deeper, wider, more gaping than anything you ever suspected existed."

There was a lot of authentic enthusiasm in Randy's delivery. I couldn't help being intrigued. But staring at the back of his glimmering skull, I felt that I had a comprehensive view of human depravity already.

We'd been on the road for hours upon hours; I'd lost track of how many beers I'd drained, but my bladder kept a running tally. "I want to stop and piss."

"Late start," said Randy. "Need to make up lost time. We can cross the Golden Gate before midnight."

"The van has double fuel tanks," bragged the shaggy kid. "We won't need any gas stops."

The thick fog cut visibility to nothing better than zero. Randy placed his face to the windshield glass and insisted the kid hold the speedometer steady at eighty. The back of Randy's bald head looked crazy. That's what had been bothering me about it.

"Piss in a can," said the kid, the shaggy fan. "If you're too ladylike to hold it."

Randy chortled, as if the kid had been funny. He knew the kid wasn't funny. Randy was being a prick because I'd mocked him internally about botching the date for his grand New Year's Eve show.

It's difficult to train a stream of piss into the opening of a beer can while you're being tossed around the back of a speeding van. The hole in the can is surrounded by sharp edges; I might lacerate my dick. The driver made the piss challenge harder than it had to be. He jerked the steering deliberately, tumbling me to my side with my penis in my hand.

I climbed back to my knees and pissed all across the back corner of the van, where the shaggy kid's clothes were heaped. Without really trying, I squeezed three or four inches of urine into the bottom of the can, most of which I splashed onto Randy's neck and ear as I tossed the can out his open window.

Oddly, Randy became jovial, almost proud of me with my piss dripping from his ear. He wrestled his laughter under control and suggested we stop to eat.

We pulled over into a pool of light surrounding an all-night café along the highway between Fresno and Bakersfield. It was an isolated, godforsaken spot where men have nothing better to do than take their honor seriously.

The café door creaked on its springs and slammed shut behind us. Obviously, we were not from around there, but the sandstorms and fog dumps dragged in all sorts of strangers. The shift workers at the counter and the scrub farmers and their families in the booths raised a couple of eyebrows and left it at that. In a weird way, we almost fit in.

We ordered burgers and coffees from a waitress who'd had enough. I followed Randy into the can. I needed to wash stray piss off my hands.

Randy huffed and puffed at the urinal. A kid, maybe ten, skinny, walked behind him toward the toilet stall.

"What are you staring at?" said Randy.

Bald head? Beady eyes? Dark streak of piss down the soft, gray back of his teddy boy jacket? The ten-year-old kid maintained the look of somebody minding his own business.

"Maybe you like me; maybe that's why you're staring at me?" Randy giggled, like when I'd slopped the urine down his neck.

The kid just wanted to crap in peace. He slid into the stall and shot the latch behind him.

"You think I'm cute?" Randy hitched himself up over the toilet stall door. Picture those beady eyes and that damp skull looming above you while you're ten and trying to settle in on a strange toilet. "You want to get it on?" said Randy.

Back at our table, burgers had been delivered. I ate without bothering to sit down.

Randy was out of the picture for a few minutes. Then we saw him at the counter, explaining that he had only been joking to some wiry shit kicker who had a protective interest in the skinny kid from the bathroom.

Randy pulled out his overstuffed wallet. He counted bills into the hands of a waitress. He shelled out a huge asshole tax, the tax for being a huge asshole. Hard-worked locals were multiplying around him in canvas and denim coats. Their shoulders jutted like shovels or pickaxes in their jackets—like sheathed weapons.

"We need to get out of here," I said.

The shaggy kid indicated Randy's burger. "What about this?"

"Leave it."

The shaggy fan and I skirted Randy's circumference of calamity and stole out into the parking lot. We started the van and did a slow roll past the "Open All Night" neon sign. Randy came sprinting out the door, what passed for sprinting with him. He had on a face I hadn't seen before: scared and lonely and certain that he was doomed to an unpleasant and well-deserved end.

The vehicle was on the move when baldy scuttled into the front passenger seat. I'd retreated to the back of the van. It seemed more difficult to place a clean rifle shot back there.

"I underestimated those people," Randy said, huffing, wheezing, spitting. He pulled the door shut and ducked down below the window. "I'm very disappointed that you two weren't there for me."

The shaggy driver gunned the accelerator and swung the wheel toward the freeway on-ramp.

Through the back window, I watched outraged locals stream out of the diner and dissolve in the fog as it closed up and swallowed everything behind us, swallowing everything all the way back to my wavering picture of Tommie alone and pondering in our Hollywood apartment.

SCENE TWO:
THE BIRTHDAY STING

A fog is not the worst. A fog is fuzzy and painless. You walk in a cocoon of watery cotton, buffered from everything, including, most mercifully, your own body and mind. A protective swaddling absorbs the bumps and jabs of being, of being the sentient creature of intellect, and emotion, and desire—all thwarted. You are out there somewhere, the active you, roaming and performing beyond the soft, wispy near-distance, seeking gratification and recompense, making up for lost time, lost causes, and lost love. But the actual inner essential you is in the custody of the fog, safely removed from that seeker—until he needs your input.

Come back!

Awareness opens up like a clearing in thick mist. It starts with a swirl. You become conscious of where you are. You see—sometimes—what needs to be done next.

This one time coming out of the fog, the time we're talking about, was around midnight, February 26, 1980.

Come back!

With no real warning, Allan MacDonell returned to life and limb, moving ahead on foot, at night. Pain locked onto me like a curse. I was staggering, doubled over. My right hand fisted in my belly; the left hand clawed at my head and neck. I had poisoned myself.

My feet flung themselves out in front of me, one then the other, slapping the sidewalk with an excruciating shock, landing just in time to keep my forward-plunging body from slamming face-first into the cement.

I put out both hands to break my fall, but I didn't fall, and I knew where I was: On a side street parallel to Santa Monica Boulevard, one block south, headed west. Home was less than a quarter mile distant. My life, the recent events and circumstances, came back to me in chunks. It was my twenty-fourth birthday.

Hey, come on back…

A few hours earlier, at home, alone in the kitchen with no birthday cake, I had realized that life descending into the future would be a continuing series of disappointments. I had sunk the boat. Twenty-five—the deadline for being a famous and rich prodigy—was only one year away. I knew, at twenty-four, that genius would not show itself to me in the next twelve months, or anytime soon after that.

This dreadful picture of my remaining life had come to me while I stood at the sink finishing a beer. No one was at home to share and soften my bleak vision. The wife had gone with purpose to a journaling workshop at the Downtown Women's Center. The last drop of beer dispersed on my unsatisfied tongue. Sadness, I knew, had only begun its lifelong momentum.

Don't go away! It's warm in the car!

I tripped on a curb, stubbed my entire foot. The jolt vibrated just short of shattering my shin. The sick swirled in my gut, and a throb spiked in my head. I couldn't throw up; I couldn't be casual about keeping my balance. I tried to make things happen. I had no business being on the street.

Back in the kitchen, I'd fished under the silverware drawer and extracted a bindle. I'd saved it for an emergency—Persian brown heroin. The Shah of Iran had fallen. The Iranian middle class was fleeing to America, packing along whatever portable wealth they could fit into an overhead luggage compartment. The market for Persian rugs had collapsed under the influx of carpet-carrying immigrants; so the émigrés had turned to bringing in Persian drugs. The stuff wasn't heroin, exactly. It was a form of crude morphine, one step away from being true H. The trick was to cook the dark granules in lemon juice, rather than water. The citric acid was said to provide that last bit of chemical processing.

Quit fucking around; come on!

I'd shot up the muck, and still—under full effect of the wonder drug—I'd seen tedium and disappointment spreading out like an oil slick on the sea of me. There was nothing the dope could do to dissipate the sludge of birthday tidings I saw and felt.

I rinsed my rig, stoned but not high. Real junkies are blessed with some extra facet of imagination that I was missing. They believe heroin will relieve their pain, even when it doesn't. I couldn't muster a blind faith in the existence of an all-powerful narcotic. That shared superstitious conception of almighty dope is what keeps novitiates scoring until the skag has them strung out and fully devout—coming back again and again to worship whether they believe in the shit anymore or not.

I'd walked out the door, every bit as miserable as before I'd put the needle in, and taken a bus to the Dangerhouse compound, a suite of storage spaces above a Santa Monica Boulevard mariachi bar. My birthday plan was to mooch weed off of Black Randy.

The flight of stairs up to the Dangerhouse quarters took something vital out of me. I slumped at a table in the Dangerhouse kitchen. I tried to put on the face of someone keeping up with the biting witticisms firing between Randy and two other people who hadn't come into focus.

A haze descended. I felt sick, so sick that I roused myself and concocted some way to say that I had to leave.

I didn't know exactly how I'd arrived outside in the thick of the fog. The walk home had marched past in a soupy mist of oblivion. That blind march had brought me to a crossroads, a dilemma, to an indecipherable perplexity, whatever you want to call it.

Get in!

I stood, doubled over, fist to stomach, claw to face, stalled in the middle of crossing the street.

A car had stopped and blocked my path. The passenger door was open, and the driver leaned across, beckoning.

"Come on over. Just get in the fucking car."

I could hear him, but I had trouble picturing him. I squinted hard. The pain in my head tripled up my vision on me. The driver needed a wash, and he was strong enough to physically overpower me. He'd turned off the interior light in his car.

I knew what he was.

He was a cop, an undercover cop on an urgent schedule. He went for the hard sell: "You need to get in this car right now, or you will have a terrible night."

Were backup cops nearby? Was he alone?

I looked up, and beyond the car. Bancroft Junior High was only a sidewalk width away; I lived half a block beyond there.

Gay prostitutes lay facedown across the lawn in front of the school building. More were caged in a temporary pen. I knew them by their low-rise jeans, crop tops, and rolled–up T-shirt sleeves. A few waved.

The vice cops had been busy. They were busy still, perhaps too busy to bother much about me. I fled, and I suppose the undercover cop didn't want to abandon the comforts of his car.

"Come back!"

Sick and poisoned from lemon-cooked dope, I forced myself over the closest backyard fence, and then over the nearest neighbor's fence. I skirted a drained swimming pool, thanking god that I hadn't landed in the bottom. I met an improbably friendly dog. I angled south, away from Santa Monica Boulevard, in the protective shadows of hedges and lights-out porches. No one had come after me, at least not with much intent.

Anyone could have caught me.

Later, I would learn two things: Addicts were going blind from shooting up this Persian shit; true believers would inject the lemon-cooked heroin, and the optic nerve would vibrate until it simply snapped from the back of the eyeball. And the Hollywood vice squad had taken forty-three hustlers off the streets, mostly along a six-block stretch of Santa Monica Boulevard, during a sweep on the night of February 26.

All I knew as I climbed the stairs to the home I shared with Tommie is that something had hit me in the head—probably a chunk of curb or sidewalk or poolside paving. Blood seeped from my hair down past my right ear and into the corner of my mouth. I threw up just inside our apartment and sprawled chest down in the shag carpet. Behind me, the door was open to the landing, to outdoors, to anyone who might walk by. There was no reaching the door to shut it.

I called, in toward the bedroom. "Help!" I didn't have much to put into my voice. "Please."

Come close this door. Do not let the night crawl in here, and lay waste, and drag me outside into the darkness, and toss my shredded and bled carcass into the nameless lime pits.

Tommie refused to acknowledge she was awake.

Twenty-four years old. Two months into 1980. I rubbed my face in the shag carpet, blind, spinning, expecting I would never see straight again.

SCENE THREE:
STRUNG OUT ON THE
GOLDEN GATE

The dark of the night was clear and perfect as the van merged onto San Francisco's Golden Gate Bridge. Lights attached to the upper spans gleamed like jeweled stars, and actual stars sparkled with clarity and proximity in the dark places between those lights, as if the stars had been strung between the support beams of the bridge. Far, far below, the cold, hard water rippled under a black diamond skin.

In the back of the van, I was all metaphorical and rich in similes because bridges give me anxiety—not photos of bridges or the thought of them, only driving across them.

The shaggy kid driver and Randy had been bickering for the past one hundred miles.

The cutoff for Tracy, a town supported by its infamous prison, had somehow started Randy reminiscing about sharing needles with Dee Dee Ramone in New York City. Randy's voice swelled with nostalgia and pride of association: "This whole punk rock masquerade you fans have adopted as your very own way of life, all that was still only a gleam in our imaginations back then."

"Fuck it," said the driver. "You must be the famous lost Ramone. Randy Ramone."

Randy went all serious—all except for that ridiculous bald head.

"You mock because you have a small penis," he said. "Dee Dee and I were large cock brothers. Tuesday afternoons in Bloomingdale's were for shopping with our dicks out. We'd try on sweaters and let our piss hard-ons twist in the air-conditioning. All the sales queens would fluster in a fainting gay panic."

"I'll ask Dee Dee about it," said the driver, a miffed fan.

Randy had photos and video to corroborate his relationship with the Ramones. I'd sat through the presentation. I'd heard the fantastical claims; that he and Dee Dee had demanded tribute from a following of callow candy-bar punks.

Like I say, I'd heard all this already. So I minded my own business and drifted off. What was Tommie doing right now? How dull life would be at home. How uneventful without me slouching on the couch, smoking weed, and wishing we had a working TV.

Tensions mounted in the van. Just past the off-ramp for Livermore, Randy and the shaggy fan shifted to yelling.

"When you OD," screamed Randy, "you go straight to hell. There's no judgment day for you. You're in hell, and you're never coming down."

"That is so stupid," said the shaggy kid. "I am looking at a grown adult who believes there's a hell, or anything after you're dead."

"There's no hell?"

"The government invented hell to keep the mud masses scared and ass-kissing."

"No hell!" Randy shouted. "Then what is this?"

Randy lunged for the steering wheel at eighty-five miles an hour. The kid—the fan—must have thought the lunge was a bluff, but a bluff doesn't adequately escalate the drama. Randy yanked the wheel like it was the leash on one of his candy-bar punks.

The van swerved and slid, and my head slammed into the wheel well. The kid switched on his emergency blinkers and stopped the van in the middle of the fast lane. Traffic sheared past us.

"You can never do that again." He shook a finger in Randy's face. "I don't care who you are. You can never do that again."

One of Randy's gifts was the ability to appear contrite, instantly and convincingly. The trick was that he truly did feel awful about the things he did. He just could never remember how awful doing his things made him feel. So he kept right on doing.

"I will be good," he said. "I promise. You have my word."

Shaggy put the van back in motion. There should have been some relaxing after that. But a bridge lay ahead. I'd heard it mentioned; I couldn't forget it.

"I will take the high road," said Randy. "The afterlife is too sensitive a topic for your shaggy head to contemplate. We will steer the conversation around to neutral ground. Like, let's stick to racial affairs. I know racial affairs are your specialty."

"My blood is pure. The pure blood is a diminishing treasure. Once the purity is polluted, it can never be pure again."

"The American Negro," said Randy, in his most agreeable tone, "was the last free-thinking person in the western world, until he bought the consumer myth. Now he's a grubbing, materialist status whore. He is slave to craven gods and false images. He makes the white man look like a corncob-smoking, cousin-fucking, hookworm-riddled rube—with a wet mop on your head."

The respectful nature of the exchange lulled me to reverie. I pictured Tommie asleep and a stack of new work on her drafting table. Peace was returned to the apartment. Peace filled the LA basin. Peace hit the highways and coursed through the Golden State's asphalt arteries, from Hollywood, to San Jose, to Oakland and beyond.

But conflict crept back in. The van's tires bumped onto the bridge that spanned the water into San Francisco, and conflict made a lane change without signaling.

Randy released his seatbelt and crawled across the gearbox. He put his mouth to the driver's shaggy ear. "Everyone you've ever fucked is there with you in hell!" He raised his voice to something like a screech. Girders flashed past like orange signposts to a plunge into hell, the hell Randy was yelling about: "Once you're dead, there's no getting away from anyone you've ever fucked. They're locked in the orbit with you. That's what makes it hell. There's no shutting them up. It's like being in county jail, only worse. It's like listening to a simple-minded cunt like you all the way from Bakersfield to Frisco."

The van jolted to a stop, midbridge. The driver swiveled in his seat. He threw a mean and precise elbow, and blood spurted across the windshield. Randy had picked up a broken nose and two stunning black eyes. His ass landed back in the passenger seat.

The red splash impressed everybody. Randy and the shaggy fan took a moment to admire their handiwork.

"Would you look at that?" said Randy, inviting me, cowering in the back, to admire the bloody visual. The image fueled my bridge anxiety. Cars were honking; vans were honking; light trucks were honking.

The speed of the van picked up, along with the physicality of the argument.

"You're stupid and you're fat," shouted the shaggy kid, slapping at Randy. "You're full of stupid superstition. You're one dumb shit in the mass of morons."

In my observation, agitated drivers should do us all a favor, stop their cars, and walk. The shaggy fan couldn't keep his vehicle in a straight line.

"I'm a boob!" yelled Randy. He slammed a beer can across the kid's shaggy ear. The van squirmed into the adjacent lane. The kid lifted a hand to defend his ear, and Randy bent back the upraised fingers. "I'm a boob!" yelled Randy.

The Golden Gate Bridge is one of the most heavily policed sections of roadway in California. The van crested halfway across the span, the point of the furthest drop. Arrest didn't worry me. Incarceration—with its ludicrous, stupid, and interminable holding-tank chatter—would come as a relief.

Randy wrapped one paw around the steering wheel. "I'm a boob!"

The kid put both his hands behind his shaggy head.

"Take your hand off the steering wheel," said the kid, "or I won't steer."

The van lurched forward. Evidently, the kid had stomped the accelerator. His fingers linked in the back of his shag.

"I'm just a boob!" yelled Randy. He released the steering wheel and brought his fist up to backhand the kid's nose. That impact would hurt, and it would make the kid close his eyes.

I looked off into the eternity of the San Francisco Bay, out to the horizon. The sky and the ocean meet way out there, out where forever and the eternal right-this-second seal their deal.

SCENE FOUR:
BLANK FRANK FACES THE END

The wife and I were leaving the Sunset Strip in the back of a stranger's car with Sheela, heading to our place at about two in the morning. The wife couldn't have thought traveling with Sheela was a good idea. Me either, if I put any honest consideration into it.

One summer Canterbury day two years before, Sheela had sauntered in from Detroit and took her time leaving. She was pale and full-faced with thick, raven-black hair. She was also loud, reckless, and what Black Randy called a butch-pussy—a bully. Someone had chipped the inside corner off one of her two front teeth. About one-third of the tooth was gone; so she had that gap-toothed allure that some people find so fetching.

Sheela's habit was to end every evening at around 4:00 a.m. in the Canterbury apartment adjacent to ours. She would open its windows and caterwaul to the moon, keening along with a stolen Teenage Jesus and the Jerks demo tape. I know the cassette was stolen because Sheela had palmed it from me after I'd pocketed it on a visit to the Dangerhouse Records compound. Night after night, the Canterbury's dead courtyard garden reverberated with loud, reckless, anguished choruses lamenting little orphans in the snow, in the snow, in the bloody snow. Nobody slept.

In 1979, Sheela did a showcase at the Roxy, singing with the Screamers. The reviews were superlative in places like the *LA Times*. It had gone nowhere. Then she moved away, to New York and New Orleans and some other new places, Las Vegas, for instance.

When the wife and I were traveling on the Strip with Sheela, all that was already in the past. It was April 27, 1980. I'd been twenty-four for two months.

Our telephone rang in the early afternoon. The wife was out at the job.

"It's me…Sheela. Go to your bedroom window."

I put down the phone, walked into the bedroom, and looked out. We had a clear view of a backyard next door and an adjacent apartment over a garage. Sheela showed her pale face in that apartment window above that garage and waved a jug of booze.

I went back to the phone.

A filmmaker from Belgium had seen potential in Sheela's Roxy showcase. He'd bought her a ticket back to Hollywood and was housing her above the garage next door.

"Allan, listen to me: Rene has left me all alone. With a gallon of wine."

The wife had some sort of unresolved beef with Sheela, separate from the 4:00 a.m. singing. The wife's beef was not technically my concern.

I walked down the alley behind our apartment and climbed the external stairs to the room Sheela was camped in. She opened the door and laughed at me, not with me, and pulled me inside. She looked cleaned-up and calm. By *calm* I mean the apparent absence of hysteria or rage. The apartment was one small square with a card table and a cot. We sat at the table, filling coffee mugs with wine.

"Allan!" She slapped me playfully across the face. "Listen to me!"

Sheela had the high-volume personality. She spieled loud and fast with a lot of facial animation. The history of Sheela was her preferred subject, a topic rich in scandal and adventure. She seldom paused to ask the listener, such as me, any personal questions, other than something like: "What is your honest opinion of how fantastic this geisha jacket looks on me? I took it off a corpse."

If Sheela turned her delivery all the way up, the venue, any venue, felt distinctly claustrophobic. But the little room didn't seem the least crowded while we drank and I watched and listened. She'd learned modulation.

She slipped a nod of the head over to the rumpled, unmade bed. That gesture puzzled me. To be presumptuous could lead to awkwardness. I looked into that pale, full face for clarification, but Sheela had moved on.

"I'm making an effort," she said. "Can you tell? This movie means a lot to me. So no drugs, no vodka; some weed would help."

She raised her wine-filled coffee mug, and I took a gulp from mine. Had she really made that nod toward the bed?

"I'm clean, too," I said. "I've been off everything for two months. A month."

"Tommie must be so happy."

Every time I'd thought of Tommie since sitting down to Sheela's card table, I'd felt a nagging pinch on my pleasure center. I shook the irritation out of my head.

"She's bringing home some weed from work today," I said.

It was dark when we'd finished the wine. We hadn't made out. I'd kept a close watch for any hanky-panky. I didn't want to miss remembering it later. Still, I couldn't pinpoint when the decision had been made for Sheela to come back to the apartment with me and make peace with the wife.

First thing inside our door, Sheela said, "Tommie! Where are all your paintings? What happened to the wall coverings? The place looks so bare."

"I took them all down," said Tommie.

If you were me, and you didn't want to see yourself in a harsh light, the removal of Tommie's artwork was a touchy subject.

"Put them back up!" said Sheela. "You are the most talented! Of everyone we know. It's so obvious. In the way you dress, and your makeup. Of course your artwork is creative beyond everyone." Sheela clasped Tommie by the shoulders. "Put them back up!"

Tommie was no pushover, but if these two ever came to physical combat, clearly my wife would land on her ass. But she would do lasting damage first; Sheela released her.

"I need empty space for new things," said Tommie, but she was smiling. "So I can see the new things."

"Come out tonight!" said Sheela. "As a favor to me. It would be a great favor. I'm going to visit Blank Frank. I'm single. He's single. He loves you. Of course he loves you, and he'd love seeing you. Come with me! We'll have fun."

Caught up in the fervor of a weed-colored reconciliation, the wife and I opened to the notion of escorting Sheela on her visit to Blank Frank. One of the Ford's tires wasn't holding air; so we hiked up Highland to Sunset Boulevard and took a bus.

Blank Frank was occupying the Sunset Strip basement squat of Lala, a Burmese drag queen. She had visions of marrying Frank for a green card. Their relationship could not be summed up at a glance. They were surprised and not pleased to see Sheela arrive, and neutral to the wife and me.

As previously mentioned, I was clean at this time, my version of clean. Blank Frank was not. He squeezed a few drops of lemon juice into a spoonful of brown sludge and put it to the flame.

He didn't sneak into the bathroom. The squat had no bathroom. Just the one concrete space with a crisscross of dripping pipes above. Basement pipes dripping fluids from above never deliver good news.

Frank cinched a skinny tie around his arm.

Lala giggled and said, "Hey, Frank. You said you were done with this shit."

"I did say that," said Frank. "And I mean it."

I watched all this despite making no real effort to do so, and I lost all sight of what the wife or Sheela were up to.

Frank took his shot. His eyes didn't change, except to brim up like he was crying from disappointment. That's the look of the burned. Imagine this: You talk yourself into putting off your resolve until tomorrow. You delay that investment in the new, worthwhile you for twenty-four hours more. Dignity, you decide, can wait. You cop. And then your guilty pleasure delivers no pleasure.

That's the worst thing about drug dependence. So often the dope is crap, and you so much need it not to be crap. You can't depend on dope, and Frank had.

He collapsed onto a pile of clothes that had been shaped into a bed. "I don't feel like going out," he said.

"I will draw you a bath," said Lala. She giggled and fussed and wrapped a blanket around Frank's shoulders. "We will have the bath together."

"Where will you draw this bath?" asked Sheela. "In a bucket?"

Frank turned his face to the wall.

Lala beamed, tonight's winner: "That's how Frank says, 'See you later.' Bye-bye, baby."

Frank's caregiver puffed up her cleavage in Sheela's face.

We climbed a set of dark stairs to the Sunset Strip sidewalk and collected ourselves out in the neon-lit night, three young tastemakers evicted from a squat.

"The Clash are playing the Roxy," said Sheela. The English insurrectionists had booked a secret show, just up the block, near the Beverly Hills city limit. "We'll find someone there to give us a ride home."

The wife, Sheela, and I crossed Sunset and walked. Sheela talked. She did about five minutes on Blank Frank and the tragedy of drugs and her relief to have put all that behind her. We passed the Whisky. She did another five minutes of material, mostly about why Russ's fears and his mother's insecurities were to blame for the tragic fact that Sheela was not yet married and raising children.

A cluster of disappointed kids came into view at the Roxy entrance. The concert was sold out, and Clash fans were being denied entrance. Sheela went silent and calculating.

Darby Crash, singer of the Germs, sat on the curb a few yards west of the Roxy, closer to the Rainbow Bar & Grill. He looked sullen and hurt, twenty-two years old going on sixteen. A half dozen of Darby's tight-lipped followers—girls with uniformly dyed and chopped hair—stood in an array behind him, silent attendants. Darby waved to us, never disturbing his air of dejection.

Sheela wedged into the disappointed cluster of fans at the Roxy's entrance. Tommie and I followed her. The *Mean*

Streets suit working the Roxy door recognized Sheela from her showcase and slid us inside.

We parked ourselves about ten yards from the stage. The band was costumed in suspenders and dress shirts with the collars raised. The shirts were in different colors, but the effect was very uniform.

Joe Strummer, the Clash's mouthpiece, yapped along while the band doled out a wan, false-funk backing track. "I just saw Lenny Bruce walking down the street," mumbled Joe. A largely unintelligible lecture followed, something about the importance of Lenny Bruce to American culture.

A row of kids three deep rained spit on the band. You couldn't really call these kids fans; they were a step up.

"Stop gobbing," protested the band's guitarist. This order triggered a fresh fusillade.

A tusk of phlegm hung from Joe Strummer's chin. The guitar player, Mick Jones, started the next song and caught a wad directly in the eye. The band kept playing. You had to hand it to them. You almost felt for them, until they stopped the music so the singer could educate the masses again.

"Who's not ashamed of who they're going to vote for?" crowed Joe Strummer. "Will anybody here care to admit who they're going to vote for?"

It was an election year, 1980. If you thought about it, you had Carter or Reagan. The lobs of spit picked up again.

"Everybody close your eyes," directed the Clash's singer. "I'll keep mine open. Who's voting for Ronald Reagan?"

Fresh launches of spit flew at the stage. Joe Strummer's face looked like the female star at the end of a porn movie.

Sheela grabbed the wife, and we stepped outside to bum cigarettes.

Darby Crash cornered Tommie in front of the club. They were friends, had been friendly at the Canterbury and at shows and parties.

"The Roxy won't let us in," Darby said.

His cookie-cutter minions kept their vigil a few steps behind. They were fresher than we were, recruits. "We have money," Darby said, "but the Roxy hates the Germs."

"The Roxy loves me," offered Sheela.

One of Darby's followers piped up: "Then why are you out here?"

Sheela stared down Darby's entire clan. She drew on her cigarette and smoked at them. "I'm out here because we hate hippies with microphones."

Darby gave his minion a scowl. She shrank back.

"Sheela," Darby said. He smiled. Conciliatory? Cringing? Mocking? The man really was an enigma. His two front teeth were as jacked up as Sheela's. That similarity didn't destine them to get along.

"Where's your Bowie cigarette?" I said. In '78, Darby had been loitering in the Rainbow Bar & Grill parking lot when David Bowie stepped from a limousine and tossed a cigarette butt into a puddle. Darby had pounced on the butt and worn it around his neck in a vial. "Do you still have Bowie's butt?" I said.

Sheela and I stepped away and left the wife and Darby to their personal whispers. The minions didn't like this intimacy between Tommie and their idol. None of the minions knew Tommie. She made them uneasy. Would she have a car? Would she take Darby away from them?

The girls could have relaxed. There was plenty of time left. Darby still had half a year before engineering his departure.

Sheela latched onto a skinny guy in a darted velour jacket. He had something to do with the movie she was in town to shoot. He owned a Volkswagen.

We pulled Tommie away from Darby, and the Germ's minions swallowed him whole. His slumped shoulders were lost in the chop-haired swarm.

The guy in the velour jacket thought he'd hit a jackpot with Sheela, until she squeezed into the backseat with Tommie and me, leaving him driving alone up front. Sheela gave him directions, and he pulled the car to a stop behind our apartment.

"You're not coming in," she said to the driver. She ran to catch up and followed the wife and me through our front door.

Sheela asked if we had a deck of cards and then pulled one out of the air, like a magician. She and I fell to the living room floor and played forehead poker. Tommie abstained. The rules to forehead poker are simple, and effective. A drunken man and an inebriated woman place a deck of cards between them. Drinks and ashtrays are to the side. The loaded man and woman each draw one card, at the same time. Without looking, players place their cards on their foreheads, live side facing out.

You can see your opponent's face value, but not your own. The point of the game is to gaze questioningly into one another's eyes in an attempt to determine if your card is higher or lower than your opponent's. You study your opponent's mouth, search for tells in her lips and eyes, lean close and try to sniff out a giveaway.

Sheela and I didn't verbalize any wager. With each pull of cards, the stakes rose toward some tacit climax. I took a hand. I took another, and one more.

The wife watched, unimpressed.

An urge to vomit swelled in me and interrupted my winning streak. Hoping not to spoil the moment or the mood, I excused myself.

"Take your time," said Sheela. "Tommie can play a few hands."

I arrived in the bathroom with moments to spare. My gut did its heave-ho. I waited to be sure everything was out. Blanking into the toilet's downward spiral, I heard voices and motion. The sounds might have been echoing from the bottom of the porcelain. Eventually, the spinning stopped.

I came out of the bathroom. Sheela had gone, and she'd left the front door open.

"What happened to her?"

The wife sat on the sofa. She had an unlit cigarette in her mouth. She snapped the lighter on; she snapped the lighter off. "I sent her away."

I went to the door and looked out, both ways. No Sheela lurking. I pulled the door shut.

The wife sat arms crossed. It had been a long night, to look at her. "If I hadn't been here," she said, "something would have happened. Between you and her."

Tommie, I saw plainly, was tired of it. Day-to-day things were wearying. Our marginal prosperity, this underemployed, poverty-teasing existence, it would wear on anyone. She had remained patient and true for so long, waiting for me to turn my act around. Other women may toy with me, or be toyed with, but Tommie had stuck seriously close, through thin and thinner. We were coming out the other side. She knew something the others didn't know, I told myself: The good times, our good times, were coming back, this time to stay.

"But you were here," I said. "You are here."

"And that's why you look so sad."

SCENE FIVE:
ENTER THE BATHS

A New Year's Eve false snow had fallen on downtown San Francisco. Three-by-five-inch sheets of white paper drifted across the ground. Thousands of floating pages blanketed the sidewalks, swirling practically knee deep, each imprinted in bold black type with a date of the year. I stepped on May 28, 1980! September 7 stuck to my shoe! February 3 scudded down toward the Bay! Random days from October, July, December, and all the other months clumped in the gutters and banked on the sidewalks.

At first, I couldn't understand. Why was I wading through past-dated litter? I looked up at the blank windows above me—portals to financial institutions, insurance companies, the entire clerical kingdom. The picture came to me. I saw the great mass of San Francisco's confined office workers spontaneously ripping the sheets from their desk calendars on the final evening of the year, opening their windows and sending the past fifty-two weeks fluttering to the streets below.

"Who thought of this, with the desk calendars?" I said. "Was it a spontaneous dump? Is it a tradition?"

"I could explain all this pointless detritus to you, Basho," said Black Randy. "Or I could locate the underground clubs that are the gateways to the kingdom of methedrine. I have only one focus, and it is our immediate future."

The immediate future was fine for Randy, but I could not ignore all those pages of bygone ambition and scheduled meetings that bald Black Randy, the shaggy fan, and I were treading beneath our wet, dirty shoes. We tramped through the discarded days of this chilly commercial district, and I reflected upon my own thrown-away year.

It really had been only twelve months ago that Girl A had come into my life and left, with a little death staying behind. There had been a tough period for the wife, and for me. I'd felt isolated at home—we can assume Tommie felt isolated as well. It seemed like scores of weeks on end had been shuttled away drinking alone in a closed-off room and doing one-hitters of street weed. I'd hardly left the house other than for the job or to re-up. That tough period had passed. I was mobile again, independent, in the world for what the universe had to offer. Who could deny my progress? I'd come all the way to San Francisco.

The shaggy fan and I stood in the end-of-December wind beside an exposed Haight pay phone. Randy pumped quarters into the coin slot—quarters earmarked for the North Beach peepshows—and dialed the desperation party line. The wind blew loose dates around us. None of us were calendared on any of them. The cold breeze whipped up snippets of conversation that were a long distance from encouraging.

"Of course I'm alone," said Randy, turning his back on shaggy and me. He hung up, flipped ahead a page in his address book, flicked another twenty-five cents into the slot and dialed desperate. If he had correct change, these calls could all be bought for a dime.

"Hey, man, it's Randy." Temporarily muted, he looked off toward where the deathly cold bay water would be happy to receive him. "But I meant to pay you back all of that—"

Randy thumbed in another quarter dollar, punched in another desperate dial.

"Hey, brother, it's Randy." He passed a hand over his blackened eyes. "That's why I'm calling. I want the opportunity to reimburse you—"

Each quarter that dropped into the phone slot was another lost snippet of filmed depravity, one less sick loop to divert my mind from the well-worn wormhole that drilled in on worry, guilt, Tommie and me. So I voiced no complaints when Randy returned his remaining silver to his Teddy boy coat pockets and announced that he had adopted a B plan for ferreting out a rumored underground bar where he hoped to gain referral to a reputable drug dealer.

"Every San Francisco person I know is running out just now to some intimate New Years affair that could not include you two," explained Randy.

We walked into inhospitable gusts, some with rain.

"They haven't even seen what you look like," said the shaggy kid. The shaggy kid had not spoken to Randy since their spat on the Golden Gate. He wasn't a Black Randy fan anymore. He had that tilted, superior disapproval of a fan who has met and been let down by his hero.

"Your friends," taunted the former fan. "Your *close, personal* friends."

Randy took the bait: "What are you suggesting?"

"Your bald head. Your black eyes. Seeing *what you look like* warns strangers away. Your friends shun you just on the force of you being you, without even seeing what you look like."

Randy mulled this over, silently, striding with purpose through the dated confetti of 1980. The shaggy kid gloated, like he'd won a battle. His eyes glowered from behind a knuckle-shaped bruise he had picked up from Randy while driving across the Golden Gate Bridge.

"If I were you," I said to the shaggy fan, "I'd keep my guard up."

Randy overheard this, and—flattered—it improved his mood.

He fixed his raccoon squint up the sidewalk ahead of us. A character in a frock coat leaned against the bricks of a boarded-up hotel. The character had flowing blond locks and a waxed mustache. His long, elaborate coat dusted the calendar pages at his feet. He seemed like any other late-night Bay Area apparition, until a rusted metal door a few feet beyond him slid open. Two dudes in disco separates and a jumpsuit girl jolted outdoors, propelled by an explosion of new wave music. The jumpsuit girl plowed into our shaggy kid and recoiled.

Randy and I turned toward the open door. I saw inebriated people cavorting inside, under colored lights. The waxed mustache stepped sideways to block our view of the interior, revealing his function.

"You're the doorman," said Randy, all popping raccoon eyes and shiny skull.

The doorman pushed the door shut and snorted hard, like he was expelling caked cocaine and wanted to ensure the pellet cleared the wax of his mustache.

Randy, in his threadbare teddy jacket, refused to accept the doorman's derision: "Is it you I talk to for scoring ups?" he said.

"You're blocking the sidewalk."

"It's a civil question, fucker."

"You want tweak? Try Animals." The mustache smirked.

"Where's Animals?" said Randy.

"Still here?" answered the doorman. "It's south of Market."

If I'd learned anything while at college in San Francisco, it was that heading south across Market Street meant crossing beyond the limits of safe and civil sexual-outlaw society. Call it homophobia, but straight-out gay dudes were afraid of being caught after dark among the shadow-dwelling predators that defined the South of Market S&M wild lands of 1980.

Almost certainly, shaggy was unaware of the region's infamy. Accounts of men-on-mook sport rape and leather-trussed, sperm-basted corpses issued from the neighborhood with startling regularity and spotty verification. Any companionable male embarking upon a trip South of Market deserved a full scouting report.

The shaggy fan and I lit silent and separate cigarettes in an adjacent storefront while Randy pressed the doorman for precise driving instructions. They seemed friendly at the end.

"Back to the van," said Randy. "We're heading south."

"Okay," said the shaggy kid.

Back in the van, Randy perked up, singing bastardized verses of the Sex Pistols song "Animals." He directed the driver to Sixth Street and we turned south.

"I'm an *an-e-mal*," sang Randy. "I'm a piggie. I'm a cock. I'm a *booooooooar!*"

The van passed Market and continued on briefly below Mission. The sidewalks were empty of everything except unseen menace. We stopped in a parking spot just beyond a plain warehouse. There was a nondescript sign: Animals.

"The fucking zoo?" said the shaggy fan.

"The *fucking* zoo!" Randy brayed with all his gut. "We're at the baths. We are fucking animals at the fucking baths!"

"The fag baths?" asked the van's owner.

"Are you coming already?" said Randy.

The driver refused to leave the familiar safety of the van. "I didn't come to San Francisco to take off my clothes with you," he explained.

"You seem very small-town," said Randy. "Provincial and timid."

The driver pulled a knit cap down over his shaggy head and sank below the dashboard. He was my alternative. If I'd opted to, I could have remained in the van and chatted with shaggy.

Randy and I walked toward the building, which gave no indication of the wonders it might contain. I understood that these places attracted a predominantly male homosexual clientele. I was prepared to encounter a three-to-one gender ratio of men to women. My mind pictured a Turkish bath scenario: Middle-class, middle-aged customers sat in private cubicles taking the steam. I would shut myself in, thaw out, and sweat away the rigors of the drive.

I followed Randy through a swinging door and we confronted a massively bored cashier inside a booth. He had pulled-back lips and a quivering neck, and mirror shades hid his eyes.

Randy fanned a hand of twenty-dollar bills. "Ups?" he said.

The cashier lifted his shades and gave us a massively withering look. He pointed a claw at a hand-scrawled sign posting the New Year's rates for Animals admission. Moneybags Randy forked over the fee.

We were each tossed a towel and a numbered locker key. The key was on a band that attached around the wrist, like at a public swimming pool. The cashier pointed his claw toward the building's interior. We followed the finger and found lockers that matched the numbers on our keys.

We seemed to be either a little late or a little early to the party. It was just Randy and flat-black walls and me there in the changing area—no menace. Excited, agitated, Randy stripped. He tossed his underwear into his locker and wrapped his towel around his belly. His towel didn't entirely close, I saw. That's as close as I needed to look.

My ardor slipped away as I stripped. The shirt came off, and I sucked in my belly. What was the hurry, really? I kept my underwear on under my towel. This was cheating, but I didn't care. I also kept on my black high-top Converse sneakers.

If there was a mirror, I avoided it. Here is what I did not want to see: The ratty hair, the shifty eyes, the grim fixed mouth, the pox-dotted pallor of the sunken chest, the gassed belly, the stick legs and knock knees, and those grimy sneakers hiding my dirty toenails. What should I be doing with my hands?

Randy started to say a few words, but appeared unable to talk, which was unusual. He croaked: "You are in for a…for a…"

I'd crashed in some strange pads, those months at the Canterbury for instance. Surely I was prepared for anything that lay ahead.

"Where do we go from here?" I said.

Randy seemed to know the layout of these places. He pushed open a black door in the black wall. The door had been invisible to me.

We entered a steam-heated warren of crowded, tight halls. Bare bulbs under tin shades hung from the ceiling, spaced to create dramatic pools of lighting. Nothing like a female was anywhere to be seen in the throng of sauntering flesh. A few towels were worn as loincloths or wrapped like turbans around the head; most were simply flung over a shoulder. If you were interested in penis watching, this was your spot. In every size and stage of tumescence, natural and cinched with cock rings, sprouting from bristle pads or swinging from a bald base, greased, oiled, or sweat-glistened, everybody had a proud one. Again, I didn't know what to do with my hands.

I wasn't the only man wearing his shoes into the showers. Army boots on the feet and a tube of ChapStick in one hand seemed to be a popular fashion statement, along with the glowing prick and a smile of reptilian satisfaction.

Cubicles with bunk shelves lined the sides of the tight halls. Dudes perched on the ledges, stroking their dicks, making the kiss face, flexing pectorals, tweaking nipples, offering ass. Hundreds of tightly grouped passersby paused; some partnered up and fucked. All kinds of penetration was going around. Not one single cubicle door swung shut for the sake of privacy.

My face worked to deny that it was being exposed to anything it was unaccustomed to. I kept Randy in sight within the crush of men cruising through the warren. His bald head and shoe-polish eyes were easy markers.

Almost right away, Randy acted up. His every stance and movement were aggressive and confrontational. I wanted to shout, "Be cool! Don't attract attention!"

Each dangling bulb set off a pool of bare light. A different, singular flexing patron occupied the center of each of these light circles. Always an idealized specimen, the illuminated studs reigned as that section of corridor's designated alpha of desire.

My understanding of the protocol, gained after about twenty seconds of observation, was that the alphas summoned anyone they deemed worthy of contact. Rings of secondary icons surrounded the primary icons and buffered them from the approaches of mere mortals.

Mere Randy refused to stand on protocol. He brushed past a protective circle of towel-flapping courtiers and cornered the most chiseled and aloof demigod in the place. Profile like a

Roman coin, chest shellacked with man sweat, throbbing while
at parade rest, a dangle like a radiator hose, this man's man was
obviously the supreme icon of Animals. He was unaccustomed
to the direct approach. Randy closed in, and the icon's cock
swung toward disapproval.

Unfazed by nicety and decorum, Randy went nose to
nose with the sun king. The king's face recoiled, lips curled in
displeased incomprehension. Randy pushed his lopsided grin
and boot-black eyes forward—he was talking nonstop. The
protective ring of towel bearers kept me beyond earshot.

The Animals king gave the slightest sniff of his fingers,
and a quartet of identical bronzed attendants stepped in like
a muscle-bound curtain. Shoulder-to-shoulder flesh moved
Randy in an impenetrable brush off. One bronzed attendant
talked while he brushed. There was a warning I didn't need
to hear to understand: One more uncool advance, and Randy
would be cast forth from Animals.

Randy slunk off from the crowned jewel. In the shadows,
between pools of light, he regrouped with himself. Regrouping
for what? I sidled up.

"Randy, I saw all that, with the sun god and all that."

After an awkward moment, he recognized me.

"Eighty-sixed from a glory hole!" He cawed. "Imagine my
shame."

"You seem to have lost sight of the mission."

"Mission?"

"To buy speed."

He laughed in a maniacal way that seemed entirely
unforced. He had become unhinged. Again, I lost the sense that
he knew who I was.

He pushed off from the wall and shambled in with the cock
walk.

SCENE SIX:
CLEAN TIME AT THE TIME MOTEL

lack Randy was soaking up inspiration at the Time Motel. The Time was the most famous lodging in Hollywood at the moment: Over the weekend, an on-premises shootout with the LAPD had been broadcast live on the local news. Western Avenue grime and little clouds of exhaust puffed in through bullet holes in the kitchenette's pulled shade. At the table window, I studied photos of a flattened gunman on the front page of yesterday's paper. He should have tried to surrender. The fusillade that had torn up the building had torn him, too.

Randy was sharing a Time Motel suite with a couple of hookers who had been middle-class punk rock girls less than a year earlier. He stood in his Pierre Cardin underwear at the sink, washing a stain from the crotch of his pants.

"Why isn't Karina here?" I said. Karina was one of the hookers. There was bad feeling between Karina and me.

"Karina and Janie are out beating the boulevards," said Black Randy. He held his wet pants up to the kitchenette light and looked for signs of success. "Karina and Janie will be bringing etchings of Benjamin Franklin back to their bad mack daddy."

Black Randy had the muscle tone and complexion of an unshaved mollusk. He was called Black Randy for his heart, not his skin tone. He had darting eyes set in raccoon frames. And then there was that hair—ratty, and sparse, and some rusty pipe color I'd never seen on him, or anybody, before.

"Did Karina dye her bad mack daddy's hair?"

Randy handed me another Coors. "She has many talents."

Karina was out beating the boulevards all right; most likely selling something she'd stolen from Randy. I couldn't remember what she had against me.

The Time Motel was a single-story structure with all its rooms in a line. The entire length had been sieved with automatic weapons fire. Randy had pointed out several bullet pocks in the kitchenette.

"A man was hit where you sit," he said. "That man's life drained right from where you are at that table—through his fingers, down his legs, overflowing his boots. He knew that flow would never reverse—and he went out, through this window, to advance upon the precipice at the end of this river of blood…"

I doubted it. The Time Motel management had slapped in new window glass, but if there had been any blood to clean up, the sloppy wiping would have smeared it in with the muck in the corners of the yellow linoleum.

"Yellow is a good color for linoleum in a place like this," I said.

"It all gets yellow sooner or later," agreed Randy.

I'd been at the table long enough to develop an urgent bladder full of Coors. Outside, the workforce, those poor saps among it, were breaking for an early lunch. Randy dollied his face in across the table and smiled—a confiding leer full of insinuations and baby teeth that made me glad I wasn't some child alone in the park.

"You're not squeamish, are you?" he said. He knew I was squeamish. I'd confessed as much the second or third time we'd met. He was the kind of guy who inspired confidences, misplaced confidences evidently. "Listen!" He lowered his voice, drawing me closer. "Can you hear that? *Squish...squash!* That's the sound of blood suction as the man who sat where you sit lifts his feet from the soles of his shoes..."

Randy saved his breath while he balanced and pulled on his wet pants; then went on as if he had not paused. "Is there a reason why drug addicts have to be so undependable? In the scheme of the universe, why can't they be more like crabs? You make contact with body lice, you enter the social contract with that species, and they show up, right when they're scheduled to. There's no waiting around for half a day wondering, *Will they keep the appointment or won't they keep the appointment?*"

Randy scratched himself dreamily, then with intent. He'd lured me to the Time Motel with the promise that Slate and Cindy—a couple who trafficked in crank—would be there when I arrived, that they had called him from the Standard Station at the Western Avenue off-ramp of the Hollywood Freeway, having just returned carrying weight from a biker clubhouse in San Bernardino.

Randy owed me for a ride I'd given him into the Deep Valley to visit a doctor who specialized in opiated cough syrup. That hadn't panned out, plus the car had blown a hose and was still down. "I look forward to making good," he'd said over the phone.

Tommie had just left the apartment when Randy called. While Randy spoke, I'd watched Tommie from the bedroom window. She walked toward our car, carrying a portfolio under one arm to hold the drawings she'd worked on the night before. Modest brown heels, slim yellow skirt, and a trim blazer—at her office, none of the men who watched as she perched at her drafting table could have pictured the havoc we'd shared. But who knows what they might be picturing, or what she might be showing them.

As I watched from our bedroom, above and indoors, Tommie pulled her key ring from her purse; then she remembered what I'd done to the car. She flipped a lustrous brunette strand behind her ear and looked up at the apartment. Those dark, swollen eyes sighted along the ridge of her nose. I knew she couldn't see me, but that's not how it felt.

Hours had died since then, the passing moments drowned in Coors and smoked in Kools.

"I hear their car!" said Randy.

He rushed from the kitchenette barefoot, then returned for a pair of flip-flops. "Slate will be here before you finish that cigarette," he said. He passed from the kitchenette into the murky sleeping quarters. He opened the outside door, and a frame of sunlight formed. Randy stepped back from the glare, girded himself against the light, and thrust forward into the world outside. The door closed, and the dark closed back in behind where Randy had stood. I hadn't heard any car.

I peeked through a rent in the kitchenette window shade— the rip might have been from a passing bullet, or just a ratty tear. The pay phone outside the Time Motel office could be kept under surveillance through the rip, no doubt a factor in why Randy had chosen this room. Under my watchful eye, he shuffled to the phone and slumped in the booth. His demeanor was apologizing to people who weren't even there. He thumbed change into the slot and dialed. In an instant, his chest inflated, and his chin jutted out, inclined to bravado. He had another sucker on the line.

I'd resisted coming to the Time Motel. My office clothes proved it. Why else would I be wearing corduroy slacks, not even black, with knockoff loafers and a button-down shirt? Because I'd made an effort to stay away; I'd exercised willpower, about half what I'd needed. My job was fairly new, as usual. Tommie hadn't heard me call in sick, but she would probably figure out how I'd spent the day.

I slouched toward the Time bathroom. The so-called suite's main room—the room that wasn't a bathroom or a kitchenette—had an unmade bed, a cot shoved against a wall, and piles of trashy female clothing. The cot, obviously, was for Randy. The room had boasted a TV at one time, high on the wall at the foot of the bed; all that remained were the signs of force with which it had been wrenched from its brackets.

A line of slutty shoes was tossed haphazardly along a wall. Karina's midcalf, red cowboy boots—unmistakable—edged me closer to the source of our bad blood. I backed away from whatever that might be, into the bathroom. The toilet, I'd been warned, was off limits; its lid was down, and I was happy to leave it down. A cold stew of nylons was brewing in the sink. The bathtub was my clear option, but its porcelain surface was unexpectedly pristine, a brilliant cleanliness that could only be the proof of proud labor. The notion of urinating on some dutiful cleaning lady's efforts shamed me. I pictured myself kneeling, scrubbing, and I couldn't pee in the tub.

Black Randy would have no such constraints. I'd seen him unleash a steaming vitamin-B enriched piss into the olive-green shag carpeting of some guy who played in the Mentors. The dude and his girlfriend had taken too long going out to buy a bag of weed. Later, after the piss had soaked into their carpet, the Mentor and his girlfriend had come back and said they'd been burned for our money. They retreated behind a locked bedroom door and refused to answer our knocking. Randy had trained a follow-up torrent directly into the couple's refrigerator. His facial expressions had fluctuated between glee and rapture.

I had to go really bad. Backing out of the bathroom, I fixed on Karina's red boots. She'd been in my apartment, hanging on with Rick Wilder and Russ on a weeknight. Tommie had come from the bedroom in her flannels, her hair knotted on top of her head, eyes sleepy and slit. She had a presentation at 8:00 in the a.m. Karina had known it was past time to leave. She'd marched around in these red cowboy boots, and a pair of ripped satin hot pants, mocking Tommie in our own place.

I hefted one of the red boots. They were real leather, not the plastic you might have expected. The Coors buzzed up in my teeth. I looked around. I was alone in the room. The decision was made before I even knew there was a question. I spread my legs to hold my unbuckled corduroys at the middle of my thighs. You never know when you'll need to pull them up real quick.

I positioned the boot, cupping my balls in the back of it, directed my nozzle toward the pointed red toe, and let whiz. The immediate joy of release—the physical pleasure of relaxing a tensed system and hearing my froth rise inside the tooled leather—ran concurrent with a separate and profound bonus satisfaction. I was the diligent husband punishing a Halloween hooker for disrespecting my wife. I loved her—Tommie—like crazy. Surely, if she could see me now, she would be awed, as I was, at how far I would go to avenge her.

I warmed inside, then my balls felt extra warm, and wet. I shut off the flow and jerked my sac out of the yellow swirl. The red cowboy boot brimmed with urine. Carefully, I stood the boot among the row of shoes on the floor. Piss seeped through the few cracks in the leather, but at a slow rate. The leather would fully saturate from the toe to well above the ankle.

And more good news! I still had half a boot's volume left in my bladder. Rushed, excited, I snatched up the second boot, and my pants dropped down to my ankles. Again, to minimize spray back, I cupped my balls inside the lip of the boot. I held the boot in both hands, head back, and gloried as my piss streamed. The outside door banged open.

Randy stood outlined, a black mass in the open doorway's square of light. My profound bliss dribbled to an end.

"Basho, are you fucking that shoe?"

I lowered the boot to the floor and tripped back, trying to keep eye contact, pulling for my pants as casually as I could. "Not exactly fucking."

Randy crossed to the row of shoes and stood over the red boots, staring down into them, like a gypsy looking for my fortune in the yellow bubbles.

He sniffed, deeply. "I'm disappointed in you. Very disappointed."

Randy took a deep sigh that pained him: "These are my friends, the people who wear those shoes. And you piss on my friendship. I had something here I wanted to share with you. Now, I don't know."

I felt as though I'd been caught doing something wrong. How could an action that felt so virtuous and correct dump me into this pit of abject shame? My best bet was to walk home and put my head under the covers. When I woke up, all this would be an absurd dream that there was no point in telling Tommie.

"Don't cry," said Randy. "Let me show you something."

I followed him into the kitchenette. He took an appraising look through the window shade and seemed satisfied. I looked out there too, again noting the direct sightline with the telephone.

"Not out there," said Randy. "Up here."

He reached into a cupboard above the microwave and lifted out a tray. He indicated I should sit, and placed the tray on the kitchen table between us. The tray was from McDonald's. A trio of plastic coffee stirrers, a pair of scissors, and a packet of children's balloons were arrayed on the tray, propped between a bottle of Ovaltine and a jar of Mannitol laxative.

"I'll get another Coors," I said.

The refrigerator had not escaped the shooting. Mechanically useless, it kept the Coors tidy and warm. I sipped pensively, the liquid going down at about the same temperature as when it would come out. Randy kept his mouth shut while he used a single-edge razor blade to chop and mix the chocolate-colored Ovaltine with the laxative powder.

"There you go," he said. "Ten bags of Mexican brown."

He tossed a package of kid balloons at me. I was getting a notion of why he'd invited me over.

"Don't just sit there. Make some Mexican brown bags."

I ripped open the packet of balloons and picked up one of the McDonald's coffee stirrers. The plastic stirrer had a tiny spoon at the end, more decorative than functional, except when it was being used to parcel out doses of LA street heroin in 1980.

I lined up the balloons. I dropped two scoops of Randy's special mix into the first balloon. The coffee stirrer is a flimsy tool, and the hole in the balloon is small and floppy. Randy watched critically. I smacked down the load into the bottom of the first balloon, tied a tight knot above the wad of powder, and clipped the excess balloon with the scissors. It's pride-building work, if you can find it. I started on the second balloon.

Randy picked up a balloon. He put in three scoops. His mind wasn't in it; an extra scoop was a generosity that would have alarmed him if he'd been paying attention. Still, he was fast, and we were almost done when the public phone outside rang. The sound came in clearly through the open kitchenette window. Randy blanked his face and looked away. The phone gave a second ring. After a moment, Randy's body relaxed. I was still waiting to hear if there would be a third ring. Randy tied up the last balloon and stashed the Ovaltine and laxative high up behind the microwave. He buried the snipped balloon remnants deep in an overflowing trash bag.

The phone outside rang again, startling me, but not Randy. This time we both knew it would ring only twice.

"Basho," he said, "I need to trust you." He indicated the ten elastic bags of fake dope. "Can I trust you not to dip into these balloons?"

"You can't be serious. Why would—"

"I have to trust you. Michael Sinatra is coming over to pick up this dope. We had an incident, and I'm making it up to him with these bags. So I do need to trust you."

"Why do I have to be the one who hands him his burn?"

Randy took on a scolding tone. "Basho, candor is not always a virtue, as I'm sure you'll agree. Your secret can be safe with me. Karina doesn't need to know. Those are her favorite boots—her high-grossing boots. I am only stepping out to make a phone call. I'll be right outside at the phone. All you need to do is answer the door for Michael Sinatra and give him his smack. When I finish this phone call, we'll have speed balls on the way."

Unlikely story, but the refrigerator still held four tall cans of Coors. I'd pretty much committed for the full shift anyway, and I had half a pack of Kools. Michael Sinatra didn't scare me. I had nowhere to go. If my neighbors saw me at home during the day, they'd suspect something. So I would wait a spell at the bullet-pocked Time Motel.

"What do I do if Karina comes back?"

"Tell her I said to comp you. On the promo account." He opened the outside door and disappeared into the light. I watched through the holes in the window shade. Randy sauntered past the phone beside the Time Motel's office. His hands dug deep in his pockets, scratching, I presume, at his crotch.

A few feet from the phone, he angled toward Western Avenue and sprinted like some two-legged crustacean. There was no clear line of sight to the street, but the taillights of Slate and Cindy's maroon '71 T-Bird moved off distinct and visible in my mind. I could see the horrible rust damage around their bumper.

*　　　*　　　*

I WELCOMED MYSELF TO a fresh beer and savored it standing in the kitchen doorway. Michael Sinatra had been an intellectual sort when we first met. I'd invented the name Michael Schmuck for him, which had stuck, but he was something of a theoretical genius, like I was. We'd spent entire nights sharing theoretical brilliance at the Canterbury until the little birds had come awake and taken the 5:00 a.m. chatter out of us and flown away with it. He'd been too smart to become addicted to a drug like heroin. Michael Schmuck had seen the dope syndrome for what it was. He was about freedom, not enslavement. I guessed that was one theory that had slipped away. I squeezed all ten of Michael Schmuck's clipped balloons into one intact balloon.

The ash on my Kool was half a cigarette long. I'd seen an ashtray in the bedroom. I stood over the girls' bed. The pillows faced in toward one another, with twin indentations. I pictured Karina and the other punk rock hooker nestled there, mouth breathing into mouth. My ash dropped. Before long, I would need to pee again.

I kneeled next to the bed, my face even with the covers, and I opened a drawer in the side table. I moved used tissues aside with an empty Marlboro pack and found what I might have been looking for all along if I'd known what to be looking for—envelopes. There was also a pocket-sized spiral notebook, the cover coated in thickly slathered purple and red nail polish—a diary. Decency told me to leave that diary where it lay, and I obeyed. A lilac bra, a black one, and a few pairs of neon panties lay on the floor. I inhaled near these items, not moving my nose so close as to be a creep about it.

The Kool had burned out. I stood it on its filter and went back to the kitchen with an envelope. I lit a new Kool off the stove, grabbed my big balloon full of fake dope and went back to the bed. I picked up a pair of underwear, folded them tightly and fitted them into the envelope. I opened the mother balloon and squeezed the ten baby balloons from it, lining them in the envelope with the panties. I licked and sealed the envelope, averting my eyes from the neon panties. I squeezed the envelope along its length. You couldn't really feel balloons in there.

Out in the kitchen, I found a felt-tip marker. A sense of security came upon me like a high. I lit one of the remaining Kools and block-printed on the envelope face: FOR MICHAEL S. Then, across the seal: FOR MICHAEL S. ONLY.

I drifted back to the bedroom, as if to watch TV, although the TV was still ripped away. The colorful bra was small—Karina's. The other girl evidently had tits. Her bra was all business. The bed sheets had been warmed by the sleeping flesh of Karina and her big-breasted friend. The covers were back. The beer had made me drowsy. I could slide right in there, into that slumber-land bedding. Then, in a week, maybe less, the body lice social contract would pay out, and I'd be scratching my scabby crotch just like Randy.

The side table drawer gaped open. I saw a corner of the diary, painted purple with glitter applied. Inside: burgundy ink and black scrawls and free verse marked with splatters and runs where tears had splashed upon the writing. Someone knocked on the door, loud and large. The diary slipped into my jacket pocket. The pounding on the door became insistent, angry.

"Don't shoot!" I called out, like I was kidding.

I opened the door slowly, shielding myself from the light out there. Michael Sinatra stood in the sunshine blast, totally alone. He was probably twenty-two or twenty-three, like me, but the poor guy hadn't outgrown his frog-eyed adolescence. His protruding gaze dragged along a heavy set of bags. About five-six and bony, he compensated in the purse of his lips and with his flared nostrils. His eyebrows were thick and active, and he spiked his hair to achieve another inch of height. He was basically a display rack for his leather-and-straps motorcycle jacket. My first impulse was to apologize for mocking his name all those years ago.

"Allan MacDonell." Tears misted Michael's eyes. "This isn't what I was hoping to see at all."

He lurched forward, lunging at me it seemed. An outsider, a manager perhaps of the Time Motel, watching from behind the counter in the office beside the phone booth, might have mistaken Michael Schmuck's lurch as a motion to embrace a cherished and long unseen friend—me. The truth was, he had a staggering case of dope sickness. And if the Time Motel manager had seen that once, he'd seen it 10,000 times, and he didn't care if he never saw it again, which is much like how Michael Schmuck felt about me.

"Is B.R. asleep? Is he in the next room? Is he coming right back?"

"He's coming right back."

"I'm fucked." Michael was a theoretical intellectual; he knew what coming right back meant. He snuffled, hard. A string of phlegm passed his mouth and headed for his Tom of Finland T-shirt. He took a swipe of his leather-clad arm across his face.

"Look," I said. "See that slice of light coming in through the wall beside the door?"

I placed my hand in the path of a swirling shaft of motes.

"If you had a time machine, Sinatra, and you put your head here where the bullet came in, all your problems would be solved."

Rivulets of tears adorned Michael's cheeks. "Randy was supposed to have ten bags for me, and the only thing here is you!" His face was a windshield of streaming pain and fury, with broken wipers.

"Ten bags!" I marveled. "God, I wish..."

Michael headed toward the kitchen. The kitchen: a place of spoons, water, and flame. Karina's boots, lopsided and leaking from the seams, caught me as I passed them. They tried to shame me. I looked away very quickly.

By the time I reached the kitchenette, Michael had all the cabinets and drawers open. He'd pulled out a chair and climbed up to reach for the cupboard above the microwave, up where Black Randy had hidden the tray, the Ovaltine, the Mannitol. I held out the envelope.

"Randy told me to give you this."

When I was a boy, in Canada, I'd been sent to live with an aunt in the country for two months to give my family a break. I'd found a sick toad under the house and attempted to nurse it back to health. The toad had not made it. On its dying day, it had looked at me with eyes bulging like Michael Schmuck's.

He sat at the table, ripping at the envelope. He unfurled the panties, paying them no more mind than if they'd been paper towels, and plucked the brightly colored kids' balloons from the neon satin. He circled his balloons on the kitchen tabletop.

His snivel turned into a sneer: "I'll do a taste here."

"Out of the question," I said. "Unless you intend to share."

"Buy a fucking clue." He moved the window shade aside and spat into the screen. "Randy said it was okay for me to fix here."

It was the afternoon, two o'clock. Tommie would be back at her drawing board, returned from lunch to the office. Her hair would be swooping down from behind her ear, angled with her smooth and steady jaw. I could watch her concentrate all day. At my job, the afternoon shift would be starting, with drowsiness and resignation. Michael Schmuck dropped two bags at once into a spoon and squirted in water. He'd brought his outfit with him.

"Two bags?" I said. "That's some habit you have there."

He heated his spoon over a low flame at the stove. He looked over his shoulder to be sure he had a clear path to the table, checked his dope, and took that path. This was as good a time as any for me to light a Kool.

"I'll need one of those when I'm done," said Michael, cocking his chin at my cigarette. He drew brownish fluid up through a pinch of cotton. I had to hand it to him; he'd come prepared for anything. He pulled back a sleeve. His face had become intent and dry-eyed. Would I be sober in time to sit at a dinner table with Tommie? Our table and kitchen were not much different from this one, really, when you came down to it. Although our refrigerator did not have a cluster of bullet holes through it, and we wouldn't have Michael Schmuck sitting across from us, his face suddenly dissolving in a wash of snot and tears.

"How is that shit?" I asked.

He checked his vital signs, his eyes tossing along the checklist. "It's not bad. I may need more."

"Can I do your cotton?" I made this request out of habit.

"I save them." He put the cotton aside, on the table top, saturated as it was with presumed intoxicants, and dumped two more balloons into the spoon. Heroin was going for 25 dollars a balloon.

"Look at you," I said, "with your 100-dollars-a-day habit!" He seemed to be showing off a bit.

"It's not a monkey," he said, "it's a gorilla. My old man locked me up in Phoenix House." He drew the brown solution into the rig, very studied in his movements, as if to correct what he'd done wrong the previous time, the mistake that had circumvented his high. "How is cleaning shit out of toilets while some ex-bank robber yells at me that I'm a vagina supposed to give me the self-esteem to stay off drugs?"

At the moment, he was doing a fine job of keeping off drugs, self-esteem or no self-esteem. He drew the needle out of his arm. He was openly weeping, wailing: "So tell me how cleaning toilets is supposed to do any good!"

"Maybe cleaning the toilets isn't about self-esteem. It could be a way to alter your—"

He shut me up with a huge slurping of snot. "It's a rhetorical question, stupid."

Hurt, I went to the refrigerator and took out a Coors. Only two were left. I put them in the warm freezer, on the off chance

Schmuck wouldn't look in there. I took a long pull of beer, washing over the sting of being called stupid.

Schmuck was back in his spoon; six empty balloons now littered the tabletop. On the bright side, he'd forgotten all about wanting one of my Kools. I blew smoke into the pinpoints of afternoon light filtering in through the bullet holes in the kitchen wall. Michael held his outfit up to the light, looking for air bubbles, looking for a sign that this shot might be different than the first two; that it might work.

"A man was shot, sitting in that chair right where you sit now," I said. Schmuck seemed to have forgotten I was there.

"That man's life began to drain from him the very instant the bullets entered. The warmth spread down his flank, soaked into his pants, trickled into his shoes, and the cold crept in and filled him from the inside."

"I don't know what you're talking about, but could you just save it?" Michael seemed to be in mourning, freshly in mourning. That shot hadn't helped him any either.

I filled him in on the news update—that the Time Motel had hosted the season's bloodiest shootout. These bullet holes were not imagined or a joke. I pushed across a copy of the LA*Examiner* front page. It showed a guest who would never check out from the Time Motel, sprawled beside the very telephone booth so easily staked out from this very kitchen window.

Michael Schmuck gave me an appraising look, summoning all his sly, cunning, and deductive abilities.

"You're not high," he concluded. "If you were high, it would make sense."

Full of resolve, he clipped open the four remaining balloons and spilled them into the spoon. His need was raw and pathetic.

You couldn't really blame him for it. Dope, if you watch its effects closely, and I don't mean the physiological reactions, but its way of pulling out the worst in people, has serious implications to such concepts as fraternity, friendship, and fair play.

I had opinions on all this, and, filled with a surge of generosity, or beer, shared my insights in a gush with sad and lonely Michael Schmuck. He loosened the tie on his arm. His eyes rolled in frustration, resignation, disappointment, betrayal, and dread of the coming hours. I'm right there with him; only a Formica kitchenette table separates us.

"Remember?" I said. "Remember how great shooting drugs was?"

He racked his eyes down from inside his skull. They wouldn't be able to hold on me for long.

"Remember how we went to parties and hung out in the bathroom shooting up while the rest of the people, the lame people, were kept locked out? It's just us, you or me, sharing this magic thing with your or my select friends. There is a feeling of solidarity and separateness. Then it sours. People turn into snakes. People turn into less than people. And it is ugly and hurtful."

My facial expressions had gotten the best of me. Pity bled into Michael's grimace, not without scorn. He pushed back from the table.

"I need to shit."

Well, of course he did. He'd been mainlining laxative for about an hour. I hid my remaining Kools inside my shirt. "I don't know how that's going to work out."

He didn't listen. He'd stopped listening when I'd tried to tell him something that I thought was important, like everybody stops listening. Hunched over, the back of his pants clingy, he scurried from the kitchenette toward the bathroom. I stood up and removed the last two beers from the warm freezer compartment.

"Oh, fuck!" screamed Michael from the other room. I hid the last two beers in one of the cupboards that Michael had previously rifled—better supplied than sorry. "Fuck. Fuck. My god, fuck," screamed Michael.

He lurched into the kitchen doorway.

I pointed to the wastebasket under the sink. "There," I said.

Later, when he'd caught his breath and rinsed his mouth, he turned on me.

"Asshole. Why didn't you tell me what was in the toilet?"

"I tried to warn you when you said you needed to—"

"You tried nothing of the kind."

He wanted to project an attitude of outrage, shooting it from a platform of moral indignation, but the illusion wouldn't hold. For one thing, the brimming tears he'd arrived with were streaming now. His upper lip was nothing but a quivering snot awning. Even the pumped up Tom of Finland characters on his T-shirt seemed to have wilted. To top it off, whatever he'd seen in the toilet had caused him to lose a grip. He smelled leaky in the ass. In short, he'd come to embody how I often felt. The acrid odor filling my nostrils is what I suspected normal people, better people, of sniffing out on me even on my best days.

Michael was leaving without saying goodbye. "Hey," I called. "Do you have my number?"

I didn't want to be alone, especially not now that I'd adopted all of Michael's depressing attributes as my own. The least he could do was sit vigil with me on our departed hopes. I shut the front door, where he'd left it open. The invading light had weakened considerably. My skull was a headache chamber—no room up there, really, for any further alcohol or cigarettes. I missed Michael. For a while, I counted down to when he would return. Then I went and pissed in the pristine bathtub. Who had I been kidding?

*   *   *

OUTDOORS, THE SUN SLIPPED away. If I'd turned on the kitchenette light, the inside of the Time would leak out through the bullet-riddled walls into the twilight at large. Maybe some ordinary Joe, heading home after the job, would catch sight of the escaping gleam and wonder: *What could be going on in that motel room? Those walls must be witnessing some extraordinary thing beyond my wildest imaginings!*

I swirled the final inch of Coors in the can. My stomach had soured. Even as I swallowed, I knew that this drink would not settle anything. I should have eaten something to soak up some of the booze. I left the empty can on the table and took the last two full ones and the cigarettes into the bedroom to work on them.

I sat in the bed, watching where the TV had been ripped from the wall. I put my feet up on the covers. Those knockoff loafers were a full size too big. In some way I couldn't fit into thought, I had put one over on my boss and coworkers. They would be clocking out about now. My advantage over them, if you'd asked me to explain it, I'd have begged off. With this headache, how could I think straight?

The bed pulled me back, deep into it. So what about the crabs? Why should I escape the crabs? The bed wasn't only a repository for the sleeping essence of Karina and her friend; it was deeper. The mattress had sopped up the dreams and sleepless sweats of so many people, you could never count them, only be one of them, just another tosser with a rank stomach dutifully laboring through his last bits of poison.

A stray thought of Karina put me on my feet. I had a swirling, painful vertigo. Karina, if she were to walk through that door, could take me in a fight. Also, there was no telling what brutal ally she might bring in with her. I was glad, after all, for what I'd done to her boots, but I knew to get out.

The walk home was hardly a mile, definitely less than two. Tommie had put stew meat in a Crock-Pot before leaving for her drawing board. There would be heat, no bullet holes, a clear toilet. My feet set down straighter than I might have expected in those oversized plastic loafers. I had one last Kool. I saved it, not for when I thought I would enjoy it, but for when it wouldn't make me throw up.

Lit windows in the bungalows and apartments lining Willoughby Avenue announced warmth inside. Walking, I saw women in kitchens, men, too. People were snug, like bugs in rugs. They lived in there together, in their homes.

It was trash night. People wheeled their canisters to the curb for morning pick up. The world insists on dumping heavy-handed symbolism on you when you're down. I looked for a match to light that last Kool, not caring if I threw up or not. My hand came up with the diary. Nail polish ridges gleamed in the streetlight. I held the secret inner workings of a life, either Karina's or her friend's. These secret workings were probably things I'd be better off not knowing, like my own secrets, for instance. I'd be closer to happy if I could let them go; instead, I kept making new ones. The next trash container that was set deep in shadow, so dark that no one could see it for sure from a car passing in the street, that's where I dumped the diary, slamming the lid on it.

A light went on in a kitchen window, and I shrank back. Having heard me in the garbage, a face came to the pane, all aglow, looking out to see if that anticipated loved one had now arrived home.

SCENE SEVEN: STEAM CIRCLES

To be factual, looking back at me circling within the steaming, congested rungs of Animals, not one swinging dick swung any interest in my direction. I was not fantasy bait for my cock-waving brethren. Here's the deflating truth: I was poxy, scrawny, shut down, and no chicken. In less than two months, I would be twenty-five, a middle-aged bathhouse virgin. No self-respecting stud or queen bothers with that shit.

Fine, for my part. I was just biding my time until Black Randy made his move to score the speed that had lured me on this trip to San Francisco.

It shouldn't matter that I was not attractive to these people, these naked and selectively rutting people. I didn't need to hog attention, not where so many others so desperately craved and depended upon it.

I lost count of how many times I'd been around the Animals block.

The layout confused me. Perpendicular corridors and parallel hallways made abrupt ninety-degree turns, intersected unexpectedly and dead-ended on whims. The cruisers were meat in the maze, but they all knew its ins-and-abouts. I was the sole clueless cow wandering the stockyard.

Marching with the livestock, approaching an unrecognized intersection, I'd take the corner in step with the shuffling sex seekers, girding myself for whatever new or different shock might veer into view. Usually, the oiled and flexed scenery coming into sight would look just like every oily flex I'd already seen.

One recurring raw, red face stood out—a stationary, ball-gagged mask of rage and ecstasy. His shaved skull and tendon-popping neck protruded like a landmark from an open cubicle. I paused and peeked inside.

The guy was in truss bondage. His aggressive, ball-gagged leer gloated at having made me stop. His wrists were bound to his ankles. His knees were bent up and attached to his elbows. A taut line ran from the cinch at his neck to a noose on his cock and balls. His asshole was plugged. Casual passersby darted into the trussed man's cubicle, reached forward and notched the masochist's crotch binds. With each added twist, the prisoner squealed around the red ball in his mouth, whether in delight or protest I couldn't decide.

I'm not an idiot; I saw the dynamic. This was a place of masters and slaves. I traced the lines of superiority and the fundamental geometry of status at Animals. The individual's position on the pecking order, I'd concluded, was not entirely elective or fully voluntary. I'd been told of heavy S&M bars where all touch is forbidden. Mere physical contact might spark the underlying raw current of sadistic sexual voltage. Not panicking became important. I concentrated on avoiding eye contact and not seeming timid while I did it.

A bundle of insecurities had shorted out just below my placid surface. This potential internal meltdown, I sensed, needed to exist separate from me, where it would not alert the orgy-maddened mob. How much more could my sangfroid withstand, wedged in among eroticized platoons of prowling male flesh, gliding chest to chest?

I glanced up and forward. Ranks of poised, brazen-eyed sensualists lockstepped toward me, marching against the flow of leering sex hunters that strode shoulder-to-shoulder with me. This opposing and uniform tide, for all their physical differences, were as alike as soldiers—except for one furtive, hollow-chested fellow who seemed to retreat as he advanced. Me. Even in this essential state, stripped to basics, I was out of step, alone, incapable of blending in.

I watched myself realize that I was fast approaching a mirrored dead end, and veer off, saved from crashing into the glass by my outstanding awkwardness.

Keeping the flat eyes and stoic face, I looked for a place to be solitary, to compose myself, gather my thoughts, take an objective assessment, and chart my next actions. Surely, some small hideaway had been provided for individual contemplation. I thought I'd spotted just such a nook, and stepped into a darkened side room.

The door closed behind me. The darkness was absolute. Where had I gone? Reflexively, I grasped and secured my towel.

Moving forward, I stepped on flesh, tripped on flesh, fell face-first into flesh, recoiled from flesh, and slid forward on flesh. I crawled on hands and knees across a naked carpet. Greased maleness slithered and coiled and grunted beneath me. I guess no one could see me any better than I could see anyone else.

If these bodies were a mix of male and female, I'd be creeping across a fifty-fifty chance of fitting arousal. I might be hoping to make contact. As it was, I belly slalomed through eager openings and protrusions with zero hopeful arousal. That zero hope went both ways: I scooted across the mass of sexualized flesh, and no hand reached out to grasp me.

A crack of light flashed. The door! I crawled toward where that light had disappeared. Elbows, asses, pectoral muscles, flexed backs, and bobbing heads paved the way for my hands-and-knees scramble. Beard stubble scraped my thigh. Just as I reached the edge of the flesh mat, the door opened again, outward. I lunged for the light.

Towel and sneakers intact, I crawled into the main warren. I stood up, readjusted my underwear and checked to see if I'd embarrassed myself. No one seemed to notice me.

By sheer happenstance, I found Black Randy in a dark corner. He had backed his ass against a wall and bunched his towel up over his waist. An idiot grin creased his face. He was crapping, right there in the baths, in a common area.

I'd never seen him happier. I moved to speak to him, but paused. To be associated with Randy might be to my detriment. Who knew what penalties might be administered for shitting on the floor? Who knew what penalties Black Randy hoped to incur? It was time to abort the mission.

I shoved off into the traffic and unsettling pools of light.

How could I hope to find my way through these black walls back to the lockers? Any portal that looked like a way out might be a chute into a deeper rung. Sex troopers shambled on every side, totally indifferent to my comfort and well-being.

Playing cool, I scanned for an exit sign.

SCENE EIGHT:
THE DAY JOHN LENNON DIED

On the morning of December 8, 1980, I was taking the march of the working poor, walking to the dead-end job. I'd had to let the Ford go. Usually, the heels of my shoes dug in with each dragging step. It was Monday. A compound hangover can be assumed. Lingering toxicity and the weekend's emotional residue gummed up my brain.

My every bouncing stride, vibrant with the elasticity of life, defied all expectations.

You anticipate the weekends will be more dramatic than the work weeks, and that usually breeds disappointment. For a string of weekends, there is no rejuvenation, no recharging; just isolated rote recreation with the wife, and only bits of that. Then an event occurs, unplanned. You hear of it late in the afternoon on Sunday. And you pick up drinking at precisely the hour of the day when normally you try to cut it off.

Someone had died, someone I knew.

My sore feet slammed into the pavement. Each step slapped pain into my head. That pain said hello to me, to me alive, hoofing to work. Overcast and cloudy; you knew the forecast. Tires hissed past on Highland, motors rumbled. One world per vehicle, and none of the drivers knew what had happened right up close to my world. I was high without taking anything. How could I be?

Darby Crash, the former Bobby Pyn, singer and lyricist for the Germs, was dead.

Darby had expired early Sunday morning from a deliberate heroin overdose in the guesthouse of Casey Cola's mother. The date was meant to go down in history as December 7, 1980.

Even as I stepped from gutter to sidewalk, trudging up toward Sunset and the building I worked in, to the desk I sat behind, details were emerging. Casey Cola had been unconscious at Darby's side when he cooked his final spoon. She had emerged from a lesser OD to find him gone.

I could not count the mornings, hiking to work, for blocks on end, that I had pictured me plunging neck first under the rumbling tires of a northbound eighteen-wheeler. For a change, I was feeling pretty good.

My job in magazine publishing was to count. I worked in the subscriptions department. I'd moved up from envelope opener to invoice counter. Each day, day after day, the envelope openers would stack trays full of subscription-order slips on my desk. The slips were bunched and trussed in rubber bands. Trays full of corresponding payment checks were stacked on the desk behind me. I would count subscription slips, stacks upon stacks of subscription slips, one by one, and tally the dollar amount of each stack.

After each stack, I would check with the twenty-four-year-old woman at the desk behind to ensure my tally of the slips matched her tally of the checks. The woman at the desk behind me was married and had a child with a man in El Monte. She was also tearing through an affair with a handsome young fellow in publishing; he might one day run the mail room.

During the moments I spent face-to-face with the woman at the desk behind, I revealed that I had been divorced, that my wife had stabbed me with a fork, that I had once hit my head on the wall and knocked myself unconscious while having sex. None of these claims were true.

What would I tell the woman behind about my weekend? That two people I knew had entered a suicide pact, and one had emerged alive? The story was unlikely and failed to paint me in a lively light.

I paused at a newspaper rack to light a cigarette. I read the huge, black headline. John Lennon had been murdered. My apartment had no working TV. Standing on the street, I learned what all those private worlds in all those private cars driving past me already knew—John Lennon of The Beatles, killed.

The Darby news had come over the phone. So far, almost everyone who knew he was dead had been informed by a phone call. I'd picked up on Sunday afternoon, to make the ringing stop. The wife was at her drafting table, mastering line, mastering form; she was mastering space.

The caller was Black Randy's business partner. He said my name. I recognized him, but not the lugubrious tone.

"Have you heard yet? About Darby?"

"What?" I said. "Did Darby change his hair back to yellow? What is there to hear about Darby? What new thing will we possibly hear about Darby?"

"He killed himself."

I repeated that out loud. There was a rush of adrenalin and excitement. A suicide! And it wasn't me! I felt like I'd made a narrow escape.

Tommie's pencil had stopped. She was motionless all over.

"How did he do it?" I asked.

"Heroin. He gave himself a huge overdose of heroin."

"I don't see how he could afford it, not in this city. You'd need like five hundred dollars worth of LA dope to put yourself under."

"Everything's a joke. I'm going now." This was Black Randy's business partner, a man accustomed to Black Randy's slanders and antics. He'd hung up on me.

Monday morning's newspaper rack held me for a few moments. I read as much as I could about John Lennon without putting in any coins. One of the world's most famous and acclaimed and beloved performers had been ambushed and shot point-blank in the lobby of his home.

Money came hard to me. For eight hours that day, I counted and tallied. At lunch, I chewed a sandwich that went dry in my mouth. I counted and tallied each bite. Walking home, step after step, count and tally. At home, in my sleep, I would count and tally. I understood how a person would want to just stop counting.

When you do stop counting, in that final reckoning, you want the stoppage to somehow count for something. Even if Darby had made the papers, which he had not, a Beatle's murder would have bumped out the notice of his death.

Dear Darby Crash: Of all the punk luck. You assume the commitment, you plan the deed, and you carry through. Then some crazed attention fiend pops out and shoots John Lennon dead before your body is even claimed.

So I'm in the apartment after work, at the dinner table with Tommie.

The Christmas holidays are gearing up all over Hollywood, and inside of our place as well. Tommie has decked the kitchen and living room with handcrafted ornaments celebrating the season. Never mind what I'd done to the festive décor the year before, in 1979.

I'm chewing and I'm counting, and I'm recounting my musing on the passing of Darby Crash. "He pulled his Bobby Pyn guts together. He took the big step."

Tommie's not eating. She has the look of a woman paying attention.

I sum up Darby's legacy as best I can: "Mr. No God took the immortal leap of faith, the leap of being young and dead and famous forever. I guess there is a God after all. And God said to Darby: 'Nice try, loser.'"

I should have known: The wife was paying attention to thoughts that had nothing to do with mine, to a life that had nothing to do with me. She was thinking of any other possible thing.

SCENE NINE:
ESCAPE FROM ANIMALS

Bobbing cocks mobbed the entrance to an extremely well-lit anteroom. Jostling hip-to-hip, bathhouse spectators overflowed the space. They seemed fascinated, mesmerized; as if by some spectacle. A few chewed on their towels.

Despite everything I had seen and touched during my wanderings at Animals, I was still susceptible to that primal urge to join a gawking crowd. I pushed in among the largely naked, completely male, and assumedly homosexual crush. To hang back might invite untoward interest.

At the center of the room, two shorthaired, sinewy showoffs were suspended side-by-side in black-leather harnesses anchored from the ceiling. The showoffs were hanging belly up; rocking in industrial sex swings about three feet from the floor, naked other than for strategic studded straps. Their knees were bent back toward their ears.

At the front of each hanging man worked a corresponding dominant stud. This pair of butch males wore tight black chaps and identical snappy leather caps. They might be twins. Their shoulders were tense and their faces intent, like a couple of doctors competing to see which could deliver the greasier baby.

It took me a while to absorb what I was seeing.

Each capped stud had a full hand up the ass of the harnessed man suspended in front of him. This was tandem fist fucking—never to be an Olympic sport, but in its own way just as breathtaking as synchronized swimming.

The hand-stuffed men in the slings grunted, jerked their cocks, and squealed out like singing pigs. The crowd groaned. No sound whatsoever came from me. The crowd moaned. In truth, I gave up breathing for a few moments there.

Were these fisted exhibitionists undergoing some punishment ritual? Had they been caught crapping in the maze? Or were they just doing what it took to be famous for that night, in that tightly packed chamber of poppers and baby oil?

I backed away from the spectacle, trying to give the impression I'd seen all I needed to see, and that this carnal sideshow was nothing I hadn't seen before. I stayed cool, I moved casual, but under my towel, my sangfroid was fried. A hasty reconnaissance circuit through the warren confirmed what I had suspected but refused to voice: *I was alone. I was in there all on my own, and I could not find my way out.*

Black Randy had disappeared. Perhaps he'd left Animals and crabbed back to the van. He and the antagonistic driver might be running red lights twenty city blocks away.

Panic would doom me. I scanned the lust-drugged throng for a face I could intimidate, for a body I could take in a fight. That person would show me the way out of Animals. All I needed was one.

Finding the right man was difficult. Looking anyone in the eye might be open to interpretation. It's hard to browbeat if you're afraid to stare down.

Another twenty minutes circuiting the maze, and I spotted a guy who didn't scare me. He was an older observer type, studious, standing alone in a shadowed corner, maybe the corner where Randy had dumped. He posed very still and fully dressed, mostly in leather. A touch of denim gave him a shrinking violet aspect. In a different compartment of his life, he might have been a junior college professor.

All my ribs showing, my hairless, tiny nipples vulnerable, I jutted my chin at the clothed observer. That got his attention. His face turned in my direction.

"How do I get out of here?"

He pointed to what looked like a slab of black wall. "There."

Was this a trick? I mocked up a hard look, out of suppressed hysteria and surging desperation. "You're sure that's the way to the lockers?"

His eyes widened, and he nodded.

I felt along the wall. My fingers found a hinge, then a handle. The door pushed away easily. I opened just wide enough to pass my body through, then quickly, quietly shut the flat-black panel behind me.

I entered relatively fresh air and half-light. The tweak freak in the cashier's booth clocked my disorientation through his mirrored shades. He pointed his claw; I followed the direction and found the locker number that matched the tag on my wrist. The key worked, the lock opened.

I dressed very fast. I pulled a shirt over my head and down past my waist and relaxed my belly. I'd been holding in my gut the whole time. My pants and my jacket and my shoes again, each shored up my confidence. These were the clothes I wore at home. I had taken off each of these garments with Tommie, sometimes drunkenly, resigned to passing out, other times in states of excitation and anticipation, tossing the pants and shirt into side-by-side piles as we flopped down on our mattress, length to length, by ourselves, slipping into sex or sleep, beyond consciousness of the raw forces dredging for bodies and release in the alien night, a night so raw and alien it might devour you.

What would protect me, when I landed back home, from lying there all alone?

Fully dressed, I had less to worry about and found myself outside in the cold San Francisco New Year.

How long have I been away?

The world outside was very much like when I'd last left it. Still, outward appearances, natural laws, none of them could be fully trusted.

The van might be parked in any direction. Who could remember? Rain was in the air. There was chill and there was wind, but the sun might show soon, might rise up between the dark buildings a few blocks over. I stepped into the empty street and walked toward where I felt the light would come from.

Two men, a pair of strangers, left the sidewalk and veered to cross my path. They were the only people out there; I was their sole witness. Their hands were up, high in their jacket pockets. Undercover cops, gay bashers, generic muggers, whoever the fuck—I didn't take to their curious glances; I wasn't lulled by their cursory smiles.

I made myself ready for whatever these next strangers might bring to me.

*Thank you to everybody who helped with this book,
especially Stefani Relles, Alex Maslansky, Sam Wohl,
and the patient, painstaking Rare Bird people.*